# Partners for the Dance

## Forming Strategic Alliances in Health Care

# Partners for the Dance

## Forming Strategic Alliances in Health Care

Edited by

Arnold D. Kaluzny

Howard S. Zuckerman

Thomas C. Ricketts III

with the assistance of Geoffrey B. Walton

Health Administration Press
Ann Arbor, Michigan 1995

99  98  97  96  95     5  4  3  2  1

Library of Congress Cataloging-in-Publication Data

Partners for the dance : forming strategic alliances in health care / edited by Arnold D. Kaluzny, Howard S. Zuckerman, and Thomas Ricketts III ; with the assistance of Geoffrey B. Walton.
    p.   cm.
   Includes index.
   ISBN 1-56793-025-5 (pbk. : acid-free paper)
   1. Health services administration—United States—Congresses.  2. Strategic alliances (Business)—United States—Congresses.  3. Health care reform—United States—Congresses.  4. Managed care plans (Medical care)—United States—Congresses.  I. Kaluzny, Arnold D.  II. Zuckerman, Howard S., date. III. Ricketts, Thomas C.
RA395.A3P27          1995          362.1'0973—dc20          94-47387 CIP

The paper used in this book meets the minimum requirements of American National Standard for Information Sciences—Permanence of paper for Printed Library materials, ANSI Z39.48-1984. ∞™

Health Administration Press
A division of the Foundation of the
  American College of Healthcare Executives
1021 East Huron Street
Ann Arbor, MI 48104-1628
(313) 764-1380

*To Edward J. Connors*

*For improving the health of the community through cooperation*

# Contents

Foreword
    The Role of Strategic Alliances in Health Care Reform
    *Kenneth E. Thorpe* ........................................... ix

Preface and Acknowledgments ................................ xv

1   Strategic Alliances: A Worldwide Phenomenon Comes
    to Health Care
    *Howard S. Zuckerman, Arnold D. Kaluzny,
    and Thomas C. Ricketts III* .................................. 1

2   Strategic Alliances: Some Lessons from Experience
    *Barry A. Stein* ............................................ 19

    The Commentaries: A Summary ............................ 35
    *W. Richard Scott* ......................................... 36
    *Tim Size* ................................................. 40
    *Gerald Martin* ............................................ 53
    *Neal Neuberger* ........................................... 57

3   The Creation of a Multiorganizational
    Health Care Alliance: The Charlotte–Mecklenburg
    Hospital Authority
    *Harry A. Nurkin* .......................................... 63

    The Commentaries: A Summary ............................ 85
    *R. Paul O'Neill* ........................................... 86
    *Paul Cooper III* ........................................... 90
    *Alan Weinstein* ........................................... 94

4  The Structure of Strategic Alliances: Evidence
from Rural Hospital Networks
*Jon B. Christianson, Ira S. Moscovice, and Anthony Wellever* . . . . . . 99

The Commentaries: A Summary . . . . . . . . . . . . . . . . . . . . . . . . . . 119
*Robert J. Baker* . . . . . . . . . . . . . . . . . . . . . . . . . . . . . . . . . . . . . . . 120
*Ben W. Latimer* . . . . . . . . . . . . . . . . . . . . . . . . . . . . . . . . . . . . . . 126
*Stephen Wood* . . . . . . . . . . . . . . . . . . . . . . . . . . . . . . . . . . . . . . . . 130
*Edward J. Zajac* . . . . . . . . . . . . . . . . . . . . . . . . . . . . . . . . . . . . . . 134

5  Strategic Alliances as a Structure for Integrated
Delivery Systems
*William L. Dowling* . . . . . . . . . . . . . . . . . . . . . . . . . . . . . . . . . . . 139

The Commentaries: A Summary . . . . . . . . . . . . . . . . . . . . . . . . . . 177
*Michael O. Bice* . . . . . . . . . . . . . . . . . . . . . . . . . . . . . . . . . . . . . . 178
*David Berry* . . . . . . . . . . . . . . . . . . . . . . . . . . . . . . . . . . . . . . . . . 181
*Stephen M. Shortell* . . . . . . . . . . . . . . . . . . . . . . . . . . . . . . . . . . . 185
*Jerald T. Hage* . . . . . . . . . . . . . . . . . . . . . . . . . . . . . . . . . . . . . . . 192

6  Implications for Research
*Thomas C. Ricketts III, Arnold D. Kaluzny,*
*Howard S. Zuckerman, and Geoffrey B. Walton* . . . . . . . . . . . . . . . 199

Appendix A
A Method for Identifying Research Issues
*Thomas A. D'Aunno* . . . . . . . . . . . . . . . . . . . . . . . . . . . . . . . . . . 211

Appendix B
Conference Participants . . . . . . . . . . . . . . . . . . . . . . . . . . . . . . . 221

Index . . . . . . . . . . . . . . . . . . . . . . . . . . . . . . . . . . . . . . . . . . . . . . 229

About the Editors . . . . . . . . . . . . . . . . . . . . . . . . . . . . . . . . . . . . 237

# Foreword

# The Role of Strategic Alliances in Health Care Reform

*The following was adapted from a presentation to the National Invitational Conference on Strategic Alliances in Chapel Hill, North Carolina, held November 11–12, 1993.*

This conference provides a unique opportunity to focus on how health care reform, and the Health Security Act (HSA), as proposed by President Clinton in Fall 1993, would affect alliances. As you know, the President has outlined several principles for his health care reform proposal. Particularly relevant to our discussion—and the objectives of this conference— are the principles of savings and new economic incentives. In terms of savings, any health care reform effort must control the growth in health care spending in this economy, in both the public and private sectors. A large component of what the President talked about with respect to savings has to do with restructuring the delivery system.

Restructuring of the delivery system and the role of strategic alliances is the issue of the day. To address these issues, three major distinctions are relevant to the concept of alliances in a reformed health care delivery system. The first is to distinguish strategic alliances within the proposed Health Security Act from the more generic configuration of such organizations. In health care reform, alliances are purchasing organizations comprised of employers and individuals that bargain with health plans. Alliances in the HSA are responsible for ensuring that their consumer members attain access to the plans' standard comprehensive benefits package. They would accomplish this largely through contracts with health plans, which represent a major restructuring of the delivery system and will have major implications for the structure and formation of alliances. This is distinct from the generic definition of strategic alliances as existing organizations involved in loosely coupled arrangements, designed to achieve some long-term strategic purpose not possible for a single organization.

A second distinction is the concept of a certified health plan, which is intended to be quite different in several respects than the concept of a health plan as we have thought about it in the past several years. First, health plans under the HSA would be responsible for delivering a comprehensive and standard benefit package to all enrollees. Competition here will be not on the attributes or characteristics of the benefit package as much as on the price, quality, and satisfaction of care delivered within the health plan itself. Second, health plans are responsible for making price and quality information available to the alliance and to members in it. Third, the president's plan puts no constraints on how a health plan could be organized. In fact, it eliminates some constraints that exist today.

The final distinction has to do with providers. Under health reform, most providers would join one or more health plans. They may be part of a single integrated health plan, such as Kaiser, or may have contracts with a variety of PPO-type health plans that have evolved through the system today. Those are the three analytic areas where substantial changes are likely to occur.

A second principle has to do with new economic incentives, in particular with respect to financing and delivery and the linkage between them. In a reformed system, relationships would move beyond linkage. In particular, under the president's plan, health plans could do more than link delivery and finance; they indeed can erase the boundary between delivery and financing entirely. As the HSA was set up, health plans would bid and be paid on a per capita basis through the alliance. As a result of this restructuring, the risk is almost entirely borne by the health plan. You can imagine that the health plan, as it restructures contracts with hospitals and providers, can pass risk on to practitioners by putting them at risk for care management decisions, as many HMOs are doing today.

How can alliances fit into this new system? The focus is really on two key characteristics of strategic alliances. First is the loose and flexible nature of alliances. Flexibility is very important because it eliminates much of the burden of capital investment and organizational restructuring. That is a major issue for health plans. Certainly alliances could, given their organizational structure, have a comparative advantage in this respect. Second, the strategic alliances could fit into a reform delivery system because they have the ability to address cross-disciplinary issues.

Consider today's alliances. It's clear that in terms of the institutionalization of the alliances, some of them will develop into more formal arrangements. The alliances of today are likely to be the networks and health plans of tomorrow. This movement will not only be driven by an actual reform proposal, as you see in the market today. In reaction to the submission of the HSA, there was substantial movement in the market already. This is more than a natural evolution. It is being enhanced by the demands and opportunities created by the health reform discussion.

Alliance participants can formalize their relationships and compete as health plans, or as health plan components. Under any type of reform, alliances would have a competitive edge in at least three respects. First, the relationships already exist. The necessary working relationships have already been forged. Second, alliances have a track record. They may have market share and even more to sell. Third—and this is the real advantage of alliances—given their flexibility and informality, they are much more prepared for innovation than more formalized structures in the market. They are more psychologically open to these types of coordinated activities.

With all of these advantages, however, alliances will turn out to be targets for takeovers or as subcontractors to health plans. With respect to existing provider networks and information systems, they will save start-up capital and help gain consumer market share for more formalized plans. As reform is developing, there will be a continued demand for primary care practitioners, so community care network alliances could be attractive targets for acquisition. One of the challenges that alliances face in this reformed market is to retain control over the most valued aspects of their alliances.

If the past is prologue, consider tomorrow's opportunities; these are opportunities that have been created by the development of alliances and plans. With respect to care delivery, the president's Health Security Act specified a comprehensive benefit package that does *not* specify how health plans must provide the benefits. Health plans are free to structure care delivery as they see fit, using any mix of licensed practitioners. This has been an important part of our discussions. Alliances offer a good vehicle for innovation in care delivery; since no major institutional reorganization or capital investment is required, they can risk trying new arrangements. In a more regulated and regulatory system, this flexibility will be particularly important. A system that developed in response to the HSA would look at innovation in areas that require the kind of cross-discipline expertise that alliances can offer. Many examples of this have been discussed as part of this conference, ranging from primary care networking to managing chronic care illnesses to using new sites of care to regional cross-alliance centers of excellence for tertiary medical care.

Alliances are also going to be important players in the new information systems needed for reform. The president's plan required a variety of new information gathering and dispersal activities. For example, information and information systems are needed to produce and provide information on cost, quality, and practice patterns of providers within and across health plans. Alliances may be well-situated to provide the cross-disciplinary expertise to collect this information, since they can combine clinical care management and data systems capability needed to develop the systems, especially in rural areas.

There are several other opportunities for existing strategic alliances created by the president's plan. One is clinical health services research. One of the more interesting things about the alliance concept is that it offers an organized population base for research. The Health Security Act also provides for new research priorities which emphasize outcome, development and dissemination of practice guidelines and quality measurement tools, as well as demonstration projects. One area ripe for a demonstration project is worker's compensation. The administration remains quite interested in fully integrating the worker's compensation system, both on the delivery and the financing side.

A second area where there is going to be a lot of interest in demonstration projects is malpractice liability. In particular, there is interest in looking at the concept of "enterprise liability," a reassignment of liability in the medical malpractice system from providers to health plans. In this way, health plans will be accountable for delivering quality care, and will have to make sure that physicians, hospitals and providers deliver adequate medical care.

As we think about and understand the notion and concepts behind alliances and health plans, several additional opportunities for alliances come to mind. One of these opportunities relates to population-based goals. Strategic alliances will have responsibilities for the health care needs of a defined population, over time. Again, that is quite distinct from the way the medical care system works today. The new system will challenge alliances to think in terms of defined populations. In addition, as mentioned with respect to research results, the existence and operation of alliances and health plans will provide new opportunities for alliances to study diffusion of research results.

There are, however, some barriers in the new system for strategic alliances, as well as the many opportunities just outlined. First, health plans, because they have a legal responsibility for providing the standard benefit package within a capped budget, may demand more formal and permanent arrangements than some alliances can accommodate. As you will see, this is going to be a double-edged sword for some alliances as they currently exist.

A second barrier is competition. Since plans will be more direct competitors, forming alliances among plans may be difficult not only due to potential antitrust risk, but also because competitors are less likely to want to share their good ideas. Working with the regional alliance may help lessen some of the antitrust risks.

As I think about some of the challenges for the future of strategic alliances both in practice and theory, it occurs to me that the life cycle of alliances may end in a final irony, one already alluded to. The greater the success of an alliance, the more likely it is to be replicated, formalized, and in many cases, lose much of the essential character it has as an alliance. Health plans may want more formality than an alliance can offer, particularly to meet their legal mandates and also to lock in market share. On the other hand, in a reformed health care system looking for new answers, alliances are an excellent format for experimentation in areas requiring cross-disciplinary expertise. Moreover, these experiments or demonstration projects can serve as templates for more permanent arrangements among health plans and regional alliances.

Given the dynamic nature of health reform and the restructuring of the delivery system—along the lines of capped entitlements, restructured purchasing power, changing the way that health plans operate—alliances, as they exist in today's market, will play a very important role in health reform at all levels of government. The future is now!

Kenneth E. Thorpe
Deputy Assistant Secretary for Health Policy
U.S. Department of Health and Human Services

# Preface and Acknowledgments

Strategic alliances in health care are growing in importance. In fact, some might say that alliances are imperative to the effective and efficient provision of health services, especially in rural communities. This book presents the proceedings of the National Invitational Conference on Strategic Alliances held in Chapel Hill, North Carolina on November 11–12, 1993, and sponsored by The Agency for Health Care Policy and Research (AHCPR). The conference provided an opportunity for dialogue among health service researchers and alliance executives. Our research colleagues were exposed to the reality of contemporary health services and executives were provided a greater understanding of the research perspective and how it might improve decision making.

While "health care reform" proved to be a nonevent at the federal level, the emergence and role of strategic alliances remain critical issues throughout the country. Health services are undergoing fundamental changes and alliances are growing in number and importance with or without the reform.

Senior health care executives, as well as health services researchers, will be the primary audience for this work. The book will also be useful in the classroom as a supplemental text to graduate and executive development courses in organizational design and behavior, and perhaps the basic health services organization and finance course. However, as the alliance movement grows within health services, the book may have applicability for classroom use in schools of nursing, allied health, and social services.

Discussions about the need for such a meeting began between the organizers and a group of alliance executives back in the beginning of 1992. This meeting, held in Chicago, and subsequent interest by AHCPR set the stage for the Chapel Hill conference. We feel we were successful in bringing together a dynamic mix of individuals from the research and practice communities as well as representatives from the insurers, suppliers, and government. At the two-day conference, the four papers which make up the main chapters of this work were presented, followed by commentaries from a panel of participants. Commentators include both managers and colleagues from the health services research community, each with the challenge to review the paper presented and to relate it to their area of expertise. These papers and commentaries were effectively synthesized from a policy, managerial, and research perspective by William L. Kissick, Edward J. Connors, and Mary L. Fennell.

The structure of the book involves four substantive chapters with respective commentaries. In addition, we have written an introductory and concluding chapter for the book. The introductory, "Strategic Alliances: A Worldwide Phenomenon Comes to Health Care," helps us set the stage for the work in relation to what is happening in other industries, as well as what we have seen in health care. The final chapter, "Implications for Research," synthesizes the material presented—as well as the ideas generated at the conference—into a set of research topics for future study. We are also fortunate to have a foreword by Kenneth E. Thorpe, deputy assistant secretary for health policy, on the role alliances will play in health care reform. At the conference we had the insightful comments of Monroe Trout and Alex MacMahon. Finally, we have an appendix written by Tom D'Aunno, that describes the process we went through in our break-out sessions at the conference where conference participants generated a list of research topics. These sessions were capably chaired by Al Gilbert, Ann Greer, Tom D'Aunno, and Laura Morlock.

Throughout this effort, we have been blessed with the support of many talented and dedicated individuals who helped the conference and this work to become reality. We thank the conference participants, in particular the paper authors and the contributing panelists, for making this project a success.

The organization of a conference and the production of the report is not the sole product of individuals, but requires an organizational context; a strategic alliance if you will. Our alliance was composed of the Cecil G. Sheps Center for Health Services Research at the University of North Carolina at Chapel Hill, the Center for Health Management Research at Arizona State University, AHCPR, and Health Administration Press. At UNC, the Sheps Center and Gordon DeFriese provided the support, flexibility, and patience for handling a conference of this size and scope. Particular thanks are given to Janice Pope for helping coordinate the conference, and Jan Pittman for her efforts in ensuring that financing and reimbursement were on time and in our budget. The secretarial assistance of Emily Revaulx, Carol Troutner, Dee Musselman, Joan Kavanagh, and Will McCann are truly appreciated. The Center for Health Management Research at Arizona State University was the second component and an equal partner in the alliance. While 2,000 miles separated the two universities, close working relationships were maintained throughout the process. Special thanks are given to JoAnn Ott for her meticulous research efforts; she undertook a comprehensive review and analysis of both the industrial and health care literature on alliances, and contributed to the summaries of the major papers.

AHCPR provided the funds and much more. Linda Blankenbacker—the executive secretary for the study section that reviewed the initial proposal—provided encouragement, guidance, and a sense of perspective that we greatly appreciated. Our project advisor, Terry Shannon, kept us on track and we commend him and his colleagues.

The final component of this alliance involves Sandy Crump, Suzanne Worsham, and their colleagues at Health Administration Press. Always helpful and supportive, they provided the guidance to transform a conference report to what is hopefully a usable, readable book relevant to both the practice and research communities. Special thanks are given to Beaufort Longest and Doug Lewis, who took the time to read the entire manuscript and make helpful suggestions "within the spirit of continuous improvement."

Finally, our thanks to Kathleen Walton for coordinating the travel arrangements for all the participants, clearly a major logistical effort for which we are most grateful. Thanks also to the staff at the Carolina Inn for their efforts in making the actual conference a success.

Arnold D. Kaluzny
Thomas C. Ricketts III
and
Geoffrey B. Walton
Chapel Hill, NC

Howard S. Zuckerman
Tempe, AZ

# 1

# Strategic Alliances: A Worldwide Phenomenon Comes to Health Care

Howard S. Zuckerman, Arnold D. Kaluzny,
and Thomas C. Ricketts III

> Companies are beginning to learn what nations have always known—in a complex uncertain world, filled with dangerous opponents, it is best not to go it alone.
>
> *Kenichi Ohmae, 1989*

In an increasingly turbulent environment, companies around the globe and across a multitude of industries are turning to alliances as a cooperative, interorganizational mechanism for adaptation. Such alliances are designed to achieve strategic purposes not attainable by a single organization, providing flexibility and responsiveness while retaining the basic fabric of participating organizations. The purpose of this chapter is to assess the development and operation of alliances in other industries and health care. To achieve this purpose, we begin with a detailed analysis of other industries and then follow with an analysis of health care, addressing questions such as the following:

- What are alliances designed to achieve?
- How do they achieve their objectives?
- What problems do they face and how they are resolved?
- How have they performed?

## Alliances as a Vehicle for Interorganizational Relations

Alliances are legion. In the airline industry, for example, Air Canada—a midsize airline—has formed alliances with carriers in the United States,

Europe, and Asia (Chipello 1992). To cut costs and increase market position, Air Canada provides maintenance services for Continental and shares schedules, reservation codes, and frequent-flyer benefits with United. Sabena, to secure needed capital, has allied with Air France. The two airlines will coordinate schedules to feed each other's flights, exchange technical and maintenance service, and jointly purchase fuel.

Several approaches to cooperation are evident in the automobile industry. For example, Jaguar–Ford and Saab–Scania–General Motors have formed alliances to ward off Japanese competition in Great Britain. Daimler–Benz is beginning joint activities to build busses with companies in China, providing the Chinese with needed production technology while enabling Daimler–Benz to expand its presence in Asia (*Wall Street Journal* 1993). Chrysler's alliance with Mitsubishi seeks to gain both product and production technology (McClenahen 1987). In planning to bring a new sports coupe to the market, Chrysler sought to gain a new product and expose its personnel to Japanese work practices and management, while Mitsubishi sought new manufacturing technologies. General Motors, Ford, and Chrysler, in a significant policy departure, are exploring an alliance to design pollution free, technologically advanced cars, building on research links among the three automobile companies and governmental laboratories (Behr and Brown 1993).

The communication and media industries likewise may be characterized by a wave of alliances as telephone, cable, and computer hardware/software companies seek to be at the forefront of rapidly developing technological breakthroughs. Pushed by changing technology, rising competition, and an EEC deadline for ending all state monopolies, European telephone companies are forming international partnerships (Hudson 1993). Alliances are emerging linking British Telecommunications with MCI, France Telecom with Deutsche Bundespost Telekom (Eunetcom), and Dutch, Swedish, and Swiss companies (Unisource). AT&T is considering allying with major cable companies to bring its customers into one interactive multimedia network, tying the current disparate cable systems into an integrated network of common switching and transmission functions (Keller 1993a). AT&T has already formed alliances with Japanese and U.S. companies—Matsushita, NEC, Toshiba, McCaw Cellular—to promote its wireless data services (Keller 1993b). Major competitors, notably the "Baby Bells" and MCI, are likewise forming alliances to develop and market cellular services. Motorola's wireless telecommunications venture involves aligning with 11 other partners in a complex consortium to provide geographic representation, telecommunications expertise, and access to markets (Grant 1993). Among the partners are Sony, Mitsubishi, Bell Canada, and Sprint, plus several Russian and Chinese groups. Time Warner and US West also plan an alliance to put both companies at the forefront of the interactive television and telecommunications market, combining resources to develop an electronic superhighway (Roberts 1993). An alliance of 11 companies, including such giants as IBM, Apple, US West, Bell Communications Research, Eastman Kodak, Southwestern Bell, and Phillips Electronics, have formed a strategic alliance to develop and market multimedia technology for the home (Pope 1992).

The evidence is clear that many companies in many industries, including former and present competitors, are entering into a variety of alliances.

## What Are Alliances Designed to Achieve?

As the examples above suggest, alliances seek to achieve sharply focused, swiftly attained goals, relying on the complementary strengths of the partners involved. The number of alliances is likely to increase for the following reasons:

- Accelerated pace of technological change
- Broader range of technological capabilities
- Industry and economic maturation
- Shorter product lives
- Larger capital requirements
- Higher risk ventures
- Entry by new firms (especially those with government support)
- Multiple proficiencies required by customers that no single firm can possess
- Deregulation and trade agreements opening previously closed markets, promoting globalization of industry (Harrigan 1987).

Alliances arise out of mutual need and a willingness among and between organizations to share risks and costs, to share knowledge and capabilities, and to take advantage of interdependencies to reach common objectives (Lewis 1990). The basic aim of alliances is to gain competitive advantage, leverage critical capabilities, increase the flow of innovation, and improve flexibility in responding to market and technology changes. For example, alliances allow participation in highly volatile industries, where knowledge spreads rapidly, at substantially lower investment and risk than would be the case for a single organization (Badaracco 1991). Alliances also enable partners to enhance flexibility and accelerate getting to the market by taking advantage of complementary strengths and capabilities in areas such as production, marketing and distribution, and technology. These characteristics are especially shared by the actors in the health care industry.

The influence of new knowledge and new technologies on interorganizational structures, coupled with the need for new ways to coordinate the complexity that comes with alliances, will be continuing themes in organizational relations. Alter and Hage (1993) propose the following outline to summarize the benefits and costs of interorganizational cooperation:

*Benefits*

- Opportunities to learn and adapt new competencies
- Gain resources
- Share risks
- Share cost of product and technology development
- Gain influence over domain
- Access to new markets
- Enhance ability to manage uncertainty and solve complex problems
- Gain mutual support and group synergy
- Respond rapidly to market demands and technological opportunities
- Gain acceptance of foreign governments
- Strengthen competitive position.

*Costs*

- Loss of technical superiority
- Loss of resources
- Sharing the costs of failure
- Loss of autonomy and control
- Loss of stability and certainty
- Conflict over domain, goals, methods
- Delays in solutions due to coordination problems
- Government intrusion and regulation.

These benefits and costs apply across industries and include service industries like health care.

## How Do Alliances Seek to Achieve Their Goals?

Alliances are established along a variety of lines—joint ventures, marketing and distribution agreements, consortia, or licensing arrangements.

Alliances require thinking in terms of "combinations" of firms. For example, Japanese firms often cooperate in order to penetrate new markets, which has often proven to be a key step to market dominance (Lewis 1990). International companies often ally with local companies to yield successful entry into new markets, drawing on the knowledge and customer base of the local company in conjunction with the capital and technological resources of the international firm. Working with competitors is often the basis for an alliance against a common enemy. Newspapers often share facilities to compete with television, Ford dealers compete yet share advertising, and pharmaceutical companies use each other's sales forces (Lewis 1990). Joining forces is further desirable in the face of difficult economic conditions or the combined power of other alliances. Alliances may also be useful in enhancing flexibility, innovation, and performance in customer/supplier relationships. Captive supply units, not subject to market pressures, tend to develop cost, quality, and technology gaps. Alliances may thus be able to secure the benefits of vertical integration, without the drawbacks associated with ownership.

Successful alliances appear to have several key ingredients, beginning with shared objectives among the participants. Commitment is based on mutual need; the alliance will endure only so long as mutual need exists (Henderson 1990). Risk sharing completes the bond, creating a powerful incentive to cooperate for mutual gain. It is important to note, however, that mutual reliability means mutual vulnerability. Relationships matter a great deal in alliances, and success requires mutual trust, cooperation, and understanding (Badaracco 1991).

Alliances have been labeled as "virtual corporations," seen as temporary networks of companies that come together to exploit fast changing opportunities (Byrne 1993). Such corporations share costs, skills, and access to global markets. Their key attributes are identified as (1) technology and information networks, (2) excellence as each partner brings distinctive competencies, (3) opportunism in meeting specific market opportunities, (4) trust as partners share a destiny, and (5) a borderless market where suppliers, competitors, and customers cooperate. The key is flexibility—absent hierarchies and vertical structures—as alliances enable companies to broaden offerings or produce sophisticated products less expensively.

## What Problems Face Alliances and How Are They Managed?

Alliances must be carefully entered into, with clear objectives, a realistic appraisal of an organization's skills and resources, and knowledge of the strengths of each partner (Wysocki 1990). Alliances should be approached carefully and systematically, often involving consideration of several potential partners with common or compatible culture and similar approaches to issues and problems is critical. Partners must understand their motivation in entering an alliance. Alliances are designed to create competitive strength or augment a strategic position, not hide weaknesses (Hamel, Doz, and Prahalad 1989). As such, they are seen by many as anticipating long-term relationships, established for strategic purposes. Further, alliances must generate tangible value, leading to win-win relationships. It has been found useful in organizations to have a "champion", or "boundary spanner" (Alter and Hage 1993), whose personal objective it is to see the alliance succeed. In many ways, the notion of alliances and the underlying premise of strength through cooperation, is hard for American companies and managers to accept. The sense of individualism, the desire for control, and the "not invented here" syndrome often makes American companies uncomfortable with alliances (Modic 1988). The close bonds required by alliances are inconsistent with traditional American business practices. For example, the IBM–Apple alliance will be successful only if the two companies are willing to place their need for this alliance above other priorities (Lewis 1991). They must learn to appreciate and adjust to each other's views, to rely on each other's information, and respect each other's need to maintain their own internal cultures.

**How Have Alliances Performed?**

Surveys indicate that CEOs of American companies tend to be much less positive about the results of alliances as compared to their European and Asian counterparts (Modic 1988). Especially problematic appear to be joint ventures. In examining why alliances are seen as unsuccessful, the following reasons have been suggested:

- Judging the alliance by short-term financial results rather than long-term strategic objectives
- Lack of trust among the partners
- Uneven commitment and imbalance of power
- Lower operating levels (who must make it work) not informed about or involved in the alliance
- Absence of clear understanding of partners' respective motivations and expectations
- Lack of mutually accepted performance measures. (Sherman 1992; Bowersox 1990)

Thus, lessons from other industries and other countries would suggest that alliances provide the opportunity and the potential to add value to organizations but that there are many challenges to be addressed in their development and operation. At issue now is how the concept of alliances applies in health care.

## Alliances in Health Care

> Health care reform is obviously driven by costs, access, and quality, but it seems the only thing we hear about today is cost . . . Let us not in our zeal to reform destroy the best health care system in the world.
>
> *Monroe Trout, 1993*

> I think the Clinton plan is like a mule. A mule has no pride of ancestry and no hope of progeny. It has no sense of ancestry since it is a strange hybrid of capitation and fee for service. It has no hope of progeny because I don't see any way that this can work its way through the Congressional process and have any rebirth in the structure in which it was presented. However, the mule does some useful things. The mule has focused in a very political way on the advantages of capitation. Second, this has taken health care reform outside of Washington. The real activity is underway in lots of places across the country . . . The message to all of you here, alliance providers and researchers, for God's sake, get on board. The world is changing and you'd better get with it because that's the way it's going to go.
>
> *Alexander McMahon, 1993*

Alliances in health care function in a larger environment, and that larger environment is likely to be influenced by the advent of health care reform, whether federal, state, local, or privately initiated. As illustrated by the comments of Monroe Trout and Alex McMahon, health care reform is a complex undertaking involving different perspectives reflecting different degrees of urgency and levels of involvement. Yet, the underlying bases for alliances in health care are fundamentally the same as those in other industries. As stated by Zuckerman and Kaluzny (1991):

> In health care, much of the development of alliances can be traced to changes in the environment. As access to needed resources is threatened and new challenges are presented to health services providers, organizations seek to reduce their dependencies on and their uncertainty about the environment by banding together. . . . While there is clearly a growing degree of interdependency, there also remains a substantial amount of organizational independence and autonomy not possible under other interorganizational arrangements such as horizontal and vertical integration. Alliances appear to offer flexibility and responsiveness, with limited effects on the structure of participating organizations. In recent years, we

have seen these new organizations become institutionalized as a form of organizational cooperation involving organizations heretofore considered autonomous, if not competitive, entities.

These conditions apply to all parts of the American health care industry but are amplified in rural communities which are faced with the further need to find a way to keep their health care systems alive. Health care providers enter into alliances in order to gain economies of scale and scope, enhance the acquisition and the retention of key resources, expand their revenue and service base, increase their influence, and improve market position (Zuckerman and D'Aunno 1990). Alliances, transcending existing organizational arrangements, permit activities not otherwise possible, link organizations through shared strategic purpose, provide access to technologies previously unavailable, and capitalize on the growing need for organizational interdependence (Kaluzny et al. 1993; Luke, Begun, and Pointer 1989). Alliances make it possible to gain access to resources without owning them, encouraging organizations to look outward as well as inward as they struggle with how to do more with less. These issues of access and the need to look beyond immediate borders and boundaries is especially important in the rural context.

## What Are the Types of Strategic Alliances in Health Care?

Alliances in health care may be categorized into two general types. The first may be described as "lateral," where similar types of organizations, often with similar needs or dependencies, come together to achieve benefits such as economies of scale, enhanced access to scarce resources, and increased collective power (Zuckerman and D'Aunno 1990). For example, strategic alliances have formed among hospitals based on common religious preferences, particular types of hospitals, or geographic distribution. These alliances serve to take advantage of pooled resources, thereby expanding the strength and capabilities of any single members to benefit the entire membership. Their domain can be extensive, including group purchasing, insurance, information sharing, and human resource management among the array of programs and services. Such alliances— defined by Kanter (1989) as "service alliances," and capturing elements of Alter and Hage's (1993) "obligational" and "promotional" networks— will receive substantial attention throughout this book.

The second type may be described as "integrative," where organizations come together for purposes largely related to market and strategic position and securing competitive advantage. Many of the attributes of such alliances are incorporated in Kanter's (1989) formulation of "stakeholder alliances," emphasizing linkages among buyers, suppliers, and customers, Johnston and Lawrence's (1988) "value-adding partnerships," and Alter and Hage's (1993) notion of "systemic networks." These alliances may be illustrated by the emergence of "corporate partnerships," linking providers and suppliers through long-term agreements and close relationships. Of particular interest will be the role of alliances as a mechanism to build integrated delivery and financing systems (please see chapter 5 for more on this subject). Such systems are defined as regional, market-based organizations, serving the health care needs of a defined population (Shortell et al. 1993). These systems are being developed to achieve vertical as well as horizontal integration, clinical as well as administrative integration, and integration of financing as well as delivery. How such systems achieve integration is a key issue. There is reason to believe that alliances will play an important role in their evolution, representing a mechanism to achieve integration without the necessity of ownership and/or control of each of the key components. These integrative alliances will likely prove especially important in the context of an already changing environment and health care reform.

There are no geographic limitations to alliances, but rural organizations often seek alliances with urban organizations for different reasons than they would with other rural providers or companies. The geography of rural America does have an influence along with the factors we have described so far. We will consider them in more depth as we look more closely at health care.

**How Do Alliances Form?**

The formation of health care alliances may be described in terms of stages of development or a life cycle model. Each of the stages or each step in the life cycle has important implications for successful development of the alliance. For example, the Kanter (1994) formulation, which appears quite applicable, proposes that alliance formation moves through stages defined as (1) selection or courtship, (2) engagement, (3) setting up housekeeping, (4) learning to collaborate, and (5) changing within. The first stage requires each organization to undertake a realistic appraisal of itself as well as of each of the potential partners. After developing the basic agreement in the engagement stage, partners next begin to experience the difficulties making the transition to a new form and relationship. They experience problems with coordinating resources, cultural differences, opposition to the alliance, lack of understanding, and dissimilarities in operating styles. Thus, the learning stage calls for building mechanisms—strategic, tactical, cultural, interpersonal, and operational—to bridge these gaps and overcome the barriers, while the final stage involves the internal changes needed to sustain the relationship over time. In a comparable approach, Forrest (1992) proposes three stages: (1) pre-alliance, (2) agreement, and (3) implementation. Like Kanter, Forrest emphasizes the importance of careful appraisal and selection of an appropriate partner, calling for a close fit in terms of expectations, values, goals, interdependence, trust, and commitment. The agreement stage serves to specify the terms and conditions of the alliance—its scope, objectives, resource requirements, management structure, mechanisms for conflict resolution, exit terms, and performance measures. In the implementation stage, emphasis is on open communication, timely decision making, ongoing review of objectives to ensure consistency with a changing environment, and strengthened mutual commitment.

Viewing the development of alliances in terms of a life cycle, steps along the way may be portrayed as (1) emergence, (2) transition, (3) maturity, and (4) critical crossroads (D'Aunno and Zuckerman 1987b). Perhaps most applicable to the "lateral" alliances noted earlier, alliances among organizations which share ideology or resource dependencies emerge in response to environmental threats or uncertainty. Members early on develop purposes, expectations, and criteria for participation, because these steps are seen as less costly organizational alternatives and providing an opportunity to reduce dependency. In the transition, mechanisms for control, coordination, and decision making are established, and trust and commitment are heightened, setting the foundation to enable the members to secure anticipated benefits as the alliance matures and grows. In reaching the critical crossroads, members face demands for greater commitment, more centralization in decision making, and more dependence upon the alliance for needed resources, which are, to some extent, counter to the reasons for initially forming the alliance and thereby raising the specter of withdrawal or creating a more hierarchical type of organization.

Moreover, public policy is likely to greatly influence the stages of the life cycle (Longest 1994). For the past decade, public policies have stimulated the growth of alliances as they have forced a health care system into greater efficiency, or at least into imposing lower costs on public and private sector purchases of their environment. These policies have presented serious threats to some health care organizations, as illustrated by the efforts of the federal prospective payment system for reimbursing Medicare services as well as state policies restricting capitation expansion in the industry.

Much of the alliance activity of recent years may have been stimulated by threats to the continued success of organizations, or at least by the perception that these threats existed or would soon exist within their environments. These policy initiatives may change over time from an essentially negative to a more positive effect. This shift will likely stimulate even faster growth of alliance phenomena in the next few years.

One clear example of a policy shift toward such supportive effort is found in the possible changes in antitrust laws. The Clinton proposal for health care reform, for example, included specific attention to the effect of existing antitrust laws on the shift to vertically integrated delivery systems. As these systems move into place, initially conforming to the cooperative spirit characterizing alliances other forces pushing for stability and accountability will influence the nature of these relationships moving toward a more permanent interorganizational relationship based on ownership among former alliance participants. As such, we may well witness the influence of public policy shifting focus from "lateral" to "integrative" arrangement.

## How Are Alliances Operated?

Sustaining strategic alliances over time requires constant vigilance. It is clear that the relationships within alliances are fragile and characterized by constant change. The belief that members are stronger together than they would be separately is required, and securing the anticipated benefits calls for ongoing commitment of time, energy, and resources. Indeed, in contrast with the long-standing control model of organizations, alliances are more appropriately defined in terms of a commitment model. As Kanter (1989) suggests, "If an increasing amount of economic activity continues to occur across, rather than within, the boundaries defined by the formal ownership of one firm, managers will have to understand how to work with partners rather than subordinates . . ." Such a model underscores the importance of designing and communicating common purposes, developing realistic expectations, and clearly framing the domain, scope, and activities of an alliance. As the purposes of an alliance may shift over time, the operating domain and the membership may also need to be reassessed. For example, as many hospital alliances evolved from "association" type efforts toward a "business" focus, areas of activity and criteria for members had to be reassessed. Likewise, as noted by Weinstein (1993), as member organizations address their attention to building vertically integrated health care systems, the role and contribution of their national alliances (lateral) will likely be reassessed. Managing these potentially profound changes and balancing the interests of multiple constituencies is a delicate and difficult task testing the commitment, openness, and willingness to share resources and information among the members, and challenging the alliance to continually add value and provide strategic benefit.

   In a major review of the research literature on factors influencing successful collaboration among organizations, Mattessich and Monsey (undated) summarized their findings into the following six categories, suggesting *membership, communications,* and *resources* are most important:

1. **Environment**
   - History of cooperation or collaboration
   - Cooperating groups seen as leaders
   - Political/social climate is favorable.

2. **Membership**
   - Mutual respect, understanding, trust
   - Appropriate cross section of members
   - Members see collaboration as in their self-interest
   - Ability to compromise.

3. **Process/Structure**
   - Members share stake in both process and outcome
   - Multiple layers of integrated decision making
   - Flexibility in structure and methods
   - Development of clear roles, responsibilities, rights, policy guidelines
   - Adaptability to change.

4. **Communications**
   - Open and frequent communications
   - Established formal and informal communication links.

5. **Purpose**
   - Concrete, attainable long-term and short-term goals and objectives
   - Shared vision with agreed upon mission, objectives, strategy
   - Unique purpose.

6. **Resources**
   - Sufficient funds
   - Skilled conveners.

Several key themes emerge in the formation and evolution of alliances over time. First is the critical nature of the selection of an appropriate partner(s). It is seen as essential that participating members or partners of an alliance are rigorous in analyzing themselves and each other as to compatibility of goals, purposes, vision, and values, and clear indications of interdependency and complementary. Next is the underlying "glue" of alliances—trust and commitment. Partners must be candid, open, and fair in the workings of the alliance, and able to recognize that maintaining the alliance over time requires continuous nurturing. In fact, the fragile nature of alliances leaves open the question of whether they will prove to be a temporary or permanent organizational phenomenon. In large part, the willingness of members to remain will depend on their perception of how crucial the alliance is to the long-term viability of their organization. Third, the terms and terrain of the alliance must be clear, the operating rules explicit, and expectations mutually understood and agreed upon. Fourth, partners must learn from—and be strengthened by—the alliance. Alliances are seen by many as mechanisms to supplement and complement the core capabilities and knowledge of an organization, not as substitutes for internal development (Montgomery 1991). Indeed, as Lewis (1990) notes, "There is no reason to cooperate unless you grow stronger by the effort."

## How Effective Are Health Care Alliances?

As is the case with health care organizations in general, defining and assessing the effectiveness or performance of alliances is now a subject of serious attention in many organizations. The performance of alliances may be viewed along either or both of two dimensions: performance as seen by those who are key internal stakeholders within the alliance, and as seen by those who are external stakeholders, outside but affected by or otherwise interested in the alliance and its impact. To date, attention has been devoted primarily to performance or effectiveness as perceived by those within the alliance. For example, Kanter (1989) suggests that effective alliances are those characterized by the following "six I's:"

1. The alliance is seen as *Important*, with strategic significance, and getting adequate resources and management attention.
2. The alliance is seen as a long-term *Investment* from which members will be rewarded relatively equally over time.
3. The partners in the alliance are *Interdependent*, maintaining an appropriate balance of power.
4. The alliance is *Integrated* in order to manage communication and appropriate points of contact.
5. Each alliance member is *Informed* about plans for the alliance and for each other.
6. The alliance is *Institutionalized*, with supporting mechanisms that permeate interorganizational activities and facilitate the requisite trust relationships among the members.

It has been proposed that the effectiveness of health care alliances should be considered in terms of both a variance and process perspective (Kaluzny and Zuckerman 1992). The variance perspective focuses on outcomes, seeking to identify variables that explain variation in alliance performance. For example, are there identifiable changes in market share or financial performance attributable to alliance membership? This perspective is appropriate for analyzing the effects of an alliance on various indicators of performance and/or factors that account for specific stages of the adoption process. The process perspective, on the other hand, focuses on particular conditions, events, or stages in the overall development process. For example, are problems faced in the early stages of alliance development different from those experienced in later stages? This perspective is appropriate in considering the interaction among various factors as alliances and participating organizations adapt over time. Further, application of both the variance and process perspectives occurs at two levels, the first being the alliance as a whole and the second being the organizations comprising the alliance. A related approach views performance in terms of an alliance's ability to achieve stated objectives, acquire needed resources, satisfy key stakeholders, and add value to the membership (Zuckerman and D'Aunno 1990). Performance would be judged in the context of an economic dimension (e.g., economies of scale, new sources of revenue and capital), an organizational dimension (e.g., market position, human resource management), and a social/political dimension (e.g., access to care, availability of services).

In the future, we may expect the issue of effectiveness to take on greater meaning and impact. With health care reform looming on the horizon, and major structural and strategic changes already underway in the marketplace, the role of alliances as a key component in the development of integrated health care systems will be scrutinized carefully. These emerging integrated systems will be held broadly accountable for their performance, not only internally but externally as well. Such organizations will continue to evaluate themselves in order to enhance operating performance, so they will continue to assess areas such as financial performance, changes in market share, and employee satisfaction. However, they will also find increased accountability in the context of public and social demands, and will be assessed in terms of such factors as access to care, availability of services, and improvements in the health status of a defined population. Further, the unit of analysis will shift to a broader perspective, centering on episodes of care and indicators defined on a per capita basis. A new era of defining and assessing organizational performance has begun.

## Conclusions

In this opening chapter, we have briefly identified an array of issues about strategic alliances in general and within health care in particular.

While it is a beginning, it is not sufficient. Managers and researchers alike face an unrelenting flow of challenges that require attention. For example, alliances have been operationalized in a variety of industrial areas; what is the applicability to health care? Are there distinct structural characteristics associated with performance, and do these make any difference? These and other questions and challenges are addressed in the following chapters.

Building on Chapter 1, where we have identified an array of issues, Chapter 2 discusses the implications of alliance structure for health care organizations. Barry Stein, drawing on experience from other industries, suggests that the fundamental American business tenet of owning and controlling as much as possible may be a competitive disadvantage in an uncertain environment. Rather, he argues that alliances, based on varying degrees of commitment and cooperation, may be a preferred innovation to address today's strategic challenges. Noting the potential benefits of alliances—flexibility, speed of response, temporary nature, and access to new resources and markets—he underscores the challenges involved in the relationships therein. Specifically, Stein points to the need for different skills and organizational orientation, internal changes, and balancing individual and alliance interests. Alliances can be undermined by uneven levels of commitment, imbalance in power and benefits, premature trust, conflicting loyalties, insufficient integration, and undermanagement.

The next three chapters focus on the development, structure, and impact on alliances within health care. The developmental issues are presented in Chapter 3, entitled "The Creation of a Multiorganizational Health Care Alliance," by Harry Nurkin. He begins with an historical perspective to the alliance movement identifying various levels of activity along with various types of alliance structures. The paper carefully assesses the process involved in the creation of alliance arrangements. Using this formulation the paper describes the development to the Charlotte–Mecklenburg Hospital Authority as a multiorganizational alliance of institutional and physician providers in urban and rural communities in North and South Carolina. The paper documents the development of the alliance and the challenges it faced in terms of integrating core facilities, physicians, urban and rural differences, and the challenges involving various payers in the formulation of the alliance.

Chapter 4 addresses the structure of alliances and provides a conceptual framework for understanding their operation and illustrates how that framework can be allied in analyzing the structure in one type of alliance—a rural hospital network. Data from an ongoing study are used to describe the structural dimensions of rural hospital networks and the interrelationships along these dimensions. Christianson and his colleagues define an alliance as a voluntary, loosely coupled interorganizational relationship between two or more organizations that are linked in ways that preserve the legal identity and autonomy of each as well as most of their functional autonomies. Using this definition they identify the key characteristics of structure to include size, number of participants, its geographic relationship among participants, and its complexity. The paper concludes with the identification of a series of research issues for future investigation.

Chapter 5, entitled "Strategic Alliances as a Structure for Integrated Delivery Systems," examines the movement toward vertically integrated delivery in health care, considering the rationale for and types of alliances, the benefits or performance of such integrated delivery systems, and the relationship between structure and performance. The paper carefully documents the pressures for vertical integration, addresses the challenges of definition, reviews the performance of systems to date, and concludes with the identification of critical success factors.

The final chapter presents a series of research issues that correspond to the substantive areas of the conference. Specific attention is given to underlying concerns, particularly as they relate to the relationship between research and the practicing managerial community, fundamental methodological issues, and finally, the substantive research questions that require attention.

Throughout each of these chapters, the term strategic alliance has been used inclusively rather than exclusively. Indeed, the term has been used to depict a broad array of informal and formal cooperative arrangements among and between organizations. Joint ventures, consortia, networks, quasi firms, and value-adding partnerships are but a few of the illustrations of types of alliances. These, and the others in use, vary as to the nature of the relationship, the degree of control and commitment involved, and the expectations.

The use of an inclusive term is not to say that a clear, concise definition is unimportant. It does suggest, however, that at this point in our understanding of the creation, structure, and impact of alliances within health care definitional rigor may be premature, limiting rather than facilitating the identification of research issues relevant to both the practice and research community.

## References

Alter, C., and J. Hage. 1993. *Organizations Working Together*. Newbury Park, CA: Sage Publications.

Badaracco, Jr., J. L. 1991. *The Knowledge Link: How Firms Compete Through Alliances*. Boston: Harvard Business School Press.

Behr, P., and W. Brown. 1993. "In Policy Departure, United States Joins Detroit in Industrial Alliance." Washington Post Service, *Washington Post* (29 September): F1.

Bowersox, D. J. 1990. "The Strategic Benefits of Logistics Alliances." *Harvard Business Review* 90 (July–August): 36–45.

Browning, E. S. 1990. "Renault, Volvo Agree to Enter Into Alliance. Japanese Expansion, Costs of Developing Products Lead to a Near Merger." *The Wall Street Journal* (27 February): A3, A12.

Byrne, J. A. 1993. "The Virtual Corporation." *Business Week* (8 February): 98–103.

Chipello, C. J. 1992. "Midsize Air Canada Plots Survival in Industry of Giants: Continental Bid Is Example of Alliances Sought to Secure Carrier's Future." *The Wall Street Journal* (12 November): B4.

D'Aunno, T. A., and H. S. Zuckerman. 1987a. "The Emergence of Hospital Federations: An Integration of Perspectives from Organizational Theory." *Medical Care Review* 44 (Fall): 323–43.

———. 1987b. "A Life-Cycle Model of Organizational Federations: The Case of Hospitals." *The Academy of Management Review* 12 (July): 534–45.

Forrest, J. E. 1992. "Management Aspects of Strategic Partnering." *Journal of General Management* 17 (Summer): 25–40.

Grant, L. "Partners in Profit." 1993. *U.S. News and World Report* 115 (20 September): 65–66.

Hamel, G., Y. L. Doz, and C. K. Prahalad. 1989. "Collaborate With Your Competitors—And Win." *Harvard Business Review* 89 (January–February): 133–39.

Harrigan, K. R. 1987. "Alliances: Their New Role in Global Competition." *Columbia Journal of World Business* (Summer): 67–69.

Henderson, J. C. 1990. "Plugging Into Strategic Partnerships: The Critical IS Connection." *Sloan Management Review* (Spring): 7–18.

Hudson, R. L. 1993. "European Phone Companies Reach Out for Partners." *The Wall Street Journal* (30 September): B4.

Johnston, R., and P. R. Lawrence. 1988. "Beyond Vertical Integration—The Rise of Value-Added Partnerships." *Harvard Business Review* 88 (July–August): 94–101.

Kaluzny, A. D., and H. S. Zuckerman. 1992. "Alliances: Two Perspectives for Understanding Their Effects on Health Services." *Hospital & Health Services Administration* 37 (Winter): 477–90.

Kaluzny, A. D., L. Lacey, R. Warnecke, D. Hynes, J. Morrissey, L. Ford, and E. Sondik. 1993. "Predicting the Performance of a Strategic Alliance: An Analysis of the Community Clinical Oncology Program." *Health Services Research* 28 (June): 159–82.

Kanter, R. M. 1994. "Collaborative Advantage: The Art of Alliances." *Harvard Business Review* 72 (July–August): 96–108.

Kanter, R. M. 1989. "Becoming PALs: Pooling, Allying, and Linking Across Companies." *Academy of Management Executives* 3 (August): 183–93.

Keller, J. J. 1993a. "AT&T, Cable-TV Firms Discuss Linking Their Customers in Multimedia Network." *The Wall Street Journal* (27 August): A3.

———. 1993b. "AT&T, Rivals Face Off in Wireless Wars." *The Wall Street Journal* (19 August): B1, B6.

Lewis, J. D. 1991. "Manager's Journal—IBM and Apple: Will They Break the Mold?" *The Wall Street Journal* (31 July): A10.

Lewis, J. D. 1990. *Partnerships in Profit: Structuring and Managing Alliances.* New York: The Free Press.

Longest, B. B. 1994. "Strategic Alliances in Health Care." Presentation at Association of University Programs in Health Administration, San Diego, CA, 11 June.

Luke, R. D., J. Begun, and D. Pointer. 1989. "Quasi-Firms: Strategic Inter-Organizational Forms in the Healthcare Industry." *Academy of Management Review* 14 (January): 9–19.

Mattessich, P. W., and B. R. Monsey. "Collaboration: What Makes It Work. A Review of Research Literature on Factors Influencing Successful Collaboration." Unpublished paper, Amherst H. Wilder Foundation, St. Paul, Minnesota.

McClenahen, J. S. 1987. "Alliances for Competitive Advantage." *Industry Week* (24 August): 33–36.

McMahon, A. 1993a. Comments at the National Invitational Conference on Alliances, Chapel Hill, NC, November 11–12.

Modic, S. 1988. "Alliances: A Global Economy Demands Global Partnerships." *Industry Week* (3 October): 46–52.

Montgomery, R. L. 1991. "Alliances—No Substitute for Core Strategy." *Frontiers of Health Services Management* 7 (3): 25–28.

Ohmae, K. 1989. "The Global Logic of Alliances." *Harvard Business Review* 89 (March–April): 143–54.

Pope, K. 1992. "Multimedia Alliance Is Formed By 11 Big Computer, Phone Firms." *The Wall Street Journal* (7 October): B4.

Roberts, J. L., L. Landro, and M. L. Carnevale. 1993. "Time Warner and U.S. West Plan Alliance. Investment of $2.5 Billion Aims at Melding Phone and TV Technologies." *The Wall Street Journal* (17 May): A3, A6.

Sherman, S. 1992. "Are Strategic Alliances Working?" *Fortune* (21 September): 77–78.

Shortell, S. M., D. A. Anderson, R. R. Gillies, J. B. Mitchell, and K. L. Morgan. 1993. "Building Integrated Systems: The Holographic Organization." *Healthcare Forum Journal* (March–April): 20–26.

Trout, M. 1993. Comments at the National Invitational Conference on Strategic Alliances, Chapel Hill, NC.

*The Wall Street Journal.* 1993. "Daimler–Benz Sets Plan to Expand Asia Presence." *The Wall Street Journal* (27 August): A3, B5.

Weinstein, A. 1993. Comments at the National Invitational Conference on Strategic Alliances, Chapel Hill, NC, November 11–12.

Wysocki, Jr., B. 1990. "Cross-Border Alliances Become Favorite Way To Crack New Markets: Mitsubishi and Daimler Are Just the Latest to See Gain In Swapping Know-How." *The Wall Street Journal* (26 March): A1, A12.

Zuckerman, H. S., and A. D. Kaluzny. 1991. "Strategic Alliances in Health Care: The Challenges of Cooperation." *Frontiers of Health Services Management* 7 (3): 3–23.

Zuckerman, H. S., and T. A. D'Aunno. 1990. "Hospital Alliances: Cooperative Strategy in a Competitive Environment." *Health Care Management Review* 15 (Spring): 21–30.

# 2

# Strategic Alliances: Some Lessons from Experience

## Barry A. Stein

What lessons can be learned about alliances in business and industry, in the hope that some may be transferrable to the world of health care? There can be no doubt about the validity of that proposition. Both theory and practice suggest enormous overlapping of different organizational realms, and the many lessons that can be drawn from one sector and applied to another—in every direction. Application is a not one-way street. We all need to take greater advantage of the opportunities presented for cross sector learning, treating everything we see as a series of "natural experiments."

Moreover, at this stage of alliance development it is probably more productive to be inclusive rather than exclusive in the definition of strategic alliances. It is important to focus on what works, seeking always to gain the level of insight and understanding that helps build systematic theory, since only theory allows us to transfer knowledge or practice from one realm to another with confidence. The central question is: What's helpful? More broadly, what sorts of things actually help us to reach our objectives? What is useful? What increases the probability of success? What makes it likelier that we will be able to do the things we want? Alliances—their forms, dilemmas, synergies, and challenges—are discussed and described from this operational perspective.

© 1994, Barry A. Stein.
Barry A. Stein is president of Goodmeasure, Inc.

## What Are Strategic Alliances?

All organizations need an assured supply of certain resources to succeed. That includes technology, information, distribution channels, capital, facilities and equipment, and, of course, people. Even though that access can be assured in various ways, long-established practice encourages firms to control as much as possible, and ideally, to do it by outright ownership. One reason is the American view of relationships.

"Good fences make good neighbors," poet Robert Frost wrote. The translation to management is easy. "Good fences make good corporations." If you don't own it, if it hasn't got your brand on it, you don't control it, and it might hurt you. What you own is "inside" the fence; everything else is "outside" and is to be treated as a potential enemy or adversary.

Paranoia aside, there are other reasons to own things. For one, there are thought to be large and perhaps even unlimited economies of scale and scope to be gained. For another, it obviously makes sense to own your suppliers because you can then guarantee nearly full use of their output, thus eliminating marketing, sales, and worry. Moreover, management skill coupled with access to capital—itself presumably subject to economies of scale—is thought to make it perfectly feasible for the same managers to manage anything, or for the same firm to do anything, because management is an abstract science, with lessons and skills capable of being applied to anything.

But there are major disadvantages to these mechanisms, disadvantages that become more visible, important, and unavoidable as the environment becomes more turbulent and unstable. Owning things outright in these circumstances is probably a bad idea, because it raises fixed costs to be covered no matter what the income. It also limits flexibility, which makes it harder to seize passing opportunities or adjust to changing environmental forces, such as new technology, economic adjustments, government regulation, and fickle consumers. Moreover, the supposed virtue of having a guaranteed use for your upstream supplies will turn into a disaster as soon as anyone else has "a better idea," as Ford likes to say. Even management itself, although certainly rooted in universal principles, depends strongly on experience and concrete knowledge, and is therefore not very universal at all in practice.

Thus, attention began to focus on the development of innovative but beneficial relationships among organizations—potential new and innovative solutions to competitive challenges that would make it possible for organizations to gain access to useful resources without "owning" them. These "strategic alliances," which were originally meant to differentiate between conventional arrangements—such as joint ventures, contracts, mergers and acquisitions—have today been stretched to cover every imaginable form of association among organizations.

Whatever the specifics, all this calls renewed attention to an old concept: relationships. The strategic alliance, and any of its variants, is preeminently based on identifying, developing and maintaining relationships. As market opportunities cross borders and new technologies cross industry lines, an old adage is gaining new adherents: "Success is not just what you know; it is who you know." Competence or know-how is one of the major intangible assets of a company; the other is relationships.

Relationships between companies are getting more attention today as a response to change. Some rapidly changing industries resemble an international dating game. Leading telecommunications companies are joining with domestic rivals to line up international partners before they are all taken. Cross-industry multimedia alliances connect telecoms, computer manufacturers, cable TV, filmmaking, software, and publishing.

Indeed, some companies compete on the basis of their connections with other companies. Mastercard International, for example, has grown dramatically by forming a network of banks who then issue Mastercards in their own name (an activity called "cobranding"). Mastercard has also pioneered in developing relationships with organizations other than banks: General Motors, General Electric, and even tax preparers H&R Block all issue cobranded Mastercards.

## What Do Strategic Alliances Look Like?

Whatever the rationale, the traditional logic led to gigantic companies, beloved by Wall Street and the stock market, although often exceedingly complex and cumbersome. Some of these organizations were bizarre by any standard. One of the favorites, Gulf and Western—skewered by Mel Brooks as "Engulf and Devour" in his movie, "Silent Movie"— bragged that its businesses ran from A to Z—and so they did, from apparel to zinc. This was, in short, the age of the giant conglomerate, and no one—well, hardly anyone—thought it curious or doubted those conglomerate virtues.

How times have changed. Today, the strategic challenge of doing more with less leads corporations to look outward as well as inward for solutions, improving their ability to compete without adding internal capacity. In the face of this pressure, many U.S. firms have established new cooperative agreements with other organizations at home and abroad that involve unprecedented (for them) levels of sharing and commitment. For example, General Motors has created a whole array of alliances outside the United States with other auto manufacturers, including Toyota, Isuzu, and Daewoo. All of them are also competitors. This sort of arrangement has become routine in the airline industry. United Airlines has just formed a marketing alliance, "code sharing" with Lufthansa; Delta has had one with Swissair; British Airways bought 24 percent of US Air; Continental now has a marketing agreement with Air France. Only American Airlines is left out, and that is a source of significant concern to the company.

In general, three sorts of strategic alliances are possible: (1) The partners can *Pool* resources with others; (2) they can *Ally* to exploit an opportunity; or (3) they can *Link* their systems in a partnership. In short, they can become better "PALs" with other organizations—from venture collaborators to suppliers, service contractors, customers, and even unions. Their benefits and costs differ. The first type involves the least overlap and smallest sphere of cooperation among partner organizations; the third involves the most. Yet that kind of partnership also seems to have the greatest potential for enduring benefits to its partners.

Such alliances became very visible as the 1980s progressed. By 1987, Ford had made more than 40 coalitions with outside commercial entities. Some—by no means all—were in Japan. Even so, there was so much traffic between Detroit and Tokyo in general that many U.S.—Tokyo flights now originate in Detroit rather than Chicago. In some sectors, there were more joint domestic ventures announced in almost any single year in the 1980s than in the previous 15 to 20 years combined.

In alliance pools, or consortia, organizations with a similar need, often in the same industry, band together to create a new entity to fill that need for all of them—an industry research consortium, for example. The service is one that is too expensive or difficult for a single organization to provide alone, and it cannot be purchased on the open market. So several ally to establish a new organization, which they control, to meet the need.

The resulting consortium requires the fewest changes in each partner of the three types discussed here, because interdependence among partner organizations is low; at the same time, the difficulty of getting the diverse partners to agree on the service that suits all of them can make these entities very hard to manage and loss of interest or commitment a common problem. Each member gains some of the benefits of larger scale, while retaining its independence with respect to every other activity. Consortia are thus especially attractive when the development of new technology is particularly important and costly.

The National Cooperative Research Act of 1984 loosened antitrust restrictions to allow joint development through the prototype stage. By 1985, at least 40 Research and Development (R&D) consortia were being organized nationwide, taking a number of forms. For example, Pradco, organized by Borg–Warner, Dresser Industries, Ingersoll-Rand, and TransAmerica to design new boiler pumps for power plants, spreads research tasks among its own members. The 33 members of the Semiconductor Research Corporation, including AT&T, GM, IBM, and DuPont, sponsor research at a number of universities, as do the seven members of the International Partners in Glass Research.

Still other consortia have created new, stand-alone organizations. Two of the better-publicized examples are Bellcore and MCC. In 1984, the regional telephone companies spun off from AT&T formed Bellcore, a research center with a $900 million budget established to carry out research and development benefiting all seven companies. In 1983, 21 computer companies formed the Microelectronics and Computer Corporation in Texas, an industrywide research center with a budget of up to $700 million over ten years and a staff of 400, drawn in part from member companies.

While R&D consortia are by far the most identifiable, they are not the only examples of this form of organizational cooperation. In 1986, 34 companies, including IBM, General Electric, and Chase Manhattan, allocated $10 million each to form American Casualty Excess Insurance Company, a company that would provide them with insurance they could not otherwise obtain. Even more significant are consortia designed to allow smaller companies to gain joint purchasing or market clout— such as the Independent Grocers of America. Of course, as that example shows, these are by no means new ideas, but their relevance and breadth of application is growing rapidly.

The second type of strategic alliance—the *Ally* in PALs—is often "opportunistic," with both its positive and negative connotations. Joint business ventures are the generic example. The partners get from each other a competence that helps them move more quickly toward their own business goals. For example, CBS formed a number of joint ventures; with IBM and Sears to develop and market Videotex, an electronic information service; with Twentieth Century Fox to develop videotapes; and with Columbia Pictures (Coca-Cola) and Home Box Office (Time Inc.) to develop motion pictures.

Another version of the allying approach is more passive; not all are aimed at immediate or specific ventures. Rather, they provide a basis for learning from one another without initially doing anything different. There are many examples in the telecommunications industry, often structured around minority investments. For example, Ameritech is part owner of a New Zealand cable system, a device that allows them to participate in a related line of business in which they have great interest but were temporarily blocked from directly operating. (Recent court rulings have probably overthrown that restriction.)

Stakeholder alliances, the prototypical *Link* form, are based on pre-existing interdependence. They are "complementary" coalitions between a number of stakeholders in a business process who are involved in different stages of the value-creation chain. Stakeholders are those groups on which an organization depends—the people who can help it achieve its goals or can stop it dead in its tracks. They include suppliers, customers, and employees.

**Suppliers.** Facing imperatives to cut costs and improve quality, leading American companies are creating closer relationships with their suppliers. Even before its purchase by AT&T, NCR had a particularly well-developed set of alliances with its key vendors, designed to ensure that the partnership works to their mutual benefit. To maintain its critical dependence on Intel, NCR established an "Intel advocate" role, which was so effective that Intel assigned its own advocate to manage its relationship with NCR.

In a variation of this, more and more organizations are forming "supply linked" alliances with other, *competitive*, organizations. IBM, in a remarkable turnabout from its traditional practice, contracted to provide PCs for Inmac Corporation, one of its direct competitors in the mail order computer business. The new computers will be labeled with the Inmac insignia, but will be publicly known to be of IBM manufacture. According to the president of Comcast Corporation, a cable operator, the same thing is likely to happen in telecommunications as alliances proliferate. "Some places you'll cooperate, some places you'll compete." These deals can get complicated. Asahi, a leading Japanese beer producer, has joined with Molson USA to help sell its product. Molson is itself a subsidiary of a Canadian brewer, 40 percent of which is owned by Foster's of Australia, of which in turn 17 percent is owned by Asahi.

**Customers.** Partnerships with customers are the flip side of supplier partnerships. There have always been strategic advantages to staying close to customers, but many newer alliance forms go well beyond traditional methods for doing that. For example, IBM won a $200 million contract for office systems at Ford by departing from its past modus operandi with customers. Ford had "asked to start with a blank piece of paper and redefine how the relationship between the two companies should work. So we did," reported an IBM executive. Under the new relationship, a team of 50 Ford and IBM employees designed the system to fit Ford's needs—and IBM's. Xerox is now actively exploring similar arrangements, seeking to shift internal functions to vendors.

**Employees.** A third form of complementary partnership is that between labor organizations and management to set policies or administer jointly an area of company operations. The planning for General Motors' Saturn subsidiary, for example, was conducted jointly with the United Auto Workers. The results included a network of management–union committees running the plant, with representatives of the UAW on all relevant committees.

## When Are Strategic Alliances Useful?

Alliances are temporary rather than permanent, they promote organizational flexibility, and their benefits are normally unavailable or more costly if each organization tries to act on its own.

These are not trivial benefits, especially in an environment that is itself changing so rapidly, in part by steadily raising the standard of competitive performance for nearly every organization, that the virtues of flexibility and access to an ever broadening array of resources and markets are important. This is not an issue for business alone. These trends are as visible in the nonprofit sector.

Alliances tend to be particularly important in unfamiliar markets. In the case of foreign companies, organizations are sometimes required by law to have a local partner. Even where that is not true, it is often still sound practice to build strong local alliances because local knowledge and connections are valuable. This is one of the most obvious advantages of alliances. Philip Morris spent $200 million to buy a minority share in Kazakhstan, its third alliance within the former Soviet Union. (The others are in Russia and Lithuania.)

Even organizations serving purely local markets can take advantage of network ties outside their traditional boundaries to tap broader or perhaps global sources of materials, capital, or expertise, as well as to nurture closer relationships with major customers. This is by no means an issue only for small organizations. Boeing, in deciding how to move forward with its new 777 airliner, developed a network of suppliers not only for actual components and subsystems, but for capital as well. The end result is that 65 percent of the costs are being borne outside Boeing itself. Companies also benefit from the endorsement of others with high reputation; organizations, like people, are often known by the company they keep.

Yet, despite examples like these, the fragility of some kinds of partnerships is as striking as their growing frequency and extent. Critics argue, for example, that many joint ventures or formal alliances are disbanded or fall short of expectations. Of course, dissolution of a partnership is not de facto evidence of failure; it may mean that the alliance *achieved* its purpose. But even for those that work, the management complexities are enormous. "The rewards of these things must be incredible to justify all the extra short-term costs that go along with them," said one participant at a seminar discussing organizational cooperation. Yet for organizations forming alliances, the long-term rewards can be very tangible.

Take for example SunHealth, one of a number of large cooperative alliances among hospitals—pools—whose benefits are very substantial. The SunHealth Alliance includes over 250 hospitals, some of which are themselves members of multihospital systems. Among the direct benefits to members are substantial reductions (over 15 percent) in supply costs. A recent example of a link alliance is an innovative arrangement among six contract metal-stamping firms in the Minneapolis area. The companies—which directly compete with one another—exchange operating information, down to the machine operator level, so that each has the opportunity to learn from the others. Here, too, the gains have often been substantial. One firm making sunroofs for General Motors' Saturn was able to increase its production from 40 per day to 400, with "only a slight increase in its work force" (Banerjee 1994). Why would competitors help one another? Because otherwise all of them might fail, in part as a result of increased competition from outside the region, and even the USA.

## How Do Alliances Actually Work?

Overall, alliances offer enough potential innovation and value to encourage organizations to seek ways to take advantage of them. However, that is not simply a matter of applying a routine formula; it requires both different skills and a different organizational orientation. Moreover, the organizations involved must themselves bring some innovative capacity of their own to the relationship with their alliance partners, both in instituting an alliance and in managing it, or it is unlikely to succeed.

Obviously, such strategic partnerships in general form because they are expected to bring value to the organizations entering into them. But there is a high possible cost. The very existence of the alliance also changes how the individual organizations operate and how their managers manage, and the stronger, more lasting, and far-reaching the alliance, the greater the corresponding internal changes. Unless partnership activities can be segregated from other organizational activities (as in the formation of a stand-alone, arm's-length unit), the need to relate to partners in ways that reap the benefits of partnership inevitably changes how each partner operates.

This creates a dilemma, a situation that requires constant management. It is, in that sense, very unlike more traditional arrangements. For example, when a company is acquired, there is ordinarily no choice about whether to stay "in the family" or not. That choice has been foreclosed by the deal. But many alliances are different. In them, there are usually choices that can be exercised by either party. There is therefore an incentive for both (or all) parties to make sure the relationship continues to provide value not only to them but also to their partners. Thus, the management focus for each has to be broader than in the usual case.

At the same time, and in other respects, members have to put their needs foremost, and in some cases alliances may even make it more difficult for them to make important internal adjustments. For example, alliances increasing vertical integration may create organizational rigidities that prevent innovation—as in the case of former external vendors who gain so much security they lose the motivation to innovate. Alliances may also make it difficult to keep up if industry technology changes dramatically—as in the case of auto makers who, because they were vertically integrated with carburetor manufacturers, were slower to change when electronic fuel injectors began to replace them. While the power to set terms and conditions may come with ownership or domination, this strategy can also limit the flexibility required for innovation and rapid technological progress.

Yet a great deal of important strategic improvement in competitiveness, both from technical and non-technical sources, may be taking place in the coalition itself—rather than "inside" the "boundaries" of one organization. This makes it especially important to understand what it takes to manage organizational partnerships—why so many, begun with high hopes, fail to produce what they promised. Partnerships, in fact, represent one of the ultimate organizational balancing acts: a way for one partner to leverage its own resources by joining forces with others, a way of encouraging others to invest in developing things that will bring future benefits to the first organization. In the future, as an increasing amount of economic activity occurs across rather than within the formal ownership boundaries of one firm, managers will have to understand how to work with partners rather than subordinates. And that alone promises a revolutionary change in the way organizations operate.

Perhaps this issue—the management difficulties they entail—is one of the major reasons that the number of interorganizational partnerships is still relatively small. For each binary partnership, there are three areas of management challenge: (1) managing the inherently fragile relationship between partners, and (2) and (3) managing the changes in each of the partners' own organizations. Until these new management challenges are mastered, organizations will not easily be able to take advantage of the benefits of strategic partnerships, or gain from them the potential benefits they offer.

But perhaps the most critical point is the inability to translate management approaches used in conventional situations, where control is legitimate and authoritative, and can be exercised over people and groups.

These situations link people and groups together only by their personal commitment. This inability to translate is both good news and bad news.

The bad news is that most people will have to learn new skills and develop new routines if they are to succeed. The old ways just won't work, and many alliances suffer or collapse because of it. Here's the good news. In most cases, the old ways aren't working too well even in conventional organizations within their own traditional boundaries, because increasingly, people's commitment is needed to get any contribution beyond the minimum—which is competitively unhelpful. And in the future, these new competencies will be absolutely necessary.

*The role of structure.* When people begin to adapt to working with a partner, they also have to recognize that the rest of their organization is subject to a different system. People on both sides look suspiciously or longingly at the arrangement. What *important external relationships* means for managers, then, is first, that they have to juggle more factors, allow for variation in their systems, and explain why people and projects are treated differently; and second, that they also have to be able to manage, under circumstances where they don't directly control the resources on which they depend. The challenge is to manage teams consisting of people from other organizations and who therefore are very independent and subject to another set of managers.

The sign of an effective relationship between organizations lies not in whether the people involved feel good about *their* relationship, but in the value of the specific operational links and activities to the organizations involved. After all, people move around all the time in business, so a relationship based purely on personal links is risky. If any one person gets too central, it's worth looking more closely to see what each organization really wants from the other. An obvious example is shown by what happened to Disney's proposed venture with Henson Associates, which fell through completely after the unexpected death of Jim Henson.

The message is simple. Be friendly, develop trust, and aim toward good working relationships with the "other" folks, but trust isn't the only basis for an effective relationship. Clear and explicit agreements, structures, and procedures are essential as well because they provide a solid foundation for the alliance. One of the most common reasons that alliances built on mainly *personal* relationships collapse is that too much is expected of them. It's a bit like the sign that used to hang in neighborhood grocery stores—when there were only neighborhood grocery stores. The sign said, "In God we trust. All others pay cash."

This is why it's so important to create formal agreements, sign contracts, create new or joint organizational vehicles, adjust compensation systems, establish formal decision mechanisms, and set up measurement and tracking devices. These are a few structures and systems that are the real heart of lasting relationships among organizations. And the more strategic the relationship is expected to be, the more important the structures are. However, arrangements that are hard to untangle or modify can undercut one of the key virtues of alliances: their flexibility.

In organizations, as in any human system, people not only get used to doing things a certain way, but they are encouraged by characteristics of the system itself in the sense that some things are easy to do—and hence become more likely to become habitual—while others are more difficult and are thus less likely to become habitual. Organizations succeed mainly when they are able to encourage good habits—habits that are helpful and constructive. Even though this is true in general, it has particular relevance where people's behavior needs to change in fairly dramatic ways, as when the system itself differs dramatically from past experience.

That particularly applies to strategic alliances, which are significantly different than conventional organizations—different in their structures, in the principles that underly them, in what is required of people who operate within them, and in their formation and management. Moreover, in actual operation, alliances cover a very wide range of variation in practice, some that constitute relatively minor adjustments from traditional type organizations to others involving extensive changes, where habits and behaviors need major and deliberate modification. For that reason, effectiveness in conceiving, setting up, and taking advantage of alliances requires consistent adjustments in many different realms.

It is not enough to simply create an excellent structure, or to train people very well, or to revise the linkages between the organization and its stakeholders, or to communicate the purposes of the new idea within and without the organization. Rather, all are necessary, and all must be carried out in concert. Change can be difficult because of these interconnections; thus, changing one thing and not others may not produce the expected results or any progress whatsoever.

*The role of management.* Many situations typical of alliances constitute true dilemmas, which can make people feel as if they were in a state of suspension between two (or more) organizations. Managing them, not surprisingly, requires more care, more sophistication, more finely tuned structures, and more management than does the state of being completely inside one organization or another. We heard someone recently say, in connection with a new alliance just in the process of being launched, that: "We're looking for this to get to the point where it won't need managers anymore." Well, that person is going to be sadly disappointed. The alliance may not need *managers* any more—that is, people with that title and its traditional perks—but it is certainly going to need *management*, and probably more of it. It is in the nature of dilemmas to need attention, and that attention requires people with new skills and competencies—for example, in building relationships and in working effectively without authority.

Of course, organizations and management issues often produce dilemmas. Success, for example, can encourage the very things that can lead to failure. These dilemmas are not avoidable. Indeed, it has been said that an organization can be defined as an instrument for the production of dilemmas. In alliances, this can be particularly tricky. For example, people often find themselves not only doing some new things, but also doing many of the same things they did before, but whereas they were once completely internal to their organization, they now involve people from other organizations. Despite the obvious advantages in leverage, in reduced fixed costs, and in flexibility, the costs may appear high (as well as eminently avoidable.) One requisite of effective alliances, then, is the ability to manage these inevitable dilemmas, and confidence in that ability is one of the considerations in a willingness to create an alliance.

Little if any of this is new. Despite all the recent talk about strategic alliances, there have always been examples of innovative organizational arrangements, but they typically emerged as solutions to specific—even unique—problems rather than as applications of a broadly useful principle. In operation, however, they provide us with a rich reservoir of experience in managing them. In one case, a firm heavily involved in sensitive government work—call it Electro—had only one customer, a unit of the U.S. Department of Defense (DoD). The stringent security requirements for everyone involved literally forced the development, over time, of an extraordinarily effective operating organization that was a de facto mixture of elements and people from both entities.

Although in principle Electro was a contractor to the DoD, which for its part was legally responsible for managing the contract and the relationship, the operational practice reflected a very different relationship. Whether paid by Electro or the DoD, and independent of their formal position in their organization, those involved in the contract were more truly members of the pseudo organization than of their nominal employer, they had much closer relationships with others in the new entity, personally and professionally, than they did with people in "their own" companies, and the work they did was not at all a function of their organizational home base.

In short, the boundary of this organization was very different than the legal one, and those inside the circle had little to do with those outside it. This pseudo organization was very successful for over ten years, until the entire project was terminated. However, it arose out of the special conditions facing the partner and was always a source of slightly forced jokes, because it was seen as an inappropriate and unmanageable accident rather than a desirable and effective innovation. That, more than anything else, may be the greatest difference between then and now. But the same lessons about the sources of both success and failure can be seen in the Electro-DoD situation as well as in the more deliberate current alliances. Chief among these are the factors that render success unlikely—call them dealbusters—and that need to be managed carefully.

## Dealbusters: Lessons Learned

All relationships have vulnerabilities. But for alliances, the issues arise more often, and their impact is more severe. Alliances are more fragile, and the vulnerabilities can threaten the relationship. They are dynamic entities, even more so than single corporations, because of the complexity of the interests forming them. They evolve; parameters are never completely clear at first, nor do partners want to commit fully at first, if ever. The sources of vulnerability turn out to be rooted in a set of common "dealbusters," identified by Kanter in her award-winning book, *When Giants Learn to Dance* (1989).

### Uneven Levels of Commitment

The vulnerability of alliances to strategic shifts simply points to another source of fragility: differences in the commitment of the partners to their joint activity. For one partner, the alliance may be central to its business, but for the other, it may simply be peripheral. Unevenness of commitment stems from basic differences between organizations entering into partnerships, and these differences can cause other inequalities of power.

*Power imbalances 1: Resources.* When richer organizations ally with poorer organizations, the richer ones often end up subsidizing the poorer ones in conducting the activities that will allow them to hold up their end of the partnership. For example, Mazda has over 100 full-time engineers who work inside suppliers' organizations, educating the suppliers' staff, making sure their procedures match Mazda's, and instituting such programs as statistical process control.

*Power imbalances 2: Information.* Two kinds of information are required for effective partnership participation: technical knowledge that permits contributions to decision making, and "relationship" knowledge—understanding of the partner, knowledge of partnership activities, political intelligence—that provides the background for successful negotiations.

A balance of power certainly helps sustain a partnership, and at least one company has taken the next step, attributing economic benefits to the avoidance of power imbalances. Corning Glass has long been known as a particularly successful practitioner of alliances, and Corning executives are particularly concerned with equalizing power with their venture partners rather than monopolizing it. "Mutuality" is the operative word. Former Vice Chairman Thomas MacAvoy declared, "If I tried to gain the upper hand in a joint venture, my boss would reprimand me."

## Imbalances of Benefits

Even if allies begin on an equal footing with all parties close together in resources and information, the structure of the deal may still favor some over others. *The New York Times* once branded foreign alliances the "high tech giveaway," claiming that they resulted in a "largely one-way flow of technology and other critical skills from the United States to foreign nations, especially Japan."

## Premature Trust: Absence of Institutional Safeguards

"Even paranoids have real enemies." Sometimes parties to an alliance are naive in trusting their partners too soon, before a solid basis for trust is established and without any legal or contractual safeguards. They give away too much. For example, Acme–Cleveland Corporation licensed Mitsubishi Heavy Industries to manufacture and sell one of its machine tools, only to watch Mitsubishi become its rival in the U.S. market. Somehow Acme–Cleveland had "understood" that Mitsubishi was going to confine its efforts to Asia.

## Conflicting Loyalties

The flexibility inherent in *allying with* other organizations rather than *merging with* them is sometimes accompanied by a singular drawback. Unless the agreement specifies an exclusive relationship, with all the additional costs that entails, each party to the partnership may still maintain relationships outside the alliance, including relationships with competitors. These other ties pose conflicts of time and attention and raise questions of how proprietary, "insider" or potentially harmful information is to be handled.

## Undermanagement

Some partnerships flounder because of difficulties of implementation and execution. They are not organized or managed well. It has been reported that nearly half the time top management spends on the average joint venture goes into creating it. Another quarter goes into developing the plan, and less than 8 percent into setting up management systems. When former Transportation Secretary Drew Lewis was brought in by American Express to head Warner Amex Cable Communications in 1983, he found "a company out of control. You had two companies with diverse views on almost everything that came up, and we had people all over us from both companies trying to call every shot."

**Insufficient Integration and the
Absence of a Common Framework**

Without mechanisms that allow the partners to work together, it is difficult for an alliance to live up to its promise. In addition to potential differences in strategies, commitment, and power, partner organizations also differ initially in organizational structures, processes, procedures, and style. Insufficient integration has both a short-term and a long-term cost. In the short run, it means that the infrastructure is not in place for the partnership to carry out its activities efficiently and effectively. In the long run, it means that the partners have not developed a sufficient stake in each other—the kind of stake built up by years of tailoring systems to fit those of the ally—to reinforce mutual commitment.

# A Brief Conclusion

What makes alliances actually work? What skills and organizational arrangements are helpful or even necessary? First, there needs to be a commitment to change, because when the deal is struck all sides of an agreement must actively live with what has been put together, even though it is almost always easier to do things "the way we've always done them"—at least in the short run. Successful alliances also require continuing change as they adjust to gain the new benefits, maneuver to take advantage of learning, respond to new contingencies or seize emerging opportunities, maintain flexibility while ensuring mutual satisfaction, and prepare themselves for the necessary rearrangement of resources or formal modification of the agreement, if need be. Alliances work best—perhaps they only work at all—when they are actively managed, when people spend time at the task of managing them, and when those management processes are structured. They do not work well—perhaps they do not work at all—when they are left on their own, when few people or components are actively involved in them, and when no time is spent and no attention paid.

The relationship between medical professionals and health care organizations provides a set of spectacular examples of interesting and unconventional alliances. In health care, the term "strategic alliance" seems very generally to be used almost exclusively for associations among hospitals or other large formal organizations, such as VHA or SunHealth, or between private practices and HMOs. But the relationship between physicians and hospitals has almost always reflected particularly interesting and exotic instances of a whole variety of alliances. These are in fact very good examples of long-standing alliances reflecting lessons that are being overlooked. Indeed, the current movement towards physicians as employees is a step toward a less distinctive, less innovative, and less flexible state. One must wonder whether this actually constitutes progress.

In short, people in health care probably have more experience with unconventional relationships and alliances than most people. This doesn't mean those arrangements couldn't be improved, because they seem to have rested on personal and collegial relationships, rooted in very strong professional and legal norms and institutions. Ultimately, these relationships must go beyond the purely personal. But alliances, like all organizations, need to work at all levels, for everyone directly involved, and for clients, patients, and other stakeholders. The course of wisdom is to develop, extend, and support systematic mechanisms and enabling structures. When alliances become institutionalized, and thus less dependent for their effectiveness on unique individuals, their survival will be more likely.

This is perhaps the ultimate dilemma: to transcend the traditional emphasis on individual relationships, by making them simultaneously less and more important—less important for the institution per se, and more important for the effective delivery of health through maximum utilization of every individual's strengths.

# References

Banerjee, N. 1994. "Firms Analyze Rivals to Help Fix Themselves." *The Wall Street Journal* (3 May): B1.
Kanter, R. M. 1994. "Collaborative Advantage: The Art of Alliances." *Harvard Business Review* (July–August): 96–108.
———. 1989. *When Giants Learn to Dance*. NY: Simon & Schuster.

# The Commentaries: A Summary

Four commentaries address Barry Stein's chapter. The first discusses the uses and appropriateness of models to guide organizational research. The other three focus on the application and implications of strategic alliances within a variety of health care settings. W. RICHARD SCOTT, in his commentary, states that "theoretical models reveal and they conceal." That is, theoretical models focus attention on some aspects of a phenomenon and thereby defocalize other aspects. Historically, our models have focused on guiding research that stresses the function of organizational boundaries—boundaries that buffer the technical core, thereby protecting the organization from uncertainty and hostile environments. More recent models have shifted attention from "buffering" to "bridging"— the ways in which organizations strategically connect to aspects of their environment. Specifically he warns that while alliances are an important bridging mechanism, they are only one of many possible bridges linking organizations. Moreover, he goes on to suggest that perhaps the notion of alliances presents a sharper demarcation between traditional organizations and outside elements than exist in reality, implies an overly rationalistic view of decision making and employs an organizationally eccentric view of the world.

The remaining commentaries provide illustration of alliance structures and operations within health care. TIM SIZE discusses the importance of alliances within health care and describes an alliance between two existing alliances, The Community Physicians Network and the Rural Wisconsin Hospital Cooperative. GERALD MARTIN suggests that alliances are nothing new at all, in fact are as old as humanity itself. He goes on to illustrate the role and development of various types of alliances, concluding with the description of an alliance involving Federal Express and Abbott Laboratories and the lessons that such activity provides within the context of health care reform. Finally, NEAL NEUBERGER takes us into the future and discusses how alliance linkages and their success are contingent on new communications and information technology.

# W. Richard Scott

Theoretical models reveal and they conceal. They focus attention on some aspects of phenomena we wish to understand and thereby defocalize other aspects. If we are smart, or lucky, our models assist us by illuminating the more significant or salient aspects. If we guess wrong, we learn little—or worse, misunderstand the situations we confront.

For many years, models guiding organizations' research have stressed the function of organizational boundaries—boundaries that buffer the technical core, that select appropriate personnel and resources, that ward off enemies and noxious elements—that, in short, protect the organization from uncertain and possibly hostile environments.

While early arguments stressed the negative features of environments and the virtues of high walls to protect organizational values and systems, more recent models have emphasized that, as open systems, organizations are dependent upon, interdependent with, and indeed, permeated by the environments in which they operate. Attention has shifted from "buffers" to "bridges"—the ways in which organizations strategically connect themselves to aspects of the environment that can affect them, either for good or ill. Not surprisingly, other organizations are among the most important connections that organizations make. (Thompson 1967).

The focus of this conference is one such connection—or, as Stein quickly convinces us, one family of connections, since strategic alliances come in a variety of forms and flavors. I suppose one issue this conference can't help but address is how widely to stretch this category. Do we include as types of strategic alliances joint ventures, affiliations, memberships in consortia or confederations, and quasi firms?

Even though the strategic alliance offers sufficient variety and complexity to occupy us fully during the conference, it is still important to remind ourselves at the outset that strategic alliances are only one of many possible types of bridges linking organizations. Others include:

---

W. Richard Scott is a professor of sociology at Stanford University.

"informal" understandings regarding such issues as domain, pricing, and market segmentation; contracts, both long and short term; hierarchical contracts that build in a variety of inspection and renegotiation rights (Stinchcombe 1985); co-optation arrangements such as interlocking directorates and external advisory boards; mergers and acquisitions; membership in industry-wide trade associations, and other field-level efforts to "concretize" activities within a given arena (Streeck and Schmitter 1985); not to overlook the wide variety of interpersonal linkages, including membership overlaps, that exist at the level of individual participants of organizations. One of the more important challenges confronting students of organizations is to explain why, when, and under what conditions one rather than another of these bridges will be constructed (Pfeffer and Salancik 1978; Scott 1992).

Returning, however, to the bridge of current interest—the bridge that has brought us together on this occasion—I believe that Stein, in his typically colorful manner, has provided us with a very useful discussion of the somewhat novel challenges posed by strategic alliances for company managers: How they must learn to manage independent partners, in contrast to dependent employees, and how they must learn to manage activities occurring across firm boundaries as well as those occurring within them. He also helpfully describes how these challenges change over time as the relation moves from romance to routine.

The implicit theoretical model employed reveals much of interest. However, it also conceals. First, his arguments assume a sharper demarcation between traditional organizations and outside elements than exists in reality. Dichotomies like organizations/environments and markets/hierarchies have done considerable mischief in this regard. They fail to recognize the variable and multiplex nature of organizational boundaries—the many significant relations and flows that cross and connect various parts of the organization to its context. The model puts too much emphasis on ownership and membership boundaries, causing it to overstate the amount of control exhibited by managers within the boundaries of the organizations and to understate how much control some organizations have on "external" units and events. Boundaries are looser and formal boundaries are less able to account for variations in influence and control than their model of organizations suggests. Most managers of most conventional organizations must attempt to manage not only within but across the formal boundaries of their firm.

Secondly, Stein implicitly adopts a strategic, intendedly rational model of decision making. In this version, managers are forming strategic alliances in order to "exploit an opportunity," to "get from each other a competence that helps them move more quickly toward their own business goals," to "obtain local knowledge and connections," and to "tap broader or perhaps global sources of materials, capital, or expertise, as well as to nurture closer relationships with major customers." Such arguments may assume more individual manager and firm-level rationality than is warranted. These are the same sorts of managers and types of firms that Stein accuses of earlier embracing a faulty logic leading to the creation of "gigantic companies." With the benefit of hindsight, we now recognize that "the logic of growth" was rational for some companies but not for others. May not the same be true for today's strategy of creating multiple strategic alliances? Alternative theoretical models, such as institutional theory, call attention to the extent that decisions are shaped by conformity to wider cultural beliefs regarding what actions are viewed by others as "rational." (Meyer and Rowan, 1977; DiMaggio and Powell 1983; Meyer and Scott 1983)

Third and finally, the model Stein implicitly employs is an organization-centric one in which the world is viewed from the standpoint of a given company and its managers. We are told that "members [the companies involved in an alliance] have to put their [own] needs foremost," and that "the sign of an effective relationship between organizations lies not in whether the people involved feel good about their relationship, but in the value of the specific operational links and activities to the organizations involved."

The theoretical model employed is one that gives privileges to *existing* organizations and asks what is in their best interests. Now if you are managing one of these companies, or if you are a consultant to one of them, this is not an unexpected perspective to embrace. But if you are an analyst attempting to understand the determinants and effects of these relations, it is a limiting one.

If we go up one or two levels of analysis to the organizational population or organizational field level (Hannan and Freeman 1977, 1989; Dimaggio and Powell 1983; Scott and Meyer 1991)—where we focus on not single organizations but on collections of similar organizations (populations) or on networks of dissimilar, functionally interdependent organizations (fields)—we may see these links not simply as bridges between existing organizations, but potentially as the beginning of new forms, as well as the end of some existing forms. Many of today's strategic alliances will be tomorrow's new companies. And could it be that the recent growth of strategic alliances represents an attempt by existing organizations to transcend the limits of their current structure and to move in the direction of becoming "network" forms: new types of organizations? (Powell 1990; Nohria and Eccles 1992). Such transformations, to the extent that they occur, will not necessarily be in the "best interests" of existing firms, which are likely to be reconfigured if not transcended by these developments, but will create new forms, and thereby new interests.

The theoretical model embraced by Stein to describe the nature, the management, and the effects of strategic alliances needs to be supplemented by other models, based on alternative assumptions and operating at different levels of analysis, if we are to better understand these complex new developments in the world of organizations.

# References

DiMaggio, P. J., and W. W. Powell. 1983. "The Iron Cage Revisited: Institutional Isomorphism and Collective Rationality in Organization Fields." *American Sociological Review* 48: 147–60.

Hannan, M. T., and J. Freeman. 1977. "The Population Ecology of Organizations." *American Journal of Sociology* 82: 929–64.

Hannan, M. T., and J. Freeman. 1989. *Organizational Ecology*. Chicago: University of Chicago Press.

Meyer, J. W., and B. Rowan. 1977. "Institutionalized Organizations: Formal Structure as Myth and Ceremony." *American Journal of Sociology* 83: 340–63.

Meyer, J. W., and W. R. Scott. 1983. *Organizational Environments: Ritual and Rationality*. Beverly Hills, CA: Sage.

Nohria, N., and R. G. Eccles. 1992. *Networks and Organizations: Structure, Form, and Action*. Boston: Harvard Business School Press.

Pfeffer, J., and G. R. Salancik. 1978. *The External Control of Organizations*. New York: Harper & Row.

Powell, W. W. 1990. "Neither Market nor Hierarchy: Network Forms of Organizations." In *Research in Organizational Behavior* vol. 12, edited by B. M. Staw and L. L. Cummings, 295–336. Greenwich, CT: JAI Press.

Scott, W. R. 1992. *Organizations: Rational, Natural and Open Systems*, 3d ed. Englewood Cliffs, NJ: Prentice-Hall.

Scott, W. R., and J. W. Meyer. 1991. "The Organization of Societal Sectors: Propositions and Early Evidence." In *The New Institutionalism in Organizational Analysis*, edited by W. W. Powell and P. J. DiMaggio, 108–40. Chicago: University of Chicago Press.

Stinchcombe, A. L. 1985. "Contracts as Hierarchical Documents." In *Organization Theory and Project Management*, edited by A. L. Stinchcombe and C. Heimer, 121–71. Bergen, Norway: Universitetsforlaget.

Streeck, W., and P. C. Schmitter. 1985. "Community, Market, State—and Associations? The Prospective Contribution of Interest Governance to Social Order." In *Private Interest Government: Beyond Market and State*, edited by W. Streeck and P. Schmitter, 1–29. Beverly Hills, CA: Sage.

Thompson, J. D. 1967. *Organizations in Action*. New York: McGraw Hill.

# Tim Size

The American experience gives us many images, often contradictory. Barry Stein in "Strategic Alliances: Some Lessons from Experience" immediately takes us back to a New England farm to emphasize our comfort with individual control and ownership: "Good fences make good neighbors." But there is more to Robert Frost's poem "Mending Wall": "I let my neighbor know beyond the hill; and on a day we meet to walk the line and set the wall between us once again. . . ." Even this American icon to self-sufficiency is expressed within the cultural context of selective cooperation being used to maintain a local sense of self.

While alliances or collaborative enterprises have not been our primary experience, strategic alliances are not new to the American landscape:

> More than 100 health care cooperatives have been formed in rural America during this century. In various forms and with varying levels of success, rural medical cooperatives have experienced periods of popularity throughout the twentieth century. Today, modified versions of the pure cooperative model are resurfacing as corporate vehicles to bring needed health care services to medically underserved regions of America. (Kushner 1991)

On the other hand, a last reference to one of our great traditional poets puts it well: "Two roads diverged in a wood, and I—I took the one less traveled by, and that has made all the difference." Those of us who have been attracted to cooperative models in health care have clearly been on a less traveled path; we have struggled to understand and develop alternatives between John Wayne look-alikes and Ivan Boesky wanna-bes. Unfortunately, in many communities, the denial of need for change has only ended when the only options left require closure or acceptance of total dependency upon a large regional or national corporation.

Stein's demonstration of the widespread use of strategic alliances in industries outside of health care is welcome and particularly timely as we examine national health reform and major shifts in our health delivery infrastructure—the experience of other major industries can help us to develop effective alternatives that balance traditional preferences for local autonomy with our country's demand that health care serve more, better, for less.

---

Tim Size is the executive director of the Rural Wisconsin Hospital Cooperative.

Providers based in rural or small communities increasingly have the choice of being part of multiple regional networks/HMOs or participating in a single public utility with state determined fee schedules and microregulatory oversight. In either event, the model of alliances is a viable alternative for rural providers to that of selling their practice or hospital to out of community corporations. Several existing alliances in Wisconsin are building on a base of earlier collaboration to develop a new and more comprehensive relationship. This paper reviews and proposes a new strategic alliance between two existing alliances, the Community Physicians' Network and the Rural Wisconsin Hospital Cooperative. *This is definitely not a plan for merger or take-over of either organization; both will continue to grow independently and form other relationships while developing with each other those selected joint ventures that are win–win scenarios for the constituents of both organizations.*

## The Critical Importance of Choice

From Washington, we have been hearing about six principles that will guide health care reform: security, simplicity, savings, choice, quality, and responsibility. Large regional or multistate medical-industrial corporations may be underestimating the importance and power of the "C" word—choice as the concept seems missing in much of their public—statements. The cultural imperative of choice is a powerful, if not defining, ally for those of us whose business it is to see the market niche for strategic alliances. The politics of reform and the marketplace are ultimately, if imperfectly, driven by the values of the voter and consumer.

Choice among alternative health plans by consumers is clearly a defining value. The end of an era of almost unlimited choice should not be mistaken with the beginning of one with zero-to-minimal choice for consumers and providers. President Clinton emphasized this point when he introduced the American Health Security Act to a joint session of Congress: "The choice will be left to you—not your boss—and not some bureaucrat" (The Associated Press 1993). It is safe to assume that the use of the term bureaucrat is not restricted to government employees, but may include staff of private corporations with a mission to acquire and control the decisions of others. He went on to say, "And we also believe that doctors should have a choice as to what plans they practice in. We want to end the discrimination that is now growing against doctors and permit them to practice in several different plans. Choice is important for doctors, and critical for consumers" (The Associated Press 1993).

However, community providers will not be left alone to do their own thing; they are unlikely to be allowed to "refuse to deal" with regional health maintenance organizations (as defined by current and future antitrust enforcement) without forcing the alternative of regional single-payer oversight. Increased and substantial accountability will be demanded. In less dense population areas, the development and maintenance of the competitive market alternative to a single-payer system will depend in large part on the ability of rural networks to balance their traditional autonomy with a need to work cooperatively with regional HMOs.

# A Requirement to Develop Systems of Integrated Care

Whether or not reform occurs or takes the direction of single payer, managed competition, or something in between, it is clear that providers and insurers will increasingly be expected to offer those patients seen at multiple sights or over multiple visits a unified or integrated experience. No longer will it be acceptable for each step along the course of a patient's care to act as if the individual was being seen for the first time. Even the Mayo Clinic has begun to accept computerized tomography (CT) and Magnetic Resonance Imaging (MRI) studies from referring physicians.

There is a real danger that the myth of service delivery integration only being possible through corporate merger and consolidation can become self-fulfilling. It is clearly an increasingly common model, but we are in danger of placing too much emphasis on this single approach. We may be artificially restricting our vision of the future by focusing on the *means* to an end, not the end itself. The end or goal should not be defined in terms of how services are owned or organized, but how they are experienced by the patient. This is not just a play on words, but something that makes a real difference in both the private and public systems we design. Systems do not design or develop themselves. If we wish to see empowered local communities, it is up to those same communities to develop the appropriate alternatives.

We know that integrated care will be an extraordinary challenge for all of us whether we work with vertically or horizontally integrated systems, whether our workplaces are characterized by a corporate culture of control or one of collaboration. The real issue is how do we integrate the receipt of high quality, cost effective services—not whether one corporation controls the delivery of care, but whether the patient experiences care as being provided with continuity, without seams.

One of many potential practical implications of the system models assumed by reform lies in an area commonly most associated with vertically integrated delivery systems—integrated health information systems. In rural areas, we must develop regional systems to access individual medical records as the patient moves among the rural clinic, rural hospital, urban specialist at a rural hospital, urban specialist at a home clinic, urban specialty hospital, and rural home health agency. The exclusive use of the "single corporation in control" paradigm inevitably tends to lead to the development of multiple, individually owned and operated regional health information system networks—duplicate systems of parallel play among competing networks. Such a system forces rural providers to support duplicate local access into competing information systems as the only alternative to exclusive contracting or merger. "Providers and payers must begin to think of an information network as a community resource rather than a way to gain competitive advantage. Other matters to be resolved include achieving technical standardization, reaching political consensus and cooperation, and resolving system configuration and ownership" (Wakerly 1993).

While supporting the development of competitive markets, we can choose to focus on the integration of the receipt of care and less on the particular ownership model of the delivery mechanism. In this example we can begin to think in terms of an openly shared electronic highway as opposed to competing private electronic networks. Just as we do concrete highways, we can govern use and access of the common arteries while retaining individual privacy. Common highways are understood as a necessary part of infrastructure support for competitive markets. The space remains public, but the choice and timing of destinations flexible. It is this latter model that I believe will be mandated by regional buying cooperatives.

Reform at any level must in every facet support the ability of rural providers to contract with multiple plans in order to not be subordinated to a declining number of increasingly larger urban based corporations. By working with multiple plans, rural providers will be able to meet their communities' needs for local access and choice among competing regional plans and their alternative specialty resources. To do this effectively, antitrust laws and enforcement must be revised in order to facilitate regional risk-bearing physician-hospital organizations that can negotiate at a level table with increasingly large health plans. While government needs to not limit network formation, the necessary networks can only be created by those with an interest in developing collaborative rather than control-oriented models of local community care.

## Background for a New Wisconsin Alliance

The Rural Wisconsin Hospital Cooperative (RWHC) was incorporated in 1979 as a shared-service corporation and advocate for rural health.

It was the major force behind the formation in 1983 of a nonstock, not-for-profit insurance corporation, HMO of Wisconsin. At the same time, community physicians organized themselves as an affiliated independent practice association, the Community Physicians' Network (CPN), in order to provide medical services for patients insured by the HMO. A parent corporation, HMO–W, Inc., was formed in 1987, when HMO of Wisconsin was converted to for-profit status in order to raise additional capital. The stock of HMO–W, Inc. is primarily held by rural physicians and hospitals and holds all of the stock of HMO of Wisconsin.

In anticipation of state and national health reform, the HMO of Wisconsin signed a letter of intent in October of 1993 to merge with Physicians Plus Insurance Corporation, a Madison-based company. "Two of south-central Wisconsin's health maintenance organizations plan to join forces next year in a merger that reflects the ripples of change that portend a possible wave of reform in the nation's medical system. The new organization would have one of the largest HMO enrollments in the state with a combined membership of 116,000" (Lautenschlager 1993). "The move will allow the health maintenance organizations to more effectively compete against DeanCare HMO, the major player in the Madison area, and give them access to markets in which they are weak or have no presence at all" (Silver 1993). "The integration of HMO of Wisconsin and Physicians Plus brings together two organizations with complementary strengths. Physicians Plus serves patients in Dane and surrounding counties, while HMO of Wisconsin provides care to individuals living in rural communities of south-central Wisconsin and the greater Oshkosh area" (HMO of Wisconsin and Physicians Plus 1993).

At the same time, the Community Physicians' Network and Rural Wisconsin Hospital Cooperative have begun movement to an expanded working relationship, to strengthen rural providers in their ability to provide community-based integrated care, in order to better work with the resulting merger of HMO of Wisconsin and Physicians Plus, as well as other regional HMOs and multispecialty group practices.

### The Community Physicians' Network

The Community Physicians' Network (CPN) is an independent practice association owned and governed by physicians. It is a partner with HMO of Wisconsin, providing health insurance and care through 400 primary care physicians in 100 Wisconsin communities and 2,000 specialists in Wisconsin, Minnesota, and Iowa. The CPN's board and committee structure ensures physician governance from each primary care community. HMO of Wisconsin provides administrative support and data for utilization review, quality assurance, and reimbursement. CPN has begun to offer volume purchase programs through medical and office supply facilities and arranges management consulting, seminars, and other practice enhancements.

Through the CPN, Primary Care Physicians (PCP) are compensated on a capitation basis for a broad array of primary care services provided to members of HMO of Wisconsin. The PCP capitation is adjusted based on age and sex of the enrollee and the benefit plan under which the enrollee is covered; a 10 percent withhold is applied to capitation payments. Noncapitated services provided by PCPs and all services provided by specialists are paid according to the CPN fee schedule; a 20 percent withhold is applied to fee-for-service payments (HMO of Wisconsin 1993).

Two mechanisms have been established by the CPN to limit the PCPs risk from capitation; the Equalization Fund and the Outlier Fund. The Equalization Fund provides supplemental reimbursement to PCPs who have demonstrated particularly effective case management. PCPs who demonstrate prudent use of referral services are guaranteed a minimum capitation reimbursement equal to 80 percent of actual charges. The Outlier Fund provides supplemental payment to PCPs whose capitation payment is adversely affected by catastrophic cases (HMO of Wisconsin 1993).

Capitation does place a degree of risk on the PCP. The risk is magnified when a PCP has a small panel of capitated patients. CPN pays PCPs on a fee-for-service basis with a 15 percent withhold until the PCP's panel reaches 100 enrollees. In rare situations where capitation is determined to be an unsuitable payment arrangement, PCPs are paid according to the CPN Fee Schedule with minimum withholds ranging from 5 percent to 25 percent (HMO of Wisconsin 1993).

## The Rural Wisconsin Hospital Cooperative

The Rural Wisconsin Hospital Cooperative (RWHC) originated in 1979 as the result of informal discussions among several hospital administrators in southern Wisconsin. RWHC is owned and operated by 19 rural acute, general medical-surgical hospitals and one urban hospital (University of Wisconsin–Madison); the rural hospitals serve a population of nearly 300 thousand people over 15 counties. The hospitals in the Cooperative are owned and governed by a variety of structures including local nonprofit associations, municipalities, counties, the state, or churches. Most members are geographically contiguous with member hospitals located in central and southern Wisconsin. The model of the dairy cooperative was chosen because it respected the autonomy of the sponsors and was a type of organization familiar to the community boards that would have to approve individual hospital participation.

The purpose of RWHC was and is to act as a catalyst for regional collaboration. Since its incorporation, it has tried to be an aggressive and creative force on behalf of rural health care. It now employs or contracts for the services of approximately 150 people (full- and part-time) with a $5 million dollar annual budget, exclusive of affiliated corporations.

RWHC staff provide services directly in areas such as advocacy, audiology, multihospital benchmarking and other quality improvement initiatives, grantsmanship, occupational therapy, per diem nursing, physical therapy, respiratory therapy, physician credentialing, speech pathology, emergency room physician staffing, and ongoing rural specific continuing educational opportunities. RWHC has negotiated special group contract arrangements for members to obtain high-quality consultant services in areas such as legal services, personnel consulting, market research, patient discharge studies, and consultant pathology services.

With private investors and operators, the Cooperative has implemented a mobile CT, MRI, nuclear medicine, and ultrasound service to rural hospitals, reducing cost and improving access to this service for RWHC members and other area hospitals. RWHC established a pilot loan guarantee program for RWHC hospitals in cooperation with the Robert Wood Johnson Foundation and the Wisconsin Health and Education Facilities Authority, which in turn was used as a model for the State's Hospital Loan Guarantee Program. RWHC developed and provided the early administration of HMO of Wisconsin.

A particularly productive and popular RWHC activity has been professional roundtables that regularly bring together RWHC hospital staff of the same discipline for mutual sharing, problem solving, continuing education, and advising the RWHC Board and staff on program and policy development. This has been recognized as one of the primary benefits of RWHC—learning from each other. The number of these roundtable groups that are active has significantly increased and now includes 22 professional groups (i.e., lab, pharmacy, and radiology).

## A New Wisconsin Alliance

Wisconsin is a health care market with a greater use of HMOs than all but a few states and is already beginning to experience the consolidation of HMOs predicted to accompany national health reform. Wisconsin also has a high concentration of multigroup specialty clinics that have been aggressively investing in the vertical control of physician practices in smaller communities, primarily through their outright purchase. Amundson (1993) makes a strong case that external forces, such as the inequity of Medicare payments and the shortage of primary care providers, are not the complete story of the challenges facing rural health. He argues that the rural providers and communities themselves have been a significant part of the problem and can become a major part of the solution.

> While the primary responsibility for the current situation resides within many rural communities, the strongest potential for sustaining rural services also resides primarily within our communities. The history of this nation is replete with documentation that the strength of community, particularly in rural America, is incalculable. The power of a group of residents, acting in concert to improve some aspect of their community infrastructure that they care deeply about, has been demonstrated for generations. It is the essence of rural America at its best to put such shared values above individual self-interests and to mount major action.
>
> *Admunson, 1993*

In the context of this environment, two existing alliances, the Community Physicians' Network and the Rural Wisconsin Hospital Cooperative, have significant long-range plans of their own but also recognize that specific joint ventures between the two alliances can foster local and regional community physician–hospital collaboration. The purpose of this initiative will be to form a united front to support community-based health care in balance with the outreach of large regional HMOs and multispecialty group practices. Figure 2.1 shows a graphic demonstration of these relationships.

For a change, seed capital may not be its usual problem: RWHC has already developed with the support of the Robert Wood Johnson Foundation a $500,000 loan reserve fund that is very suitable for the envisioned projects. The current holding company of HMO of Wisconsin, HMO–W, Inc. will be asked to invest in the maintenance and strengthening of the regional network of community providers that constitute its stockholders. Both organizations will be positioned to work with the merged HMO as well as with other regional HMOs.

The Community Physicians' Network has significant experience organizing physicians around the negotiation of HMO contracts, and the Rural Wisconsin Hospital Cooperative primarily has experience with shared services and advocacy among multiple partners. Both organizations have begun a discussion to explore the possibilities of developing selected joint ventures in the following areas: (1) rural network negotiations, (2) network-based practice support, (3) local infrastructure development, and (4) rural network advocacy.

1. *Rural network negotiations:* negotiating equitable relationships with regional and multistate insurers, networks, and regional purchasing

**Figure 2.1**   Proposal for a New Strategic Alliance: An Independent
Practice Association and a Cooperative of Rural Hospitals

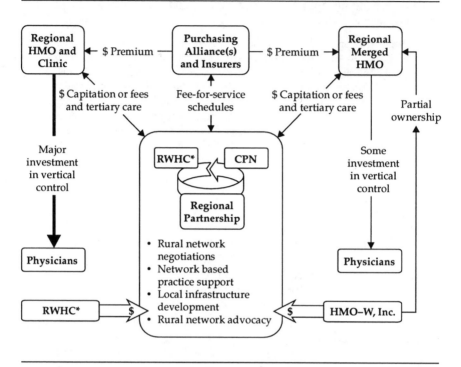

*RWHC = Rural Wisconsin Hospital Cooperative.

alliances. "Where network arrangements among rural providers already exist, health plans (health maintenance organizations) seeking
to serve these areas likely will attempt to take advantage of existing
networks in establishing their delivery systems. This could, in turn,
cause existing rural networks to organize more formally to function as
contracting entities for negotiating with health plans." (Christianson
and Moscovice 1993) "During the transition to the new health care
system, physicians and other providers may require some protection
to negotiate effectively with health plans. To protect physicians and
other providers from the market power of third-party payers forming
health plans, providers are provided a narrow safe harbor to establish
and negotiate prices if the providers share financial risk." (Clinton
Task Force 1993)

2. *Network-based practice support:* developing an alternative for community physicians to that of selling their practice to large regional multi-

specialty clinics. Extensive surveys by RWHC indicated that the availability of practice support and employment opportunities is a major factor in the decision in a physician's site selection decision. In 1992, a written survey was conducted by RWHC of over 1,000 physicians who graduated from Wisconsin's two major medical colleges during the years of 1983–85. With an impressive response rate of 44 percent (usable surveys) RWHC obtained valuable information regarding in-state practice site selection factors that are important to physicians. Four key areas of importance surfaced as: assistance with malpractice premiums (66 percent of all respondents), practice management support (52 percent), practice set-up assistance (47 percent) and retirement/benefit packages (36 percent). In most cases, family practitioners, physicians practicing in small towns and small cities had higher percentages ranking the above areas as important.

Malpractice premiums were felt to be amenable to immediate intervention, RWHC is working collaboratively with Physician's Insurance Corporation of Wisconsin to develop a unique professional liability policy with rates reflecting a purchasing pool discount. The purchasing pool will consist of RWHC related health providers (hospitals and physicians). It is envisioned that this prototype will be expanded to all members of the partnership with CPN. Research and development is also underway for local practice management support that goes beyond a "consulting" relationship, providing support typically obtained only through joining a larger clinic. Various models, such as clinics without walls, are being explored. A partnership between CPN and RWHC will allow many of the physician services to be fast-tracked and the critical volume to support a shared service will be easier to obtain.

3. *Local and regional infrastructure development:* supporting the integration of high quality, cost effective services within and among communities as noted earlier in this paper. In addition, we need to go one step further. Again I would like to quote President Clinton's address to the Joint Session of Congress: "Responsibility also means changing the behaviors in this country that drive up our health care costs and cause untold suffering. It's the outrageous costs of violence from far too many handguns, especially among the young. It's high rates of AIDS, smoking and excessive drinking; it's teenage pregnancy, low-birth weight babies, and not enough vaccinations for the most vulnerable." (Clinton Task Force 1993)

Hospitals and physicians must break out of their traditional isolation from the community at large. Partnerships must be aggressively pursued with a variety of public and private community based organizations that do not lend themselves to a system of regional or intracommunity vertical integration—schools, city councils, local public health agencies, community development agencies, churches, to name just a few. From the perspective of community oriented primary care, one can argue that compared to intercommunity networking, an equal challenge and perhaps greater payoff will be the development of broad based intracommunity partnerships.

4. *Rural network advocacy:* advocacy for community based primary care and working with state organizations to create a more favorable environment for primary care and rural health.

CPN and RWHC leadership have traditionally been very active in the development of broader strategic alliances with many state-wide organizations in order to better serve Wisconsin, CPN and RWHC interests in primary care and rural health. CPN and RWHC has helped to develop the Wisconsin Primary Care Consortium, the Area Health Education Center System, the Wisconsin Rural Health Development Council and worked as part of major advisory committees or governing boards with the University of Wisconsin Medical School, the Wisconsin Department of Health and Social Services, the Office of the Commissioner of Insurance, the State Medical Society, the Wisconsin Academy of Family Practice, the Wisconsin Hospital Association, and the Wisconsin Health and Education Facilities Authority.

With reform, additional organizational linkages will have to be developed in order to achieve the appropriate resolution of a series of reform issues critical to the future of community based health care:

- Employees and individuals should be assured an unrestricted choice among all eligible plans offered through a regional health council. This is good politics because it maximizes individual consumer choice. It is good public policy because it reduces the likelihood of monopolistic systems forming based on a coercive claim that they can exclude nonparticipating providers from multiple employee groups.

- Systems or HMOs, at least in rural counties, should be precluded from requiring participating rural providers to sign exclusive contracts.

- If regional alliances will set fee schedules for self-insured and indemnity plans, assurances must be given that the negotiation process is not dominated by a few large multispecialty clinics—that the interests of individual physician and other primary care providers and networks are fairly represented.

- The shortage of primary care providers is expected to get worse before it gets better as we are faced with (1) the loss of a large number of retiring rural providers, (2) an increased demand for primary care providers due to the shift towards HMO delivery systems, and (3) an increased demand for primary care services resulting from a larger insured population. This issue must be aggressively addressed and funded if rural areas are not to be made worse by the reform initiative.

- More explicit language is needed regarding the scope of and development processes for retro-adjustments or risk-adjustments on payments from regional health clinics to networks and from networks to individual providers. The market needs to be managed so that networks compete based on the quality and cost of their services, not on their ability to avoid sick people.

- "Charity care/bad debt" and losses stemming from government payments (at a level below reasonable cost) tend to make rural and inner city providers less competitive than they otherwise would be. To create an equal playing field, Councils should be required to spread these losses equally across all providers in a region so that competition is based on quality and cost and not one's ability to avoid the poor and elderly and uninsured.

## Steps to Developing a CPN/RWHC Alliance

After the initial work group finalizes its sense of what specific activities are appropriate for a joint venture between the CPN and RWHC, the focus will shift to the development of an initial business plan that will include at a minimum the following:

- Conceptual approval by RWHC and CPN boards
- Development of an initial partnership agreement
- Draft development on an initial operations plan
- Investigation of corporate alternatives for joint activities
- Securing commitments for initial capitalization
- Establish parameters of current Wisconsin limits to joint negotiation
- Approval and formation of the corporate structure for joint ventures
- Approval of an initial partnership work plan by new corporate governance
- Implementation of the initial operations plan.

# Summary

While leaders of both organizations are optimistic about both their individual futures and possibilities for joint action, neither minimizes the challenges to be faced. The development of strong mutually beneficial physician-hospital relationships at the local level are not easy, the are no more so when aggregated at the regional level. Experience within and outside of health care indicates that community based providers can develop effective alternatives that balance traditional preferences for local autonomy with our country's mandate that health care serve more, better, for less. In Wisconsin, two existing strategic alliances, the Community Physicians' Network and the Rural Wisconsin Hospital Cooperative, have significant individual objectives but are also committed to the development of welcomed joint ventures that can foster local and regional community physician-hospital collaboration to the advantage of both parties and the communities they serve.

# References

Amundson, B. 1993. "Myth and Reality in the Rural Health Service Crisis: Facing Up to Community Responsibilities." *The Journal of Rural Health* (Summer): 182.

Associated Press. 1993. Prepared text of the speech delivered by President Clinton to Congress. (22 September)

Christianson, J. B., and I. S. Moscovice. 1993. "Health Care Reform and Rural Health Networks." *Health Affairs* (Fall): 61.

Clinton Task Force. 1993. Working group draft, 7 September, p. 170.

HMO of Wisconsin and Physicians Plus. 1993. Press release, 18 October.

HMO of Wisconsin. 1993. "Primary Care Physician Compensation Arrangements." Occasional paper, Madison, WI.

Kushner, C. 1991. "The Feasibility of Health Care Cooperatives in Rural America: Learning from the Past to Prepare for the Future." Working paper series, University of North Carolina Rural Health Research Program. Chapel Hill, NC, May, p. 5.

Lautenschlager, S. 1993. "Two Area HMOs Planning to Merge." *Wisconsin State Journal* 21 October.

Silver, J. 1993. "Physicians Plus, HMO of Wisconsin Plan Major Merger." *Capital Times* 20 October.

Wakerly, R. 1993. "Info Networks to be Integral to Reform." *Modern Healthcare* (25 October): 54.

# Gerald Martin

I would like to put a slightly different perspective on the issue of *strategic alliances* by suggesting that they are nothing new at all. Alliances are perhaps as old as humanity itself. The very emergence of the earliest tribes or clans and their evolution into villages, then cities, states, and then nations would suggest that alliances are a part of social, organizational, and geopolitical growth. Certainly in recorded history we can find innumerable examples of these alliances and their subsequent evolution. Medieval Europe was a patchwork of small, often isolated pockets of governance that formed alliances with others for protection or prosecution of war. The alliances eventually knitted together into the fabric of nations that is Europe today.

On a more recent scale, the advent of the twentieth century saw most of the nations of the world divide into one of two powerful alliances—the East and the West. These alliances were built on fear of a common enemy and protection which led to the military alliances of the '40s: NATO and the Warsaw Pact.

These alliances were so powerful and had such fearsome weapons of war at their disposal that most of the rest of the nations of the world aligned themselves with either the East or the West. Even the normal conduct of human commerce was polarized along an east-west axis.

If you accept this thesis of the antiquity of alliances, then history must provide some lessons of why they were formed, why they endured, or why they failed. In simplest terms, these alliances came together for one basic reason—they had a common goal. Often, that goal was nothing more complicated than survival, mutual protection. Other times it was to wage war, or to conquer a common foe. A common goal, however, was fundamental to the formation of these alliances.

In forming the alliance, there was a cost to the parties. They had to surrender part of their autonomy to the greater good of the alliance. If one member was attacked, the others were obliged to wage war as well. Was this cost worth it? This is the fundamental question that is key to whether alliances survive.

Let me then apply this very simple question to two geopolitical alliances of today: NATO and the European Economic Community. One is in the ascendant phase, while the other could be at the edge of the slippery slope to oblivion. NATO was formed to protect us from an enemy, a common foe. Every nation behind the iron curtain—members of

Gerald Martin is divisional vice president for corporate hospital marketing at Abbott Laboratories.

the Warsaw Pact Nations—were the enemies. Today the Eastern Alliance is in disarray and decaying rapidly. Is the common goal for forming the NATO Alliance still valid? Are we going to receive value from the NATO Alliance that balances the cost of maintaining it? Time will tell, but it is safe to say this question will be asked.

On the other hand, the EEC seems to be growing stronger. Why was this alliance formed? *Survival*, in an economic sense.

The United States and Japan are formidable business competitors, and in order to compete on the same footing, each country in the EEC had to give up some of their national autonomy to form a more powerful market. Are the financial cost and surrender of some autonomy offset because they receive something of greater or commensurate value? The survival of the EEC demands a positive answer. The debate here at home on the North American Free Trade Agreement (NAFTA) is raising the same question: Is the value received worth the cost? Obviously the Labor Unions in the United States think not.

How does this historical or global perspective translate into modern health care in America? Let me share some experiences of a health care company that conducts business worldwide.

Abbott is a 105 year old, multinational producer and marketer of a diverse portfolio of products. Our current annual revenues are $8 billion and approximately 35 percent of that revenue comes from overseas markets. Those facts alone would hint that we have been involved in a significant number of different relationships from acquisitions, to co-marketing ventures, to joint ventures, to strategic alliances, and perhaps a few that defy description. Most of our experiences have proven valuable to us, and I presume for our allies or partners as well. The good relationships have brought value to all sides, and the bad ones taught us at least how *not* to form one in the future.

International marketing, at least in health care, demands doing business differently than in the United States, and from country to country. Our ability to grow worldwide required us to "partner" with other companies or organizations in these various countries. And those "partner" relationships reflect the spectrum that Stein alluded to.

More interesting perhaps, is what has been occurring in U.S. operations since the mid-'80s. We have been changing, and we believe improving, the way we conduct our business. For instance, we have forged important alliances with our key suppliers, such as Federal Express and Eastman Kodak, both Baldrige Quality Award winners. We have learned from each other and are stronger for it.

For example, we have had a contract with Federal Express since 1989. This contract only establishes the framework of an agreement however. The working relationship between Abbott and Federal Express has as its goal maximizing quality by integrating and streamlining our mutual operations. Federal Express has 15 of their own employees working in our warehouse, who sort and load their products into trucks. The high priority products are shipped by air each night to Memphis. The rest goes by truck to Memphis for shipment the following night. By working together, we ship a majority of the products by truck, thus saving both companies money.

Federal Express has allowed Abbott to link our computers into its customer service data base. We are able to track the location of all of our shipments from our own computers without having to call Federal Express. This allows us to know when there are weather delays or other problems, and we are able to call our customers and alert them.

This relationship has benefited both sides, and we continue to seek ways to reduce the costs of doing business together. At one time, Federal Express had 11 salespeople calling on Abbott. Today there is only one, and he has an office to work in at our main facility. Moreover, Federal Express now participates in Abbott-sponsored supplier certification workshops, where we work with our hospital customers to help them define the parameters of forging their own alliances with their suppliers. One of the more important lessons we have learned from this integrated distribution alliance is how to judge whom to partner with, at least in the distribution area.

The financial strength of our potential partner, their management skills, and the quality of their service are the first three criteria we evaluate. Only after we are satisfied with these points do we consider price. The cost of doing business with a weaker partner, regardless of their prices, is too high of a risk for us. We are changing the way we relate to our customers as suppliers as well, to develop relationships similar to those we have with our suppliers. Even the way we develop contracts with customers has changed.

There was a time when we sold our products on an individual basis to individual accounts. Today, more and more of the prices of our products are constituted under long term, portfolio-type contracts with national purchasing groups or alliances. These national hospital groups were formed with group purchasing as one of their common goals. Unlike the automobile industry, where the Big Three manufacturers are giants compared to their much smaller suppliers, hospitals in this country buy most of their products from suppliers who are much larger than themselves. Their common goal for forming these alliances was in part to pool their buying power to achieve the best price possible. To do this, they were obliged to surrender some of their individual autonomy in product selection. Have they received value commensurate with the cost? I think the answer has generally been *yes*.

But health care is undergoing a fundamental change, and will continue unabated even if Congress doesn't act. What is interesting is that the new emerging integrated health care systems are themselves alliances that bring together physicians, hospitals, alternate care operations, and some financing vehicle. Why are they forming? What is their common goal? *Survival!* More and more of health care will be awarded in large blocks to providers by the payers, often in the form of capitated contracts. The amount of health care delivered outside these contracts will continue to shrink. Thus, the motivation to form or join these alliances by these independent entities is *economic security.* Whether these regional alliances survive or not will be determined, in large part, by the members using the same value-received equation.

While these new regional alliances are forming and spreading, they pose a challenge to many of the national alliances. If a regional alliance can develop the skills to negotiate large scale contracts with the payers, could they not use the same clout to form new relationships with their suppliers independent of national contracts? The answer will probably in time be *yes.*

What, then, is the need for national purchasing organizations? Those organizations which have built their entire existence solely around group purchasing functions may be the first to be challenged.

On the other hand, there are other organizations, national alliances of hospitals, who are beginning to transform themselves into national health alliances. Many of the leaders of these organizations are at the conference. The leaders of these organizations have had the wisdom to apply one of Stein's tenets—flexibility. They have been steadfastly seeking to develop programs for their members that go beyond their purchasing programs. These are the organizations or alliances to watch. They are mindful of that pervasive equation of cost verses value, and are seeking to develop programs that constantly enhance the value received.

History then has taught us some valuable lessons about alliances:

1. They can be powerful entities that yield benefits for the members beyond the costs of constituting them. On the other hand, they have the potential to fail dramatically often resulting in painful and costly readjustment for their members.

2. They can be powerful forces of change—or equally powerful in slowing change.

3. Alliances are fragile entities. Their success or failure is dependent on a number of variables, but I would emphasize two which I believe are key: a common goal that is clearly defined and agreed to by all members and strong commitment that is shared equitably by all members.

4. Pick your partners well. Stein alluded to the need for new relationships based on trust. These relationships may never evolve if you and your partner's cultures and values do not line up well.

Our industry is challenged as never before and strong alliances will surely be part of the new health care delivery system.

One note of caution, however. Health care has at times been a victim of management by fad. The challenge for all of us in this industry is to avoid the tendency to form alliances simply because that's what everyone is doing. There are valid reasons for forming new strategic alliances—the herd instinct is not one of them.

Abbott is proud of its relationship with several of the finest national and regional alliances in the country. Within those structures, we have forged many outstanding relationships with health systems.

We have learned with time that there is no "cookie-cutter" approach, that successful alliances require a customized plan with constant attention to the uniqueness of each relationship. We know we do not have all the answers, but we believe alliances can be enormously successful as long as there is a genuine desire to bring real value to the relationship from both sides.

These relationships require a long-term perspective and work to develop the trust required to overcome the inevitable differences of opinion that will arise. A shared goal or vision and the willingness to work together to achieve that goal are absolute necessities. While we are aware of the barriers to success in alliances, we are also aware of the mutual rewards that are possible. Thus we have a positive attitude about participating in or with alliances.

# Neal Neuberger

In his chapter, "Strategic Alliances: Some Lessons from Experience," Barry Stein stresses the importance of business relationships in forming alliances. Companies are competing on the basis of their connections, and these linkages are being enhanced by new communications and information technologies that can open up new cross-industry and cross-border opportunities.

Neal Neuberger is senior partner at the Center for Public Service Communication.

No clearer example of this phenomenon exists than in health care. Emerging "systems" of care—alliances, health purchasing cooperatives, networks of care—will be held together by new ways of providing clinical services, administration and management of care, education of providers and patients, and all aspects of financing and reimbursement of services.

In order for these systems to most efficiently impact access to quality health services—information sharing using existing and evolving communications technologies will be required. "Informatics"—electronically controlled systems of all types, including advanced electronic interfaces both within individual hospitals and among institutions—will determine the success of the health care alliances of the future.

Once the application is defined, electronically mediated interactive sharing of data, voice, and video exchanges of a clinical, educational, scientific, and administrative nature help determine the terms of systems development.

The proliferation of legislation and public sector interest in the convergence of the telecommunications and health care industries is considerable. Proponents of two of the nation's major domestic agendas—development of the information superhighway and health care policy reforms—are each searching for ways in which new technologies can be brought to bear toward the more effective delivery of health care services.

In his message to a Joint Session of Congress, President Clinton (1994) prominently referenced reform measure provisions establishing programs to link "providers in underserved areas with each other and with regional health care institutions and academic health centers through information systems and telecommunications."

At the same time, the information superhighway bill, (§ 4, The National Competitiveness Act of 1993) gives considerable weight to development of applications by the Department of Health and Human Service's (DHHS) existing High Performance Computing Center Program which can produce significant savings in national health care costs.

Attorney General Reno has proposed revisions to the so-called "Safe Harbor" regulations that would ease the antitrust barriers that otherwise exist for some of the potential linkages.

Beyond these flagship efforts lay no less than a dozen other pending bills to provide start-up funding for various uses of information technologies in the health care field.

Notwithstanding policy considerations in Washington, the field of telemedicine is moving ahead rapidly. Examples include uses in rehabilitation medicine, reconstructive surgery, burn management, psychiatry, sanitation and epidemiology, preventive medicine, and post-traumatic stress therapy.

So much has been happening that policymakers find it difficult to catch up to the myriad of tested and other demonstration programs which have been in place over the years.

Much of the current Telemedicine work in underserved areas of the United States was pioneered by NASA in the late 1960s as it positioned three satellites in geosynchronous orbit to demonstrate the delivery of education and health services in remote areas of the world. In one of the earliest health applications, NASA and the Lister Hill Center for Biomedical Communications (under the auspices of the Indian Health Service) helped provide teleconsultation services to Native Americans in scattered small villages in remote regions of Alaska. During the first year, contacts between doctors and health aids in the field increased by 400 percent. NASA extended its work to the Papago Indian Reservation in the Sonora Desert of Arizona between 1973 and 1978.

Today, NASA is helping to further demonstrate international applications in telemedicine, working to provide long-distance medical assistance via satellite to health care providers in Moscow. This follows on the heels of successful efforts to mitigate some of the effects of the devastating Armenian earthquake in December 1988.

From NASA's pioneering work, domestic demonstrations throughout the United States have proliferated. The Office of Rural Health Policy, DHHS funded the Texas Tech MEDNET program to create linkages to rural hospitals for purposes of continuing education, clinical oversight, and consultations in patient care, and to help evaluate and certify telemedical training and equipment.

The University of Washington School of Medicine has a state-of-the-art medical and telecommunications infrastructure and expertise in medical imaging. The University's Department of Radiology has a history in teleradiology dating to 1978.

Kansas University uses compression technology to link three sites for consultations in endocrinology, neurology, allergy, and oncology. Recently, the West Virginia University Health Sciences Center received an $800,000 grant from the Office of Rural Health Policy and $28,000 from the Appalachian Regional Commission to use T-1—for higher speed—phone lines for linking three remote sites to its Morgantown hub. The University of North Carolina is operating one of five high-speed testbeds, organized by the Corporation for National Research, linking a supercomputer, image processing unit, and medical workstation. The school is also testing the "Medical Information Communications Applications Program designed to conduct research into remote consultations."

In 1991, a human services consortium in Eastern Oregon received a 36-month, $700,000 grant from the Resources and Health Services Administration to link 13 rural counties to improve care for mental health patients, using the State's two-way interactive television network. The Medical College of Georgia links several facilities via T-1 lines for interactive programs in cardiology, dermatology, pathology, radiology, urology, and orthopedics consultation.

Many other exciting domestic and international initiatives are well underway.

Despite all of the many important demonstrations and experiments over the past 20 years, there is little validated national evidence of the large-scale benefits of applying data, audio, and video technologies to the provision of both acute and chronic care services. The problem has been that telemedicine applications have been of short duration, and without sufficient validation to overcome the skepticism of an understandably cautious and often conservative health care provider and patient community. Because of this, telecommunications and information technologies have not yet found their way into routine practice on a wide-scale basis.

In the near term, outcomes research of several types must be conducted. Facilities' administrators' and clinicians must be convinced that specific applications can indeed lead to both improved access and management savings, without any compromise to accepted standards of care. Moreover, mechanisms for recovering costs of capital investment and payment for services employing these technologies must be identified and sanctioned by appropriate administrative bodies. From a national perspective, private sector accreditation organizations like the Joint Commission or the Accreditation of Healthcare Organizations and third-party payers like the Health Care Financing Administration will pay more attention to determining the effectiveness of various telemedicine applications as they determine their policies with respect to licensure and reimbursement.

While these and other issues of regulation, jurisdiction of practitioner license, and matters of liability are sorted out, the technology continues to march forward. Increasingly, health care administrators and caregivers will of necessity become familiar with the language of the telecommunications industry as new and unique partnerships are forged between these sectors.

In hospital board rooms, discussions concerning "modes of transmission"—including a working knowledge of the differences between satellite, optical fiber, microwave, cable, and T-1 phone lines—will ensue. Board members will also find themselves discussing methods of access, hardware and software costs, protocols for equipment, institutional capacity and interoperability, and the licensure of their staffs with respect to the use of these new technologies.

From a business perspective organizations will be concerned about the opportunities and challenges which the new technologies present. If the local information highway bypasses them in favor of their chief competitor down the road, they will undoubtedly be placed at an immediate disadvantage to their neighbors. If, on the other hand, they are included simply for the purposes of some short term strategic alliance, they will want to be cautious about preserving the integrity of proprietary information regarding their business practices. Either way, the new technology poses a series of daunting questions they must face. Just as the automobile interstate system created "boom towns" and "ghost towns," so too could the new health care information highways.

For these and other reasons, the widespread acceptance of these technologies will not come easily to health care communities which have gotten used to business as usual. Health care leaders will need to move quickly but cautiously into all of these areas. The successful introduction of clinical applications will similarly require a process of consumer education. Patients must be assured that there are many occasions when a remote consultation can effectively substitute for the interpersonal interaction of an on-site specialist visit.

Arthur D. Little, Inc. (1992) has estimated that use of new technologies in health care holds significant promise for the following:

- Improved claims management
- Better materials management and inventory control
- Home health uses of an extended nature
- Improved emergency room utilization and outpatient visits
- Video conferencing for education and clinical purposes.

All told, the Little study has estimated that as much as $36 billion in health care system savings might be achieved annually. With these applications in mind, it isn't hard to imagine how telemedicine could be used to help develop and manage alliance-type structures.

In order to do so, policies must be thought out carefully yet quickly with respect to these new technologies. Acceptable and appropriate applications must be determined by the users—health care providers and patients—who will work in tandem with technology companies on particular products and new technologies.

In any case, the electronic highways are going to descend on the delivery of health services and the field is going to change forever. I predict that when that day comes, terms like "point of service" will have a changed meaning because patient consultations, routine, and even more complicated procedures will be performed on a remote basis, with primary care givers in rural or underserved areas linked to medical specialists sitting in another state or halfway around the world.

The process cannot be reversed. Health care leaders are better off waking up to the new reality sooner rather than later, so that they may be able to take full advantage of these new opportunities and use this reality to better manage strategic alliances in health care.

## References

Arthur D. Little, Inc. 1992. "Telecommunications: Can it Help America's Health Care Problems?" Report, Boston, MA, (July).
Clinton, W. J. 1994. "State of the Union Address."

# 3

# The Creation of a Multiorganizational Health Care Alliance: The Charlotte–Mecklenburg Hospital Authority

## Harry A. Nurkin

The emergence of alliances among health care organizations signals a dramatic shift in the structure and operation of previously independent and fragmented entities that have been described as organized health care. Health care alliances can take multiple forms and have differing purposes. The causative factors influencing health care alliance formation vary, and the chronology of alliance formation may be years or decades. Due to laws and regulations impacting entities that join together in various alliance structures, the process of health care alliance formation may vary considerably depending upon factors such as size, geographic location, market share, competition, and legal interpretation. Therefore, it appears timely and relevant to chronicle health care alliance creation, structure, and operation in order to determine the relevance to other health care entities.

Kaluzny and Zuckerman (1991) identified alliances among and between hospitals, physicians, and other related parties as strategic in purpose and emerging rapidly. Kanter (1989) attempted to rationalize such multiorganizational structures as postulating three categories that alliances may be grouped in for clarity and understanding: service, opportunistic, and stakeholder.

Observers of health care organizations have correctly identified a recent flurry of multiorganization arrangements that have been labeled

Harry A. Nurkin is president and CEO, Carolinas Medical Center.

*strategic alliances*, for lack of more innovative description. The genesis of this phenomenon occurred over a decade ago. Others have attempted to compare and contrast alliances in order to determine causative factors, as well as to try to predict chances for success of these often unique relationships.

It is remarkable that health care alliances have emerged during a period when the need to contain health care costs has become one of the most dynamic and powerful of all the forces affecting the health, economic, and political stability of our nation.

The debate over whether the creation of alliances is an industrywide reaction to dynamic pressure to alter the system or part of an evolutionary process seems capricious and simplistic.

The issues of costs, access, and quality are essentially strains of the DNA of health care. Such issues are latent genetic artifacts that have been observed throughout the lifeline of organized health care, periodically mutating to cause acute symptoms of disease within health care organizations. Throughout history, when these symptoms have become acute, changes emerged to abate the symptoms. These therapeutic measures have altered organized health care structurally, philosophically, and pragmatically.

The interorganization alliance is not a new concept. It is a refinement of the obvious and basic elements of human interaction emerging at a time of great concern and often unfathomable complexity in health care organizations. Basically, the interorganizational alliance is a corporate extension of human behavioral theory. Perhaps, a reexamination of the human need for affiliation can better explain the phenomenon.

In addressing the complex problems of health care, organizations have begun to choose the sobriety of basic human interactional theory as an alternative to the intoxication of recent data-based, competitive models of organizational development. In the management of complex organizations, computerized data analysis has never succeeded in replacing the human mind and spirit, nor can it ever truly satisfy any hierarchical level of human or organizational need.

Montgomery (1991) commenting on Zuckerman and Kaluzny (1991) points out that alliances are merely vehicles for expressing the core strategy of aligned organizations. Without the compatibility of redefined core values, alliances are little more than reactive configurations of various successful and unsuccessful health care business entities. Such reactive configurations are placebos for fractures in the current system. Through the definition of compatible core values, separate and often competitive health care business entities can combine into alliance structures to accomplish the vital purposes of the alliance subsets or component parts.

The decade of the '80s can be described as a period when hospitals, physicians, third-party reimbursers, and ultimate payers grew more remote from one another. To a great extent, the remoteness and isolationism were caused by eclectic alternative payment schemes and organizations designed to do little more than reduce revenue to providers. These alternatives failed to reduce overall expenditures for health care, but clearly succeeded in multidirectionally antagonizing and further separating the various participants. To the extent that institutional and physician providers, insurers, and ultimate payers have grown remote from one another, understanding the values and needs of each is necessary to provide mature symbiosis. Understanding the attitudes and problems inherent in creating alliances made up of institutions, physicians, insurers, and ultimate payers can improve communication and enhance the possibility of truly collaborative efforts to resolve the problems caused by the separation and fragmentation within the health care system.

## Historical Perspective

The participants are descendants of a common progenitor. The source was a desire to ease the process of death and to improve the health of the living. As these processes have grown more complex and costly, so have the subsystems of institutions, physicians, insurers, and ultimate payers. The once symbiotic relationship, based on similar values, has to a great extent grown separate.

We are now in a period of profound change initiated to correct the chaos created by separateness and fragmentation within the health care system. Like a three-dimensional game of chess, participants exist in an environment that is constantly moving on multiple planes, at different speeds, in different directions.

At one level, hospitals are restructuring and redefining their functions to compensate for reduced income, reduced occupancy, rapidly declining lengths of stay, and the need to demonstrate higher outcome values through more competent and more highly compensated workers. Each day, traditional boundaries and relationships that have maintained hospitals as separate, autonomous entities are being breached.

On another level, physicians face new questions of motives, ethics, and competency while struggling to retain the valued elements of control and autonomy. RBRVS and other payer-structured programs have begun to control and reduce payments to physicians, while the expense of medical practice has increased. Traditionally, boundaries and relationships were built to insulate physicians from the business aspects of organized health care, but now are being breached.

On a third level, ultimate payers, insurers, and the government are altering their reasonable and customary attitudes toward health care funding while attempting to regain economic security harpooned, in part, by inflationary health expenditures.

For patients, change in a familiar, if not understood, system affects them with surprising regularity, and the whole notion of what constitutes health and health care is being reexamined by politicians and journalists regularly.

While these changes are painful, they are still part of a necessary adjustment process that is essential if the United States is to continue to care for its sick and maintain a strong economic position for the future. The changes will not only make the health care system stronger, but also will make managing the microcosmic parts of the new system more challenging and exciting than ever before.

In an era of rising costs, providers of care are struggling to find ways to control cost, improve access, and document quality. One way for participants to attain such goals is through the formation of the multiorganizational health care alliance.

Health care providers are forming alliances in an attempt to deal with a multitude of environmental pressures. These pressures include increasing costs, reform, and the changing needs and values of societal clients. Providers are feeling pressure from what is perceived to be inadequate reimbursement from government and other third party payers. To deal with the constantly changing external environment, providers may choose to enter into alliances. Observers of the formation of alliances have described the phenomenon using the Kanter (1989) categories of *service, opportunistic,* and *stakeholder.*

The multiorganizational *service alliance* is defined as a "consortium model wherein a group of organizations with similar needs band together to meet that need (Kanter 1989)." The goal of such an alliance is to pool resources in order to obtain economies of scale. Group purchasing is an example of this pooling. Service alliances also provide a means for idea and knowledge sharing. Such sharing is done through alliance meetings, forums, and educational programs. Alliances also help in the recruitment and retention of employees, as well as participating in other human resources activities (Zuckerman and Kaluzny 1991).

Joint ventures best describe the second type of alliance, an *opportunistic alliance.* This type of alliance exists when two organizations form a joint venture that relies on the unique strengths of both organizations to create greater success for the participants.

The third type of alliance is the *stakeholder alliance.* The stakeholder alliance is a "value-adding partnership." Stakeholder alliances usually are created by long-term agreements between hospitals and vendors.

Such long-term agreements can foster close relationships between the two entities. Regional or national networks, such as the Voluntary Hospitals of America (VHA), are an example of stakeholder alliances (Zuckerman and Kaluzny 1991).

As noted above, alliance formation is not confined to institutional providers. Alliances may occur between hospitals and physicians, hospitals and businesses, hospitals, physicians and third party payers, and among and between various combinations of all participants.

One goal of providers entering alliances is to create a more integrated health care system that provides multidirectional benefits. Theoretically, participants in alliances can benefit from lower cost due to economies of scale and shared resources. Seamless, integrated, efficient groupings of health care providers may improve their attractiveness to third party payers. Physicians may be attracted to alliances as a means for preservation of income in an uncertain market. Hospitals benefit from alliances through a strengthening of ties with other providers. Providers may benefit through cost reduction by the elimination of redundancies. (Anderson Consulting 1993). Patients may benefit in many ways from these new provider relationships. Conceptually, benefits to the patients can include less price escalation and improved coordination of care.

Hospital–hospital alliances can be found in many forms, from totally integrated models to loose affiliations. Two models of hospital–hospital integration are *super parent* and *limited parent*.

The *super parent* model requires all organizations involved to give up individual control of operations. Control is given to a new organization that runs the alliance. The new organization, or super parent, has the right to elect the boards of each of its constituents. The super parent also approves budgets, negotiates managed care contracts, and approves long-term strategic planning (Anderson Consulting 1993). The advantage of the super parent model includes flexibility, reduction of duplication and overhead, and greater access to capital. The super parent alliance requires member organizations to cede individual control. Often, ceding control is difficult politically. It is also difficult to discontinue the new organizational relationships, once power is given to another organization (Anderson Consulting 1993).

The *limited parent* model is a scaled down version of the super parent model of integration. In the limited parent model, a new organization is formed among the members. Unlike the super parent model, the individual members have control over the new organization (Anderson Consulting 1993). This type of model reduces duplication of administrative effort.

The various models of integration have the same ultimate goal: to provide service through an integrated continuum of preventive and primary care, inpatient hospital care, alternative inpatient care, ambulatory care, transitional care, and long-term or chronic care (Philbin 1993). The objective of an alliance is to create a seamless, vertically integrated system of care that improves quality while controlling costs.

The phenomenon of alliances appears to be one of the results of an identifiable process that has occurred and recurred at regular intervals in the history of organized health care. Much of the rhetoric currently at play is similar to the rhetoric that preceded the enactment of Medicare and Medicaid legislation in the mid–'60s. Issues commanding attention today are similar to the issues that lead to health planning, certification of need regulations, Medicare DRGs, alternative delivery systems, HMOs, PPOs, PHOs, and other such attempts to address problems inherent in organized health care. The case can be made that the issues of cost, access, and quality were the causative factors in the advent of health insurance, Hill–Burton legislation, and other historical changes in organized health care.

The process of change is a reaction to cyclical forces. The depth and breadth of this change related to the length, depth, and breadth of public dialogue regarding the issues rather than the specifics of quality, dollars per capita expended, or access to care.

The resulting actions within organized health care are rarely inventive or innovative. Rather, they are akin to the administration of increasing doses of anesthetizing drugs designed to abate pain. Organized health care, physician and institutional providers, and users devise and administer increasing doses of change to the system until the debate about problems within the system is abated. Historical patterns indicate that the greater the intensity of debate, the greater have been the changes.

Unfortunately, palliative changes in organized health care, like pain medication, cannot and do not address underlying disease.

The phenomenon of strategic alliances is a heavy dose of social, economic, and structural alteration to organized health care that merits examination. Changes currently underway may for the first time consolidate the multiple, fragmented subsystems that comprise organized health care in the United States.

In fact, strategic alliances are attempts to consolidate the previously separate and often antagonistic social and economic subsystems of physician providers, institutional providers, insurers, and those who actually pay for health care services.

## Relationships of Subsets to the Greater Organizational Set

For a so-called industry that prides itself on scientific achievement, organized health care has consisted of separate, boundaried subsystems with minimal information or knowledge exchange among the subsystems in the health care organizational set.

A number of researchers have attempted to describe the process through which subsystems may be linked through information flow (Duncan 1972; Churchman and Schainblatt 1965; Dykeman 1967). Perry and Angel (1979) developed a model for subsystem boundary spanning interaction, using specific individuals called boundary role persons (BRPs) and collective bargaining techniques. Duncan (1980) identified linking agents that facilitate the spanning of subsystem boundaries. In these studies, the identification of linking agents and barriers in the information flow process were considered critical. Aldrich and Herker (1977) found that an organization's ability to cope with environmental constraints depends in part on the ability to achieve a compromise between subsystem maintenance and environmental constraints.

By definition, subsystems are independent, autonomous entities functioning separately or within a larger set. Physicians, hospitals, and ultimate payers have traditionally functioned as independent, autonomous entities within the larger set of organized health care. Insurers, no matter what form they take, have functioned within the set as a subset of entrepreneurial brokers. The essential parts have fostered and perpetuated the growth of insurance broker subsets due to the inability of physicians, institutions, and ultimate payers to communicate in a common language, cooperate, and effectively coordinate the provision of health care services to shared clients.

In part, physicians, institutions, and ultimate payers have remained remote from one another because of the myth and fear of financial risk. The fear of financial risk has caused these payers to abdicate a significant part of the system to insurance brokers. Managed care is little more than a tightly controlled, financially insured risk.

An alliance can serve as the collaborating mechanism in the transfer of information among physicians, institutions, insurers, and ultimate payers. Alliances can cause providers, insurers, and ultimate payers to communicate and to work collaboratively on the same issues together rather than separately.

## Collaborative Alliances in Society

In the world of business, corporate collaborations are a familiar phenomenon. Industrial affiliations and/or mergers occur for purposes of diversification of product line, improved market penetration, financial advantage through the use of economies of scale and for basic corporate strength and survival. While some industrial mergers are characterized as "unfriendly takeovers," for the most part, the joining of two or more businesses, or the merger of smaller businesses into larger corporate structures, is considered to be routine and often healthy. One also sees corporate alliances occur in other stable institutions and enterprises in our society. For example, institutions of higher learning join together for economic reasons as well as for the more effective provision of the process of learning and the development of new knowledge. Churches and religious orders affiliate or merge for the purpose of creating larger and stronger congregations in order to carry out, more effectively, the mission of the particular denomination or church. Human beings marry for a variety of purposes, but such unions are generally based on a mutual desire to live, work, and love together, so that the parties of the union benefit far greater than they would have as separate individuals.

But when hospitals, physicians and other healthcare entities consider marrying, or other types of symbiotic relationships, unusual emotions erupt, and there is a rush to chronicle the activity, as well as to determine the strategic or competitive relevance of the union. Perhaps such mergers, marriages, and other strange relationships involving hospitals and physicians engender emotion and lengthy discussion because such activity is a relatively new phenomenon in organized health care.

Hospitals have been created for social and scientific purposes in over 6,000 locations in the United States. Hospitals are the most unique of modern enterprises according to management theorist, Peter Drucker. They provide services that most recipients would prefer not to need. Most activities carried on in hospitals place the recipients of care in an atypical and unnatural environment. In this unnatural environment, the recipient's bodies, internal chemistries, organs, and personalities are examined, probed, punctured, and excised, in an attempt to resolve and/or cure afflictions that cause great anxiety and fear. In addition, hospitals are unique enterprises because of the myriad of formal and informal relationships brought to bear at the point of service. Physicians, with the exception of teaching physicians and hospital-based specialists, are private entrepreneurs who practice voluntarily at hospitals. In this capacity, physicians interface with a variety of workers in health professional and support capacities to carry out orders to diagnose, examine, and provide therapeutic modalities for the care and treatment of patients.

Hospitals and physicians are the prime example of a service industry. Generally, the products of hospital and physician activities are human-to-human interactive encounters as compared with manufacturing or sales of products in the typical industrial setting. Most patients leave the hospital or physician encounter without tangible evidence of the experience, other than a general feeling of well being and the elimination of anxiety and fear related to disease and injury. Unlike institutions of higher education, diplomas are not awarded. Unlike sales companies, no product can be viewed, used, or worn by the purchaser of the health care service. And, unlike most other economic exchanges, the recipient of the service rarely pays at the point of service.

## Health Care Alliances Create Emotion

In recent years, hospitals and physicians have become the subjects of much discussion related to the cost of care. Headlines proclaim that health care costs, of which a sizable proportion relates to physician or hospital expenditures, have risen at a rate greater than inflation, to the extent that almost 12 percent of the gross domestic product of our country can be related to expenditures for keeping our populace healthy. Of course, such dramatic increases in the cost of health care create additional anxiety on the part of citizens in communities throughout our country. These increases also produce anxiety in business leaders who buy health insurance for employees, tax payers who sponsor health care through governmental programs, insurance companies who provide various types of health care insurance, and others who are generally concerned about the rapid increase in health care costs.

In addition to such broad and varied emotional responses to hospitals and physicians, a broader social view of health care in our country has been difficult to define. Because of the increasing cost to provide care, our nation has wrestled with how this societal need should be balanced against other needs in light of available financial resources. Generally, Americans accept a social philosophy that supports the "highest possible quality" and "unlimited access." Americans also believe that such quality and access should be provided at reasonable costs. Obviously, "reasonable costs" may be defined in a number of ways.

In a strained economy, emotional responses to health care force us to examine our collective social and philosophical conscience and determine if the traditional system of organized health care should continue or if new formats should be created to provide necessary services at the highest possible quality with unlimited access, but at a controlled cost. These are difficult and often unanswerable dilemmas.

The most pressing issue facing the family of health care relationships today is the issue of cost. If, indeed, appropriate health care is a basic human right, how much money can we afford to spend on this right as opposed to other human necessities and societal needs?

One of the ways to address these dilemmas is to determine whether more efficient systems can replace what we have known to be the organized health care system in our country. The multiorganizational alliance can take the form of alliances, mergers, partnerships, and other intimate relationships among and between hospitals, physicians, insurers, and ultimate payers. In the decade of the '90s, we will see a change in the corporate structure of organized health care. Because most hospitals have operated as singular corporate entities, little in the way of economies of scale to contain costs have been available.

Until the burden of regulated payment systems and the advent of for-profit multiple hospital systems emerged in the 1960s and 1970s, singular hospital units attempted to survive financially and provide all elements needed by physicians and patients on a continuing basis. The decade of the '90s will witness a proliferation of new corporate designs as hospitals discover that "going it alone" does not work, and hospitals begin to maneuver for secure positions in a highly competitive marketplace filled with increased risks and continuing complaints about efficiency, effectiveness, and high cost of care.

Alliances and other innovative structures will be based on the need of the singular hospital to protect or expand its market to achieve economies of scale by spreading the high cost of personnel and technology.

The reasons are easy to understand. In addition to economies of scale, singular hospitals that merge into larger corporate entities will also have greater access to capital, increased reimbursement from cost-based payers, reduced regulatory constraints, and to a lesser degree, limited liability for certain operations within the hospital organization. In addition, hospitals in collaborative affiliations and alliances will find it easier to enter nontraditional businesses as a way to offset the high cost of health care and limited reimbursement from regulated governmental agencies and commercial insurance companies.

Similar to human bonding through marriage, alliances, mergers, marriages, and other affiliations will not occur without trauma. For centuries, hospitals have been singularly owned and operated, and the community pride and spirit of those singularly owned units will be forced to give way to the good of a greater need: to provide high quality and access at reasonable costs for multiple, sometimes conflicting constituencies with conflicting missions.

What does this portend for the future? For smaller hospitals in rural or suburban areas, the current economic facts of life are not promising for long-term survival. Access to capital, patient referral patterns, and the recruitment of primary and specialty physicians continue to be problems for smaller communities. Hospitals in smaller communities will find it increasingly difficult to stay abreast of technology and to provide to physicians, and their patients, the type of technology and care required to deal with current diseases and injuries at reasonable costs.

Alliances, mergers, and other formal and informal interactions can be attractive to those who pay for care. Employers and insurance companies encourage the amalgamation of health care entities in order to reduce fragmentation, duplication, and therefore, the cost of health care.

The problems are obvious. No singular hospital or physician, with the pride of history and performance, wishes to give up identity to a larger group. Physicians have reasonable and unreasonable anxieties regarding such activities because there is no guarantee that the essential elements of pride and quality will be maintained as alliances, mergers, and other relationships continue to consolidate hospitals and physicians.

## The Charlotte Experience

The opportunities to alter our microcosmic part of organized health care by creating better outcomes at controlled costs came to be viewed simply as a better way of doing business. The better way could also guarantee not just survival, but integrated success for provider, payer, and patient in our environment.

When we looked at truly integrated systems, we discovered that the best organizations took the time to select from a larger universe—the subset of physicians, and institutional partners for whom collegiality and values were higher priorities than autonomy, status or the ability to buy expensive toys.

This led the board and management team of the Charlotte–Mecklenburg Hospital Authority (CMHA) to a renewed understanding that identification is the most important factor in any individual's association with an organization. Being a member of something good, something that matches one's own values, can greatly influence one's self-concept and attitude, as well as serve as a motivational force to improve performance.

If any integrated health care system, or network, or partnership is to achieve "self-actualization"—the realization of full potential, creativity, and development—it must allow the members or partners to first achieve self-esteem or use of one's skills, confidence, independence, recognition and appreciation from others.

After we redefined, with our board and key physician leadership, the value system we wanted our network to stand for, we went about searching for those physicians and institutions that had similar goals, values and needs.

We found that the opportunities for collegial, value-based partnerships are plentiful. Partnering simply to increase, or prevent loss of, admissions or revenue does not work, just as marriages of necessity or for financial gain usually do not last.

Our network functions without walls. It is diverse geographically. It does not operate under one unifying name and logo. We have not yet advertised the network.

We also understand that this is not a one-act play. We will mature in structure and in quality and cost of our products as time goes on. Patience and tolerance for ambiguity, defining similar value systems, and collegiality are crucial to a successful collaborative effort among hospitals, physicians, insurers, and ultimate payers.

CMHA is a multiorganizational alliance of institutional and physician providers in urban and rural communities in North and South Carolina, direct and indirect purchasers of care, insurers, and managed care companies. CMHA does not conform to any previously reported specific description of an alliance. Rather, CMHA combines elements of alliance models known as consortium, opportunistic, and shareholder.

CMHA serves as the coordinating alliance entity and, as such, may be described as super parent (Anderson Consulting 1993).

## CMHA Alliance Development

The genesis of the multiorganizational alliance known as the CMHA was the passage of the North Carolina Hospital Authority Act in 1943. The forward-looking statute established the structure for the operation of singular or multiple hospitals and related health care services. The structure is quasi-governmental in form, combining elements of both private enterprise and governmental entities.

Originally, the only entity within CMHA was the Charlotte Memorial Hospital which had been constructed in 1940. The hospital authority act created a self-perpetuating governing board and established a broad array of activities and powers available to CMHA.

In the 1960s the second phase of alliance formation occurred. Three smaller hospitals, operating in Mecklenburg County, North Carolina, were added. Huntersville Hospital, Charlotte Community Hospital, and Charlotte Rehabilitation Hospital joined Charlotte Memorial Hospital as members of the Charlotte–Mecklenburg Hospital Authority.

Each of the facilities operated independently, with separate boards appointed by the board of CMHA. The function of the authority was, primarily, to act as the facilitating agent for the several units to general obligation bond funding. Bond funds were dispersed to the separate units for capital improvements and equipment. Each facility was managed independently by administrators reporting to each facility's board. Little in the way of coordination among the facilities occurred.

In the late 1970s, Community Hospital and Huntersville Hospital experienced massive financial losses. Charlotte Memorial Hospital and Charlotte Rehabilitation Hospital continued as marginal successes financially. In 1981, Community Hospital closed its doors and Huntersville

Hospital was in jeopardy of following its sister facility due to low occupancy and eclectic management.

In the third phase of alliance construction, the board of CMHA changed the format and structure of the organization in an attempt to salvage remaining institutional members. The boards of the remaining three facilities were disbanded, and a CEO was named to manage all of the facilities. A long-range plan was developed to solidify and expand the Charlotte–Mecklenburg Hospital Authority into a multiorganizational alliance.

The plan, approved in 1983, had the following goals:

- Creation of a fully integrated health care delivery system
- Creation of financial stability without reliance on tax-based funding
- Maintenance of medical and allied health educational programs
- Competition based on clinical competency, organizational efficiency, and growth of facilities and programs.

To accomplish the creation of a fully integrated health care alliance, and other goals, four initiatives were established. The initiatives were as follows:

1. Establishment of a core group of facilities to provide stability through institutional integration.
2. Establishment of a core group of primary care and subspecialty physicians to provide physician integration.
3. Establishment of value-added relationships with nonurban hospitals in the Charlotte region to provide urban-rural institutional integration.
4. Establishment of value-added relationships with third party payers, managed care companies, and direct purchasers of health care services to provide for provider-payer integration.

The four initiatives were designed to create a multiorganizational integrated alliance. The purpose of the formation of these disparate, and often separately operated activities was strategic for survival in a health care environment that had begun to identify duplication and fragmentation of the various components of health care as the primary cause of cost escalation.

Regulations promulgated to attempt to constrain health care cost escalation rarely apply uniformly to all participants. For example, initial efforts aimed at cost containment were directed toward institutional providers in the 1960s and 1970s. However, to CMHA planners, it was clear that, ultimately, control of cost could not be accomplished by regulatory and management alterations to institutional provider operations alone. Full integration of institutional providers, physician providers, insurers, and ultimate payers offered the only real opportunity to provide a seamless system of quality health care services while concurrently controlling the escalation of the price for services.

The ambitious undertaking was not uniformly applauded by observers. The motives behind CMHA attempts to establish integrated alliance initiatives were not understood by the general public. Changes to the cultures and established relationships among and between health care institutions, physicians, insurers, and ultimate payers created anxiety. Although the multiple initiatives formed a linear plan for the CMHA, alterations to the established systems appeared to occur in a haphazard and uncoordinated manner.

## Core Facility Integration

Alterations to the structure and operation of CMHA core facilities occurred first. The Charlotte Memorial Hospital had transitioned from a 200-bed community hospital in 1943 into a 777-bed medical center with 12 medical and dental residency programs and services equal to those provided at medical school based medical centers. Inexplicably, clinical and environmental changes did not attract insured patients. A multiyear cultural transition was implemented by management to change the format and function of Charlotte Memorial Hospital.

Today, known as the Carolinas Medical Center (CMC), the entity is recognized by the state of North Carolina as one of five academic medical center teaching hospitals. CMC is financially sound and carries a "AA" rating from both Standard and Poor's and Moody's Investor Services. The CMC medical teaching faculty has expanded to 120, and the James G. Cannon research center carries on basic sciences and clinical research. CMC has the region's only level-1 trauma center and also houses the Carolinas Heart Institute, the Children's Hospital, the Carolinas Neurosciences Institute, a cancer center, and the Carolinas Diabetes Center.

Alterations to the physical facility and the creation of a TQM-based corporate culture have attracted insured patients to CMC.

The Charlotte Rehabilitation Hospital has grown from 88 beds to 143 beds and now operates a physical medicine and rehabilitation residency program with a full-time faculty of ten.

Huntersville Hospital was closed. Today, on that site a 377-bed nursing home functions in support of acute facilities within the alliance.

Other CMHA core facilities, added under the institutional integration initiative, include the following:

- University Hospital and Medical Park—130-bed primary and secondary hospital with five physician office buildings
- Amethyst—94-bed substance abuse facility
- Center for Mental Health—66-bed community mental health facility
- Sardis Nursing Home—130-bed nursing home
- Brookwood Retirement Community—60-unit facility.

As a subset of the institutional integration initiative, outpatient facilities were established in North and South Carolina to provide diagnostic radiology, home health services, physical therapy, radiation therapy, surgery, work hardening, health promotion and fitness, and medical equipment supply.

## Physician Integration

The physician integration initiative was premised on the simple fact that neither physicians nor institutional providers can function alone. Although institutional and physician providers have functioned separately, the fragmentation has caused duplication, cost escalation and antagonism. CMHA believed the vital purposes of physician and institutional providers are similar. Creating the environment and structure to accomplish physician integration forced the reality that relationships are more successful if the value systems of the parties in the relationship are compatible.

Beginning in 1984, CMHA sought integrated relationships with groups of primary care and subspecialty physicians. Primary integrated relationships took the form of merger or acquisition with each physician group retaining clinical decision-making responsibilities and corporate name for identity purposes. Secondary integrated relationships with subspecialists took the form of agreements or contracts for services. No agreement or acquisition was based on patient shift.

Early on, CMHA adopted a clinic-without-walls philosophy of physician integration. This philosophy has proven to be more acceptable to physicians in the alliance than more traditional models such as PHO or MSO.

Today, the integrated physician division of the CMHA contains the following components:

- Pediatric Group             6.5
- Family Practice Group       5
- Family Practice Group       3

- Family Practice Group        1.5
- Urgent Care Group            2
- Internal Medicine Group      19
- Internal Medicine Group      22
- Internal Medicine Group      3
- Internal Medicine Group      5
- Ob/Gyn Group                 10
- Rheumatology Group           2
- Primary Care Facility        47
- Subspecialty Facility        25

      Total              151

# Urban-Rural Institutional Integration

It seemed clear to the integrated alliance architects that singular hospitals could not survive alone in a highly competitive, cost conscious environment. Obviously, management expertise and economies of scale can best be used to reduce cost if several institutions combine efforts. Elimination of fragmentation, duplication of effort and services, coordination of patient care, recruitment of physicians and other key personnel, and information processing and exchange are several of the benefits of singular institutions joining an alliance.

Rural hospitals are handicapped by geography, demographics, and economics. An alliance combining urban and rural hospital services and systems can insure survival for both urban and rural institutions.

The Charlotte–Mecklenburg Hospital Authority was awarded a $3 million grant from the federal government to plan an alliance format among urban and rural hospitals. Utilizing the data base and analytical capacity of the Cecil G. Sheps Center for Health Services Research at the University of North Carolina at Chapel Hill, CMHA has created an alliance comprising fifteen nonurban facilities and the Carolinas Medical Center. These members include the following:

| Institutions | Type | Total # Beds |
| --- | --- | --- |
| **AMI Piedmont Medical Center**<br>Rock Hill, South Carolina | Joint planning | 276 |
| **Bruce Hospital System**<br>Florence, South Carolina | Affiliation | 193 |
| **Cabarrus Memorial Hospital**<br>Concord, North Carolina | Joint planning | 284 |

| Institutions | Type | Total # Beds |
|---|---|---|
| **Chester County Hospital** Chester, South Carolina | Affiliation | 163 |
| **Cleveland Memorial Hospital** Shelby, North Carolina | Affiliation | 278 |
| **Florence General Hospital** Florence, South Carolina | Affiliation | 172 |
| **Kings Mountain Hospital** Kings Mountain, North Carolina | Strategic Assessment | 102 |
| **Lincoln County Hospital** Lincolnton, North Carolina | Affiliation | 75 |
| **Mercy Hospital** Charlotte, North Carolina | Affiliation | 97 |
| **Richmond Memorial Hospital** Rockingham, North Carolina | Affiliation | 129 |
| **Scotland Memorial Hospital** Laurinburg, North Carolina | Affiliation | 143 |
| **Stanley Memorial Hospital** Albemarle, North Carolina | Affiliation | 124 |
| **Union Memorial Hospital** Monroe, North Carolina | Affiliation | 195 |
| **Watauga Medical Center** Boone, North Carolina | Affiliation | 98 |
| Total affiliated beds | | 2,605 |

The urban-rural alliance members individually determine programs and strategies appropriate for their facilities. Community-based health agencies and local governments also participate in planning through the alliance. The alliance goals are perpetuation of appropriate institutional activities and elimination of fragmentation and duplication of effort and cost. Alliance activities include jointly negotiating managed care agreements, physician integration through the CMHA network, and the assistance of alliance institutions in the recruitment of primary care physicians. Subspecialty duplication in nonurban areas is unnecessary due to alliance enhanced relationships and communication with Carolinas Medical Center specialty faculty and other subspecialists in the integrated physician network.

The greater alliance set functions as a result of the integration of the subset: the alliance of core facilities, the alliance of primary care and subspecialty physicians, and the alliance of rural hospitals.

## Indirect and Direct Payer Integration

For full integration to occur, an initiative to establish closer relationships with direct and indirect payers of care was initiated. Direct payers were defined as businesses that buy care directly from the greater alliance set or an alliance subset. Indirect payers were defined as third party insurers or managed care noninsurers. Ultimate payers are businesses that purchase care through insurance companies or managed care brokers.

The most delicate relationships in the entire alliance integration were those initiated with direct, indirect, and ultimate payers due to the competitive nature of multidirectional providers and payers. So long as no party dominates the direct or indirect payer market, achievement of symbiosis is possible. Contracts have been negotiated directly with businesses for agreed upon prices, services, and outcome measures. Similarly, contracts with insurers and managed care noninsurers have been negotiated. The essence of these fragile relationships is communication and long-term contractual agreements that provide incentives to all participants to stay in the relationship and make it work to the satisfaction of all parties and patient clients.

After ten years of effort on four initiatives, the integrated alliance shows promise of surviving post–health care reform because of its participant-inclusive integration, successful maintenance of relationships among participants within the alliance, and the flexibility of its structure. The weakness of the alliance is also the flexibility of its structure.

## Unanticipated Affiliations

Early in 1993, while the four strategic components of the CMHA integrated alliance were not only taking shape, but also coalescing, an unanticipated alliance segment developed. Mercy Health Services (MHS) is a catholic organization operating two private, not-for-profit hospitals in Charlotte, NC.

Independently, MHS had evaluated its current and future options and had concluded that a collaborative affiliation with a larger, multidimensional health care organization could provide elements of clinical, organizational, and financial stability, if not security, for its future.

The CEOs of the Charlotte–Mecklenburg Hospital Authority (CMHA) and Mercy Health Services (MHS) entered into conversations regarding the values, goals, and missions of each enterprise. Interestingly, value-system compatibility outweighed the previously competitive nature of the two organizations.

Fully cognizant of potential questions regarding the collaboration of previously separate health care systems, and with the frequent advice and overview of legal counsel, CMHA and MHS arrived at a format to work in a collaborative way to eliminate fragmentation and duplication of effort with the goal of achieving functional integration of services to create a more seamless, cost-effective approach to the provision of health care services. Both CMHA and MHS had separately developed integration of institutional and physician providers.

The boards of CMHA and MHS agreed to develop a collaborative relationship for reasons enumerated earlier. The ongoing relationship is based on value-system compatibility and trust.

While the collaborative effort continues, the demonstration of alliance benefits pertain to and ultimately will provide a more cohesive, cost-effective system including institutional and physician providers, insurers, and managed care companies, as well as ultimate payers.

## The Future

Obviously, the details and implications of reform are unknown. In all probability, such details will not be available until debate ends in one to three years. The CMHA multiorganizational alliance of urban and rural institutional providers, primary care and subspecialty physician providers, and direct, indirect, and ultimate payers may well mature in the interim. Statistical indicators of success are few, but length of stay, cost per discharge, and other frequently used measures are positive. Elimination of duplication of effort, personnel, equipment, and other expense through alliance coordination has occurred. The use of economies of scale in purchasing, production of supplies and laundry, and distribution has begun to impact cost, service, and quality. The use of primary care to manage the cost of disease and injury has promise. Ultimately, the alliance must be flexible enough to serve single payers, managed competition, state buying consortium, price caps, and/or capitation. Depicting the Charlotte–Mecklenburg Hospital Authority multiorganizational alliance structure may be helpful in understanding the interaction basis for relationships among the alliance subsets (Figure 3.1).

The decade-long Charlotte–Mecklenburg Hospital Authority experience in multiorganizational alliance construction has revealed key elements inherent in alliance formation success. They are as follows:

**Figure 3.1**    Charlotte–Mecklenburg Hospital Authority
Multiorganizational Alliance Structure

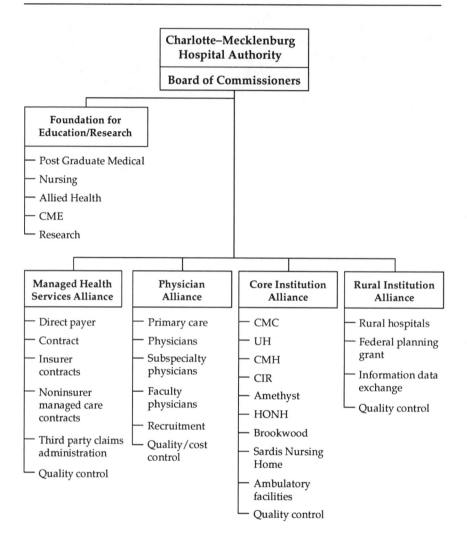

- Corporate governance structure and attitudes conducive to non-traditional approaches to policymaking

- Flexible, nontraditional approaches to managing diverse, often conflicting enterprises and personalities

- Financial stability of the coordinating entity in the greater alliance set
- Value system compatibility among and between alliance subsets
- Ability of management to negotiate for centrality of organizational purpose without requiring loss of identity of alliance subsets
- Serendipity
- Patience
- Tolerance for ambiguity.

In an era of increasing pressure for providers, insurers, and ultimate payers to control costs and improve quality, alliances will continue to thrive. Alliances offer a stable structure in which participants have an opportunity to survive while controlling costs. Alliances provide participants a chance to share in economies of scale and avoid duplication, while providing a fully integrated, seamless system of health care. Most importantly, properly structured, value-system based alliances create an environment of multidirectional trust through participation of the subsets in the future of the greater organizational set of organized health care.

# References

Aldrich, H., and D. Herker. 1977. "Boundary Spanning Roles and Organization Structure." *Academy of Management Review* 2 (April): 217–30.

Anderson Consulting, and Ropes and Gray. 1993. *Winners and Losers—Redefining Relationships Under Health Care Reform.* VHA Carolinas: Tennessee Performance Workshop.

Churchman, C. W., and A. H. Schainblatt. 1965. "The Researcher and the Manager: A Dialectic of Implementation." *Management Science* 11 (February): B69–87.

Duncan, W. J. 1972. "The Knowledge Utilization Process in Management and Organization." *Academy of Management Journal* 15 (September): 273–87.

———. 1980. "Knowledge Transfer in Administrative Science." *Public Administration Review* 40 (July–August): 341–49.

Dyckman, T. R. 1967. "Management Implementation of Scientific Research: An Attitudinal Study." *Management Science* 13 (June): B612–20.

Kanter, R. M. 1989. "Becoming PALs: Pooling, Allying, and Linking Across Companies." *Academy of Management Executives* 3 (August): 183–93.

Montgomery, R. L. 1991. "Alliances: No Substitute for Core Strategy." *Frontiers of Health Services Management* 7 (3): 25–28.

Perry, J. L., and H. L. Angle. 1979. "The Politics of Organizational Boundary Roles in Collective Bargaining." *Academy of Management Review* 4 (October): 487–96.

Philbin, P. W. 1993. "From the Ground Up: Planting the Seeds of Network Development." *Hospitals and Health Networks* 67 (June): 46.

Zuckerman, H. S., and A. D. Kaluzny. 1991. "Strategic Alliances in Health Care: The Challenges of Cooperation." *Frontiers of Health Services Management* 7 (3): 3–23.

———. 1992. "Strategic Alliances: Two Perspectives for Understanding Their Effects on Health Services." *Hospital & Health Services Administration* 37 (4): 478–88.

# The Commentaries: A Summary

Three panelists respond to the Nurkin paper providing illustrations and a perspective to the challenges facing the development of alliance structures within health care. R. PAUL O'NEILL begins with the description of the process and players involved in the formation of the Yankee Alliance. Yankee Alliance is a group of noncompeting hospitals in the Northeast and this description outlines its rationale, its early challenges, and its current-day mission and values.

The last two papers provide a perspective to the alliance movement. PAUL COOPER III addresses the issue of different types of alliances and the factors associated with their success. Attention is given to vertical versus horizontal integration, the importance of competition to assure quality performance and the role that employers in data base models will play in the development and management in both vertically and horizontally integrated alliances.

Finally, ALAN WEINSTEIN reminds us of the importance of definition and the dimensions, components, and levels involved. He talks about the evolution of alliance functions, and the shift from emphasis on economics of cost and cost containment to the emerging emphasis on revenue and the inclusion of suppliers and physicians as they participate in the challenges of preserving revenue.

# R. Paul O'Neill

Nurkin defined strategic alliances as, "Little more than reactive configurations . . . placebos for fractures in our current [health care delivery] systems." He said, " . . . hospitals that do not wish to merge with larger systems may attempt to form alliances with other singular hospitals in an effort to find the benefits of marriage without actually consummating the marriage." The following is my description of how a group of noncompeting hospitals in the northeast put together their placebo. My intention is to give you an idea of why Yankee Alliance was formed, its early challenge to add membership while defining its purpose, selecting its tasks, and establishing a modus operandi.

The transference of knowledge and sharing of demonstrated expertise were early goals of the organization along with revenue generation, cost reduction, and the ability of doing things better collectively than hospitals could do individually.

To share services among members on a regional basis had some appeal to the original membership. Diana Barrett of Harvard, Howard Zuckerman from the University of Michigan, and Montague Brown had consulting roles to play in the early planning of the organization along with Karl Klicka of the Kellogg Foundation. By 1982 a group of five CEOs were meeting sporadically during New England Hospital Assembly gatherings to put flesh on the bones of the concept.

A list of potential projects and joint venture opportunities was constructed with Barrett's help (using the Delphi method), suggesting some initial projects for the then group of five to consider. A $13.8 million bond issue, jointly issued by four hospitals through Yankee Alliance, resulted from the identification of the need for short-term capital. The unique issue, a variable rate demand note, pooled capital debt financing offered through three state HEFAs, gained Yankee some national attention.

Eastern Maine Medical Center had positioned itself for membership in United Healthcare Systems of Kansas City during 1983. However, United and Associated Healthcare Systems of Phoenix froze their membership recruitment efforts in 1983 pending an exploration of the potential for merger of the two hospital systems. With the Eastern Maine entree, Yankee positioned itself for membership in the emerging American Healthcare System, the merged United and Associated Healthcare Systems. An exception to the membership criteria was sought by Yankee, in that, unlike all other AmHS shareholder members, Yankee did not and had no intentions to, own its member hospitals. As an alliance, we are

R. Paul O'Neill is president of Yankee Alliance.

now unique among the 40 shareholder members, in that Yankee does not own its member hospitals. All the other 39 shareholder systems own two or more hospitals. In 1985, AmHS approved Yankee's shareholder/member status at which time we became the 27th shareholder/member—the second organization to join AmHS following the merger.

In the spring of 1985 Yankee began offering its then three member hospitals purchasing contracts for medical-surgical supplies and pharmaceuticals in conjunction with AmHS. Though the program was far from developed at that time, it showed promise. With the assistance of Health Center Corporation, the rudiments of a regional purchasing program were put in place for the then three Yankee Alliance member hospitals in mid-1985. Membership increased from three to five members by the end of the year. Six months later, three additional members were added and Yankee began to establish the critical mass necessary to strike out on a number of programs development projects, including a managed care development program.

From the beginning, Yankee's founders had intended to link hospitals in New England and upstate New York with other strong hospitals. Managed care was seen as "glue" which would bind the membership closer and more firmly together. A triple option product consisting of an indemnity, a PPO, and an HMO product was developed over a 15-month period. The Provident and Transamerican insurance companies, along with the AmHS proposed PPO product, were committed to underwrite the respective elements of the Yankee health insurance product.

At a point when the managed care product was to be capitalized, a wise decision was made by the board of Yankee to cease the project due to the failure of the Provident to honor its investment commitment and AmHS's decision to get out of the PPO business. In addition, Yankee members had significant concerns about their chances to adequately penetrate a very competitive managed care market in New England.

The experience of research and development of the managed care product added glue to the Yankee organization. Though the product never went on line, members saw the positive aspects of researching and developing a product or service regionally. Despite the nonoutcome, the shared-experience and shared-risk aspects, the regional research and development project was beneficial to the membership. Each was not independently responsible for the cost of the research, educational, and developmental aspects of creation of a managed care product; rather, the members shared the risk.

Following studies in 1987 and 1988, the first conducted by the staff and the second by Touche Ross (Deloitte and Touche), the Board approved the development of a collection agency to collect the overdue patient accounts of member hospitals. Ultimately, two corporations were

**Table 3.1**  Yankee Alliance Goals, 1994

| *A. Take Costs Out* | *B. Put Revenues In* | *C. Learn as You Go* |
| --- | --- | --- |
| **Mission** | **Mission** | **Mission** |
| Yankee Alliance, a 4,000-bed health care system, will develop and implement collaborative processes to achieve significant cost reductions for member hospitals. | Yankee Alliance will identify common needs of member hospitals and research, develop and implement strategies designed to augment revenues and to maintain and expand markets. | Yankee Alliance will create a learning environment to support the transformation of knowledge, skills, and attitudes needed to master the demands of the new health care world. |
| **Goals** | **Goals** | **Goals** |
| 1. Continue with what is working now.<br><br>2. Gain consensus and commitment to a collaborative process:<br>• Working with each department head, identify cost savings opportunities and objectives<br>• In collaboration with senior operations managers (COOs) identify cost savings objectives hospitalwide | 1. Vigorously pursue the development of a primary-care physician entity that will be instrumental in helping hospital members establish a dedicated primary care network.<br><br>2. Information Systems—development of a managed care world. | 1. Because we believe the speed of learning is today's primary source of competitive advantage, we pledge to make our time together learning time.<br><br>2. Board meetings will be held through teleconferencing. |

- Develop and implement measuring/reporting tools to monitor progress towards goals
- Focus always on successes of the "Yankee Process" and seek to identify additional opportunities.

3. Develop a simple project/planning tool for CEO oversight and reinforcement back at the hospital.
4. Learn how to relate Yankee efforts to compressed time, restructuring of work programs at the hospitals.
5. Bring COOs together.

3. The board members will meet for action learning sessions on a quarterly basis. The format will be seemingly chaotic, interactive dialogue—not formal presentations—because we must learn from the actions we have taken in the face of gross uncertainty. (These sessions might include other hospital members, especially trustees, as appropriate.)
4. We will encourage and provide support for any kind of ad hoc learning efforts. Our collective size provides preferential access to scarce expertise.

Notes: Cross Cutting Goals for Yankee:
1. Create and provide a budget for a Yankee Alliance reward, recognition, and incentive program.
2. Develop a leading edge competency in distributed site work (e.g., "working together, apart"). Put the capability into practice to overcome the long distance between members.

formed: a not-for-profit cooperative to collect member hospital accounts and a standard business corporation to collect physician and nonhospital accounts. Six member hospitals became owners/members/customers of the not-for-profit cooperative in the fall of 1988. Currently, all but two of the members are participating in the collection program. Accounts placed annually amount to in excess of $14 million. The collection agency is rapidly transitioning into a service bureau, offering a wide array of patient account personnel, insurance, and legal and educational services to eleven member/customers.

Gerry McManis of McManis Associates was a key person urging the Board to explore managed care as a regional group of hospitals. He went further to encourage a geographic clustering of other services at member hospitals.

Clustering has historically had two meanings in Yankee. The first holds that members may select, based upon their needs, from a menu of services (other than core services such as the purchasing program which is mandatory for all to participate in and be in compliance with). The second meaning of clustering has to do with a membership strategy whereby members look to cluster affiliate hospitals of interest to them within some relevant geography, offering them access to Yankee Alliance and AmHS services such as the purchasing program.

Yankee has always taken the position that members should not have overlapping service areas. The membership has benefited from this policy in that open, frank discussions can occur in our forum. From early on membership was restricted to 200-plus bed hospitals serving distinct geographies which have good financial positions and a CEO who will "fit" as a Yankee Board member.

Yankee Alliance is maturing and metamorphosing. It presently concentrates on missions geared to assist its members in establishing cost reducing and revenue enhancing integrated delivery systems for their communities. Table 3.1 describes our current missions and goals.


# Paul Cooper III

I haven't studied the literature of human and organizational behavior and certainly not to the extent that Nurkin has. I come to this discussion

---

Paul Cooper III is chief operating officer for HealthSpring.

strictly as a manager. I've been involved with a number of things I think most of us would call strategic alliances, as a manager and from the inside—some involving HMOs and insurance companies, some involving physician groups and HMOs, some involving HMOs and hospitals, some involving employers and managed care companies.

I have taught health care administration at the graduate level for one memorable semester and I think how I came to do that is a story worth telling. In 1979, I went to Oklahoma City, working for the Prudential Insurance Company to develop a group practice HMO program, which I proceeded to do from scratch. We acquired medical facilities, recruited primary care physicians, built a medical group from the bottom up, contracted with a hospital (later more than one hospital), got licensed from the state, and put the thing together. I had been there three or four years when the head of the Health Care Administration Program at the OU Health Sciences Center approached me about teaching a course in Ambulatory Health Care Administration. I felt I really had a lot of strikes against me. My academic background was in English literature, relevant perhaps in the long stretch; and second, in Oklahoma, I was a Texan. Now from here Oklahomans and Texans may look quite similar but, in fact, they respect their differences down there. Oklahomans tell a story about Texans and how Texas came to be settled. It was during the Land Rush of 1889; when some of the Sooners went off course, and drifted south across the Red River, some of them encountered a sign that said "Texas Begins Here." So, of course, all those who could read, turned back.

As if those two crosses weren't enough to bear, I was in the pay of an Eastern insurance company, which is not an instant ticket to friendship anywhere anymore, and certainly not in the Oklahoma City of 1979. But they had this course in the catalogue, "Ambulatory Health Care Administration," for three years. They said, "Nobody here feels qualified to teach it. All of us are hospital by training, by background. You've been doing it. We'd like you to teach it." So I did. Fifty students signed up and all 51 of us worked very hard. I don't think the academic community today behaves as if hospitals were the center of the universe. But I think we're still coming off that mind-set, which has something to do with how we think about strategic alliances and how we think about the health care system. As a manager, I'm not going to enter the definitional debate either. In the tradition of Stein and Nurkin, I spend most of my time thinking about what works and what doesn't, rather than what you call it.

I will start with some observations about different types of strategic alliances, which ones I think are the most significant, and some thoughts on what will determine success.

I submit to you that between vertical integration and horizontal integration, I think vertical integration is the phenomenon to watch. I think that is the central one, the most important, and I'll tell you why I think that. First, as Nurkin said, to make any of these types of alliances work, significant behavioral changes are necessary. I think he referred specifically to physicians and the need for physicians in this context to learn to behave more as members of a team, as sharers of responsibility and authority with other kinds of providers. I think that's less likely to happen if you only horizontally integrate physicians or physician groups.

A very compelling economic point is that if we're looking for value in health care, for the best clinical outcome, and at the same time, the best available economical outcome in doing that, it has to be the case that savings in one sector of the delivery system can be credited against another. I think vertical integration with an integrated budget makes that possible. For example, you can string together as many hospitals as you want in horizontal integration, and yet if you move a patient from the inpatient setting to some outpatient setting, that's a loss of revenue if the budget is defined as the hospital piece. You need this broader budget so that saving here is credited here.

A second example—you can string together as many surgeons as you like in horizontal integration and yet if a decision is made to manage a patient's problem medically, with prescription drug therapy, as opposed to surgery, that's a loss of revenue to the surgery line unless the surgery and pharmaceutical budgets and all those pieces are together. I think that's a very compelling argument for vertical integration. I think vertical integration will drive horizontal integration, but not the other way around. As organized systems of care that are responsible and accountable for providing the whole range of health services to patients, among other things, seek the optimal service mix and the optimal mix of providers. To do that will cause the right kind of horizontal integration to occur in hospitals to think about how they can share resources as well as physicians and medical groups.

We will see in the future a variety of sponsorships and alliances or accountable health plans or whatever you want to call them. We'll see hospital-driven alliances. We'll see physician-driven alliances. We'll see payer-driven alliances. My company is involved with what I would call a joint-physician group and payer-strategic alliance in a northeastern city. There is a large Blue Cross plan that has hundreds of thousands of HMO members in a network, but wants also to bring a group practice-based product to the market. We are in an exclusive relationship with that payer. We are going to develop a full-time primary care group practice of salaried physicians to be the core of the delivery system for that new product. Again, we need to think about the alliance phenomenon as one that will involve a multiplicity of sponsors. I think the physician-driven and payer-driven alliances are probably as important as the hospital-driven alliances.

Health care organizations, or alliances, that compete for patients with other alliances are likely to reach higher levels of performance than those that do not. We'll have both situations. We'll have rural or smaller communities, where for a variety of reasons maybe there is only one integrated health care delivery organization. I think there are some compelling considerations that make choice, or competition if you like, something that drives us towards higher performance. It's going to take tremendous incentives to change behavior in the ways that will be required to make vertically and horizontally integrated alliances work. Incentives are going to be required. A market gives choices to the consumer, and that calls for meaningful comparisons in the job that various alliances do in taking care of their population, and will produce a more aggressive benchmark performance than either regulation or collegial self-discipline will.

I've spent my entire career, basically, focusing on the private-sector employer-driven market. One of the strongest forces driving change in our health care system, totally irrespective of the White House and the Congressional debate, is the growing ability and the growing awareness of employers that it is becoming possible to measure the value of what they receive in health care. There are emerging techniques for measuring the outcomes that occur (I am speaking of population-based statistics, for those of you who are not familiar with HEDIS) that make it really possible (for the first time) for major payers to specify and demand levels of performance from a health care delivery system.

Nurkin's response makes a reference to our intoxication with the data-based competitive model. We don't want to get drunk on it, but I think the data-based competitive model is here to stay. Are all the measures valid? No. We're a long way from having scientifically or clinically valid measures to really make all the adjustments we need to evaluate the performance of one health plan against another. But it's critically important that employers, who pay for a large part of the health care in the system, are starting to ask the right question: What are we getting for what we spend? That's the central question in health care reform. Politically, the debate will always gravitate towards what are we spending and how can we get somebody else to pay for it, or who can persuade the largest number of voters that someone else will pay for their health care.

Finally, in evaluating and studying this alliance phenomenon, we need to look not only inside at the stuff that holds strategic alliances together, but look outside as well at the circumstances that brought them together. Introspection can always be dangerous in excess and there are as many outside factors as internal ones that would bring alliances together. It's important to consider that it's the comparison to others that spurs being the best you can be in health care or anything else.

# Alan Weinstein

What struck me when I was asked to respond to some of the early comments was that as much as we don't want to discuss definitions, it's pretty tough not to. It's really a question of where you are coming from in terms of your own personal experience. We've talked about multihospital systems, we've talked about multiprovider networks, and we've talked about alliances. We've talked about local, regional, and national; and if you put all those cells on a chart, it's pretty tough to not come away saying there needs to be some type of clarification and definition but I'm not going to try to do that.

In thinking back to the paper which was talking about a system's development in a particular community, I was struck by a couple of things. It was referencing an inpatient focused, hospital administration approach to economies of scale and, short of the explanation that we've just heard, it was mostly geared toward cost containment. I think if you look nationally and over a period of time, this is exactly also what's occurred. That, back in the '50s and '60s, you had groups coming together, either for a single purpose in the purchasing area, or in other cost-containment areas. That's all that they were about. They were also just hospital groups and they were looking at the cost-containment side of the equation. I believe what's really thrown everybody on their head in the last number of years in the alliance movement, and in the hospital industry locally, is that people are now saying you've got to take a look at the revenue side of the equation. You've got to take a look at the way you can collaborate together on the revenue side. So the risks now are a revenue risk rather than just the risk of reducing cost. I think a lot of the alliances that are going to continue to be successful into the future are going to have to bridge both the cost side and the revenue side. That can be through a local mechanism, or it can be as a national organization, or a regional organization like the Yankee Alliance.

---

Alan Weinstein is president of Premier Health Alliance, Inc.

It was mentioned earlier that you needed to constantly bring value back to the members; this could be in a multi-institutional system or it could be with a single hospital and its medical staff. But, if you don't quantify on a regular basis the types of things that you are bringing back, in terms of both hard tangible dollars as well as the soft qualitative stuff, you're going to have problems over time. Alliance members around the table frequently have different views of what they want to get out of the relationship even though in these relationships we want to align everybody's incentives up front. As separate legal entities, alliance members over time are going to find different things coming up that are tugging at them, bringing them together and also pulling them apart. If you can't, as an organization, constantly validate what you are doing for your members, you are going to start seeing that fragile structure start falling apart.

In national alliances we do not get involved in the direct provision of patient-care services. We leave that up to our own constituents and members who in their own local markets are doing their own thing. I think we all (AmHS, VHA, Premier, and others) from time to time have kind of skirted into this area but we've stayed away from direct patient care. What's starting to confuse the issue significantly right now has to do with a lot of the regional activities that are occurring among our own members who are getting together with members of other organizations who traditionally we viewed in competing camps. In St. Louis, for example, three hospital shareholders in three different national alliances are basically coming together under one umbrella—it just doesn't make any sense for that new entity to have three different alliance affiliations. This brings into question the whole selection process of how the network will decide whom to affiliate. They might throw the three of us out and bring in a fourth, who knows? But that raises the issue of would it be better for the alliances and in the three hospitals to try to do something new and different? In the past, we would have never thought about allowing those other providers to gain access to our programs or to work together with one of the other national alliances specifically in a specific local market. But as the providers out there at the hospital level are starting to hook up in some strange relationships, we too in the future might find ourselves putting together a joint venture with one of our traditional competitors in a local market to serve common members who would then become members of a new joint venture.

Many managed care issues that our own members are confronting, such as being part of a PPO network where you've got competitors historically now coming together, are confronting national alliances. Where it gets further complicated for the national alliances is the fact that we're involved in providing managed care consultation and direct management expertise to our members at the local level, and they are bringing to us providers in other national groups that want to be part of the local group but they don't want to join Premier at a national level. It gets back to the earlier point that you've really got different spheres here—things going on locally and other things going on nationally and regionally.

From our perspective at Premier, we are recognizing that a lot of the traditional policies that said if you are a part of VHA you can't be a part of Premier, AmHS, or whatever are now changing. I see that changing even more dramatically in the future, just as those relationships have been changing at the local level. Where this gets particularly confusing is with the supplier community. And again it was mentioned earlier and I concur, that a very significant income stream for alliances comes from the supplier community through group purchasing. If you have a particular hospital provider that's involved in multiple groups because of the blurring of these relationships, it's very, very confusing and troublesome to the suppliers out there who want to know are you in this group or that group. That's an issue that in the next few years will have to be sorted out.

The last point that I don't think anyone has really discussed at any length, is that we should not forget that the suppliers are part of this whole equation. As you start talking about capitation and subcapitation of managed care plans in the future, you have to start thinking that the suppliers ought to be responsible for both the good and the bad financial outcomes; perhaps as a quasi-provider or as a sub-capitator, along with those who are involved in direct provision of services. The alliances should not always just be thought of as provider groups, they should also involve the supplier side of the community.

Another observation in Nurkin's paper had to do with alliances of hospitals getting together with their medical staff and thinking that everybody has aligned incentives. I believe the only reason in many communities the medical staff is getting together in this day and age with the hospitals, has to do with the issue of preserving revenue. The physicians fear they are going to lose revenue and not be able to compete on managed care contracts. The physicians come at that alliance relationship looking at the revenue side and don't expect the hospital to do much for them on the cost side. If you look at why hospitals in recent years have come together, it was to address economies of scale on the cost side of the operation, although in local markets now that is also changing. My point here is that when you bring together parties to come under an umbrella of an alliance, you absolutely have to know what their expectations are, what their incentives are, what they expect to take away from the party, and I think we gloss over that much too quickly.

Finally, Nurkin mentioned issues of the community, how difficult it is for hospitals to start getting together or for a community to give up a particular facility or service because of the pride that they associate with that facility. I don't think that we can lump communities all together. I think it's a very different situation in the urban areas than it is in the rural areas. In the urban areas, there isn't anything near that sense of community when it comes to preserving the services or the structure of a facility, as it might be in a rural community where the hospital and the medical staff represent perhaps the only alternatives for the community and also represent the largest employer in the community. The urban areas are a very different setting from the rural areas.

# 4

# The Structure of Strategic Alliances: Evidence from Rural Hospital Networks

Jon B. Christianson, Ira S. Moscovice, and Anthony L. Wellever

The purpose of this paper is to provide a conceptual framework for understanding the structure of strategic alliances and to illustrate how that framework can be applied in analyzing the structure of one type of alliance—the rural hospital network. Data for the empirical analysis were collected through a survey of rural hospital networks throughout the United States. These data are used to describe the structural dimensions of rural hospital networks and the interrelationships among these dimensions. The paper concludes by identifying several potentially fruitful areas of empirical research relating to the structure of alliances in health care.

## The Structure of Strategic Alliances: Definitions and a Conceptual Framework

The terms "strategic alliance" and "organizational structure" are used in many different ways in the literature. Therefore it is necessary to begin by defining how these terms will be used in this paper.

### What Is a Strategic Alliance?

An alliance, as we use the term, refers to a voluntary, loosely coupled interorganizational relationship between two or more organizations that

---

Jon B. Christianson and Ira S. Moscovice are professors at the Institute for Health Services Research, University of Minnesota. Anthony L. Wellever is a research fellow at the Institute.

are linked in ways that preserve the legal identity and autonomy of each, as well as most of their functional autonomies (Longest 1990). As such, an alliance is an intermediate organizational form that falls between the hierarchical organization on one extreme and the market at the other extreme.

There is agreement in the literature that exchanges between organizations are managed differently by markets and hierarchies. Markets are the most common way in which linkages are established between organizations. In the simplest "spot market," exchange takes place based on the "market price," both parties possess adequate information about the characteristics of the good or service being exchanged, and organizations are linked as "buyers" and "sellers" in this single exchange.

Market failures and high transaction costs limit the utility of markets for some interorganizational exchanges. Williamson (1975) has argued that the limitations inherent in market mechanisms as means of organizing production and exchange explain the presence of hierarchical firms. And Powell (1990) noted,

> . . . transactions that involve uncertainty about their outcome, that recur frequently and require substantial "transaction specific investments" are more likely to take place within hierarchically organized firms. . . . transactions are moved out of markets into hierarchies as knowledge specific to the transaction (asset specificity) builds up. When this happens, the inefficiencies of bureaucratic organization will be preferred to the relatively greater costs of market transactions (296–97).

Hierarchical firms are seen as one means of addressing the problems of "bounded rationality" (the inability of parties to an exchange to write contracts that cover all possible contingencies) and "opportunism" (the potential for a party in a transaction to use information asymmetries to their advantage in a market exchange). The "boundaries" of the firm (which activities the firm will carry out internally) depend on how the firm weighs the relative inefficiencies of each alternative across the myriad of decisions critical to the production process.

While the concept of the hierarchical firm and the market as extreme forms of organizing exchange is useful, there are clearly a large number of examples of organizational linkages that fall between these extremes (Borys and Jemison 1989). Organizational theorists are currently devoting considerable attention to the development of theoretical models of these intermediate organizational forms that address questions such as: Why do intermediate forms exist? What motivates their participants? How do they develop over time? How should their success be measured? However, with few exceptions, relatively little attention has been devoted to describing and understanding the structure of intermediate forms. The effort devoted to this end has focused primarily on those intermediate forms, such as the "quasi firm" and the "joint venture," that most closely resemble the classical firm (Luke, Begun, and Pointer 1989). The structure of more loosely coupled intermediate forms including, we would argue, the "alliance," has been the subject of much less discussion. This is perhaps understandable, since the term "strategic alliance" seems to imply a temporary linkage of convenience among organizations (or countries or individuals) that would possess a relatively flexible and easily altered structure. Yet, a case can be made for the potential importance of structure in differentiating among alliances, understanding their actions, and predicting their performance.

Obviously, a wide variety of organizational linkages fit our broad definition of strategic alliance, including long-term contractual relationships between sellers and buyers. Therefore, to focus this discussion, we will consider only a particular type of strategic alliance—one that involves " . . . similar organizations operating in the same industry which serve geographic markets with roughly equivalent products" (Longest 1990, 21). In the health care industry, examples of strategic alliances that will not be addressed in this paper include alliances between physician groups and hospitals aimed at achieving increased vertical integration of service delivery, or long-term purchasing relationships between hospitals and suppliers of pharmaceuticals, equipment, and so on. However, the discussion in this paper will encompass, for example, "horizontal combinations" of physician group practices, of hospitals, or of community health centers.

## The Structure of Strategic Alliances

Organizational structure refers to the internal differentiation and patterning of relationships among participants in an organization (Thompson 1967). A key characteristic of organizations, structure creates a stable context for the functioning of the organization; it relieves participants of the need to define each situation anew.

We hypothesize that a key element in understanding the structure of an alliance is the motivation for its formation. This hypothesis is based on the assumption that an alliance is the result of strategic adaptation. It can be viewed as the outcome of an attempt by managers of one or more of the participating organizations to manage the organization's environment more effectively (Shortell, Morrison, and Friedman 1992). This is consistent with a "resource dependence" model of the organization which, as described by Kimberly, Leatt, and Shortell (1983):

> . . . portrays the organization as an active agent of change, capable of altering the environment as well as responding to it. Administrators regard

this as a crucial activity that involves the management of a complex set of exchange relationships designed to acquire the resources necessary for survival. These exchange relationships often entail ties of mutual dependence and, in the face of few alternatives, asymmetric power relations that result in dependence upon more powerful and potentially controlling elements in the environment. The manager's strategy therefore becomes a balancing act of obtaining necessary resources without making unnecessary commitments or weakening the power of the organization to manage its own affairs. This model further assumes that a variety of possible actions and resulting structures can lead to organizational survival; in other words, no single structure will yield optimal environmental fit. (p. 340)

This description of the manager as change agent could serve equally well as a general summary of the motivation for the formation of alliances—they are relationships that result from the actions of managers in balancing the need to obtain necessary resources without making unnecessary commitments or weakening the power of the organization to manage its own affairs. Viewing the alliance as the result of an adaptive activity suggests that the structure of an alliance will reflect the goals of the participating organizations for that alliance. This assumes that in forming the alliance, the manager(s) has specific objectives in mind for it and the structure of the alliance is designed to facilitate the achievement of those objectives. How conflicts among objectives of the organizations forming the alliance are resolved is usually not explicitly addressed in the literature.

According to a rational model of behavior, alliance participants would recognize that cooperation is in their best interest as long as all have some expectation of securing benefits from cooperation over the long term. Under these conditions, the structure of the alliance will be chosen so as to maximize the expected joint benefits for the participants, with written or unwritten rules established to allocate those benefits among participants over time. However, some analysts might argue that the structure of alliances is essentially the result of a political bargaining process among members. Pfeffer (1978), for example, takes this approach in explaining the internal structure of firms, with employees as the "members" or "participants." This political model would argue that alliance participants cannot be expected to view the alliance from a global perspective, making "rational" decisions about the structure that would maximize joint benefits for all members. Therefore, the goals of an alliance will reflect the goals of its individual participants, weighted by their political power within the alliance. Viewed from this perspective, the structure of the alliance will reflect the resolution of political struggles among members, rather than their intendedly rational, cooperative efforts (Kimberly, Leatt, and Shortell 1983). A major purpose of the structure of an alliance, according to this model, is to reduce the potential for conflict, since conflict is costly and limits the ability of the alliance to deliver benefits to its members. In either the rational or political model, organizational structure is hypothesized to depend on the goals of participants, although the way in which conflicts relating to organizational goals are resolved differs between the models.

The literature cites a variety of possible motivations for the formation of loosely coupled, horizontal, cooperative arrangements among organizations (Oliver 1990). The economic view of the alliance emphasizes its ability to minimize transaction costs for all parties involved. Jarillo (1988), for instance, suggests that an alliance will be formed if the costs of transacting (carrying out an exchange) within the alliance framework are less than the costs of transacting and organizing without it. Under this view, an alliance is a tenuous form of organization that will be displaced by any other organizational form that promises lower transaction costs. Its structure is extremely fluid and is subject to repeated alteration in response to changes in environmental factors or the characteristics of organizational participants that might influence transaction costs.

Other theorists believe, however, that there are objectives other than the minimization of short run transaction costs that motivate the formation of an alliance. Powell (1990) summarizes this view as follows:

> In only a minority of instances is it sensible to maintain that the genesis of network forms is driven by a concern for minimizing transaction costs. Strategic considerations—such as efforts to guarantee access to critical resources, to obtain crucial skills that cannot be produced internally, to pacify the concerns of professional communities or national governments . . . certainly seem to outweigh simple concern for cost minimization. (p. 323)

This view clearly emphasizes the "strategic" dimension of an alliance. It suggests a longer-term relationship that is more stable than that based on cost minimization alone and possibly less clearly defined and measurable objectives for alliance participants.

While alliances may have similar goals, they may differ in the activities they adopt to reach those goals. Variation in activities could occur because of differences in environmental conditions and in the characteristics of participants in the alliance. Different structures may be more effective at supporting different types of activities even when, ultimately, the hoped-for outcomes of the activities are the same. Therefore, in addition to the goals of the alliance, the nature of the activities chosen for pursuit of those goals could influence the structure adopted for the alliance.

## The Dimensions of Structure in Strategic Alliances

In the previous section we argued that alliances resulted from the purposeful, goal-directed activities of organizational managers. In this view, variation in the structure of alliances could be expected because the participants in different alliances have different goals; conflicts among the goals of participants are resolved in different ways; participants face different environments and have different organizational characteristics; and participants choose different activities to pursue the goals of the alliance.

The purpose of this section is to identify the relevant dimensions of the structure of alliances. Our fundamental hypothesis in this discussion is that, since alliances are "hybrid" organizations on the continuum between markets and hierarchies, their structure can be described by drawing from the literature on the structure of markets and on the design of organizations. Therefore, we begin by briefly discussing the commonly employed descriptors of market structure and of organizational design. We then propose a conceptual framework for classifying and measuring the dimensions of the structure of alliances that combines elements of both perspectives.

In describing and contrasting different markets, the classical literature from industrial organization distinguishes between the concepts of structure, conduct, and performance. The *structure* of a market is a term encompassing market features such as the number and size of sellers, the degree of differentiation among products, the presence or absence of barriers to the entry of new sellers, and the diversity characterizing firm product lines. The conduct of sellers in a market refers to pricing policies, advertising, legal tactics, and so forth. Performance relates to the ability of a market to generate the outcomes desired by society.

Alliances contain clear counterparts to the concepts of market conduct and performance. The parallel to conduct consists of the activities that the alliance undertakes, while the parallel to market performance is the ability of the alliance to achieve the goals it has established for itself. More importantly, some of the dimensions of market structure would appear relevant to the structure of alliances. For example, the structure of an alliance can be described, in part, by the number and relative size of its participants. However, unlike markets, this element of structure for an alliance is the result of decisions made by the founders of the alliance or, subsequent to formation, by its members. What are termed "barriers to entry" in describing market structure could be termed "conditions of membership" for the alliance. Thus the number of alliance members and their relative size are elements of the design of the alliance. They can be expected to influence the costs of transacting within the alliance and the nature of the exchanges that take place.

In addition to size and number of participants, an implicit element of the structure of some markets, particularly markets for services, is the geographic relationship among market participants. Firms are included in the description of a market's structure, or excluded from a market, based on their physical proximity to other sellers. The geographical relationship among members of alliances is similarly an important dimension of alliance structure. It influences whether alliance members are competitors in the sale of their products and it affects the programs that alliances undertake. For instance, if alliance members are located quite far apart from each other, they may not be able to undertake projects involving the sharing of productive inputs, but they may still be able, for example, to combine their political lobbying efforts effectively.

A fourth element of structure relating to membership characteristics has been termed "complexity" by Kaluzny et al. (1992) and "homogeneity" by other authors (Powell 1990). In general, complexity refers to variation in the types of organizations that participate in an alliance. Even though our focus is on alliances consisting of organizations producing "roughly similar products," the degree of homogeneity can still be an important characteristic of the structure of these alliances. Powell (1990) suggests that the more homogeneous are organizational participants in networks with respect to their cultures and experiences, the greater the trust among members, and the easier it is to sustain network arrangements. Size (1993), in summarizing the experience of a rural hospital cooperative, concludes that trust among members is the "first principle" of successful collaborative arrangements. Similarly, D'Aunno and Zuckerman (1987a) hypothesize that when members of alliances share values and goals, transactions costs in the formation and operations of an alliance are reduced.

Just as the dimensions of market structure suggest relevant descriptors of the structure of alliances, so do the dimensions of organizational design within hierarchical firms. As defined by Kimberly, Leatt, and Shortell (1983), "The term organization design refers to the way authority, responsibility and information are combined within a particular organization" (p. 293). In discussing the organization design of hierarchical firms, the components of organizations are often identified as top management, middle management, the technological structure, the support staff, and the operating core (or workers). Different designs can then be described in terms of different configurations of these components. Because alliances are more flexible, informal organizations than hierarchical firms there are specific elements of their design that are critical. Particularly important aspects of the design of alliances, that have counterparts in the design of hierarchical firms, are " . . . the degree to which rules are formalized and procedures standardized, where and how decisions are made, how communication takes place, how coordination is accomplished" (Kimberly, Leatt, and Shortell 1983, 293). These elements of design relate directly to the governance structure of the organization.

Within strategic alliances, there are two critical dimensions of governance structure: the governing board and the executive director, or coordinator. The existence of a governing board indicates a degree of formalization in rules and procedures relating to the operations of the alliance and its decision-making process. The existence of a paid director or coordinator suggests that a formal management structure exists, separate from the structure of any of the alliance participants, to carry out the day-to-day activities of the alliance and to coordinate communication among alliance members. Provan (1983) has highlighted the importance of what he has termed a "Formal Management Organization" in distinguishing among different loosely coupled organizational forms. Loosely coupled organizations without formal management have sometimes been called "coalitions" in comparison to similar organizations with formal management, which have been termed "federations."

In summary, any conceptual framework for the analysis of the structure of strategic alliances must take into account the fact that alliances are loosely coupled, hybrid organizations, which exist on a continuum between markets and hierarchical forms. As such, their structures can be described using the language of both economics and organizational theory. Just as the relationship among organizations is important in describing the structure of markets, so too is the relationship among the multiple organizations of an alliance important in describing its structure. This suggests that number of participants, relative size, homogeneity of membership, and spatial relationships among members are relevant descriptors of alliance structure.

However, alliance structure is not limited to these market structure characteristics. Alliances provide an organizational framework for enhancing the welfare of their members. In this regard, they differ from markets where each organization is assumed to pursue its own goals independent of other organizations. To accomplish the goal of enhancing member welfare, information must be exchanged and activities must be coordinated, tasks which imply some degree of organizational governance and management. These necessary activities suggest that the existence of a formal governing board and the existence of a designated, paid director or coordinator are also relevant descriptors of alliance structure.

# The Structure of Strategic
# Alliances among Rural Hospitals

There has been relatively little empirical work performed relating to the structure of alliances. A major reason for this is the lack of published sources that document the existence of different types of alliances and present data on their characteristics. In this section of the paper, we utilize survey data collected as part of the evaluation of the Robert Wood Johnson Foundation's Hospital-Based Rural Health Care Program (HBRHCP) to describe the structure of rural hospital networks, a specific type of alliance. Using simple, bivariate correlations, we examine the way in which the different elements of structure are interrelated. This analysis is explicitly exploratory in nature and should be considered a first step toward gaining a better understanding of the relationship between the different structural dimensions of alliances. In a concluding section of the paper, we suggest areas for future research.

## Data Collection

Rural hospital networks were surveyed twice in conjunction with the HBRHCP evaluation. The first survey was conducted by telephone during December 1988 and January 1989, and the second, also by telephone, in April and May 1991. The analysis of rural alliances for this paper used only data collected during the second survey. However, the data collection procedures of the first survey helped establish the sample frame for the second survey.

The American Hospital Association (AHA) defines a hospital consortium as a formally organized group of hospitals or hospital systems that have come together for specific purposes and have specific membership criteria. This definition served as a starting point for our identification of rural hospital networks. In developing our survey, we narrowed the AHA's broad definition through several decisions. For example, we did not include individual rural hospitals working with nonhospital organizations; groups of rural hospitals that met sporadically for discussion purposes only; groups of hospitals that collaborated under the ownership umbrella of a multihospital system; groups of hospitals that pursued only legislative liaison activities; groups of two hospitals pursuing only a single activity (which we considered a joint venture); and groups of rural hospitals that were connected only through participation in a university-based education program for staff.

For the first survey, 269 potential networks were identified, 180 from a list of organizations that had applied for participation in the HBRHCP, and 89 identified through telephone conversations with hospital association staff in all 50 states. Telephone contacts were made with 266 of the 269 potential respondents (a response rate of 99 percent). Based on these contacts, we identified 127 groups of rural hospitals that were meeting or working together and met our definition of a rural hospital network. Complete survey data were obtained for all of these networks.

For the second survey, our list of potential respondents began with the 127 networks surveyed in 1988. Forty-six new organizations were identified as possible networks through a repeat survey of hospital associations. All 46 were screened for participation, and eleven were included in the second survey. Of the networks included in the first survey, we were unable to contact four network respondents and we found that 36 were no longer in operation in 1991. We also determined, on reinterviewing, that 13 of the hospital groups identified in the first survey did not, in fact, meet our network definition, primarily because they had not instituted programs in addition to legislative lobbying activities or university-based staff educational efforts. We completed interviews with respondents from 85 rural hospital networks in 1991.

## Structural Characteristics

The survey data were used to describe the structure of rural hospital networks and to explore interrelationships among different dimensions of structure. A description of rural hospital network structure, using the six dimensions of structure identified above, is presented in Table 4.1. The measures used to operationalize the dimensions of structure and our basic descriptive findings are discussed briefly below.

*Size.* The size of rural networks varied greatly, with some having as few as two members and others having almost 100. Larger networks are less common than smaller ones. Ninety-two percent of rural networks had 25 or fewer members. The average size of a rural hospital network is 15.7 members.

*Concentration.* Concentration was measured as the "single firm concentration ratio:" the percent of total acute care beds in the network that are in the largest hospital in the network. This measure may reflect the degree of political/economic control the largest member is able to exert on other members or, alternatively, the ability of a large member to satisfy operational needs of smaller members from slack resources. Generally speaking, it is expected that larger networks will have smaller concentration measures. Concentration ratios range from a low of 3 to a high of 83. The average concentration ratio for the networks surveyed was 32.7.

*Homogeneity.* We utilized two dichotomous measures of homogeneity. If a network contained an urban hospital or a rural referral center (a rural hospital with urban hospital characteristics) it was considered less homogeneous than a network containing only smaller rural hospitals. Using these simple measures, rural hospital networks are generally not

**Table 4.1** Descriptive Characteristics of Rural Hospital Network Structure, 1991 ($n$ = 85)

|  | Mean | Standard Deviation |
|---|---|---|
| **Market-related dimensions** | | |
| • Total number of members | 15.7 | 17.5 |
| • Single-firm concentration ratio* | 32.7 | 17.0 |
| • Homogeneity | | |
| Percent with urban hospital | 58.8 | |
| Percent with rural referral center | 21.2 | |
| • Standard distance in miles† | 72.1 | 57.3 |
| **Governance-related dimensions** | | |
| • Percent with board of directors | 75.3 | |
| • Percent with paid director | 60.0 | |

*Total number of acute beds in largest participating hospital as a percentage of total acute beds summed across all hospital participants.
†Square root of the average square of the distances from every network member to the "mean center" of the network; mean center consists of the arithmetic mean of the spatial coordinates of the participating hospitals.

homogeneous. Eighty percent of the networks contain either an urban hospital or a rural referral center. This raises a host of issues concerning motivations for forming rural hospital networks and the ways in which conflicting goals among network participants are reflected in other elements of structure.

*Standard distance.* Standard distance was used to measure the geographical extent of rural hospital networks. Standard distance is a measure of spatial dispersion of a locational pattern that is the counterpart of the standard deviation in statistics. It is defined as the square root of the average square of the distances from every hospital participant location to the "mean center." The mean center consists of the arithmetic means of the spatial coordinates of the participating hospitals. To calculate the standardized distances, hospitals in rural hospital networks were located according to their spatial coordinates using data provided by a private vendor. The mean standard distance for rural hospital networks is 72.1 miles. The range of standard distances among rural hospital networks is quite large, varying from a low of 1.13 miles to a high of 241.9 miles. Networks with small standard distances are more tightly grouped around a hypothetical network center.

**Board of directors and paid director.** Approximately three-quarters of all rural hospital networks are governed by boards of directors, and 60 percent of rural hospital networks employ a paid director.

**Associations among structural characteristics.** One of the purposes of the empirical analysis is to determine whether there are any systematic relationships between different dimensions of network structure. To do this, we estimated simple correlations between structural characteristics (Table 4.2). Correlations for dichotomous variables (such as the presence of an urban hospital and rural referral center in a network) were calculated using phi coefficients. Correlations for one dichotomous variable and one continuous variable (for example, presence of an urban hospital in a network and standard distance) were calculated using point biserial correlations.

Several of the associations among the structural dimensions we defined are statistically significant. Size is positively correlated with heterogeneity (the existence of an urban or rural referral center in the network), standard distance, and the employment of a paid director. Two possible explanations for the correlation between size and heterogeneity are (1) rural hospital members of networks are less threatened by the participation of larger, more complex members when there are more hospitals to offset their influence, and (2) larger, more complex members play key roles in the development of rural networks, but, in order to achieve an adequate return on investment, a greater number of participants is required. Larger networks may have greater transaction costs (the costs of coordination) than smaller networks, and these transaction

**Table 4.2**    Correlations among Characteristics of Network Structure, 1991 ($n = 85$)

|  | Size | Concentration | Homogeneity | | Standard Distance | Board | Paid Director |
|---|---|---|---|---|---|---|---|
|  |  |  | Urban | RRC |  |  |  |
| Size Concentration | −.528** |  |  |  |  |  |  |
| **Homogeneity:** |  |  |  |  |  |  |  |
| Urban | .3244** | −.1649 |  |  |  |  |  |
| RRC | .5032** | −.2848** | .3166** |  |  |  |  |
| Standard distance | .6299** | −.4956** | .2961** | .3554** |  |  |  |
| Board of directors | .0711 | −.1313 | .0750 | .0966* | 0090 |  |  |
| Paid director | .2946** | −.2029 | .2440* | .3056** | .2845** | .4232** |  |

*Indicates significant correlation at the .05 level.
**Indicates significant correlation at the .01 level.

costs may be reduced by employing a paid director. Size is negatively correlated with concentration, since any single hospital is likely to have a larger percentage of the total acute beds in a network, the smaller the number of participants in the network.

Concentration is negatively correlated with standard distance, which might suggest that "nondominant" members in highly concentrated networks tend to cluster in a tight orbit around the "dominant" member. However, this correlation could simply reflect the indirect effect of network size. The concentration measure is likely to be larger in small networks because of the way it is constructed, and small networks may also consist of hospitals located more closely together.

Finally, the existence of a board of directors is positively correlated with the employment of a paid director. The chief executive officers of network hospitals, who often serve as network board members, may hire professional management (i.e., a paid director) when the tasks of coordination become too time consuming, when special expertise is needed, or when it is desirable to shift network authority to a neutral party. Alternatively, the hiring of a paid director may precipitate the formalization of network governance, leading to the establishment of a formal board of directors.

# Areas for Future Research

The primary purpose of this paper is to introduce the structure of strategic alliances as a topic that is worthy of further research. We presented a conceptual model for thinking about the structural characteristics of alliances and suggested how these characteristics might relate to other dimensions of alliances. We illustrated the conceptual model using data on the structure of rural hospital networks.

The purpose of this section is to provide a framework for thinking about future empirical research relating to the structure of alliances and to suggest specific research questions within this framework that are especially deserving of attention. Building on the discussion in the first part of the paper, we offer the schematic in Figure 4.1 as an organizing framework for future research. (The linkages between concepts that do not involve structure directly are suppressed in this figure, as are possible "feedback loops.")

## Defining and Measuring Structure

We have suggested that the dimensions of structure in alliances be based on a combination of concepts used to describe structure in markets and

**Figure 4.1**    Framework for Future Research on Strategic Alliances

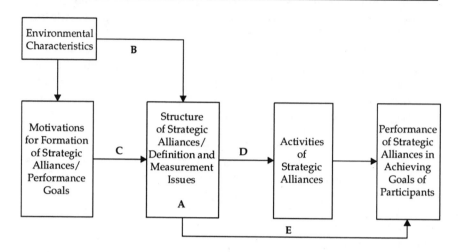

A. How should the structure of strategic alliances be described and measured?
B. How does the environment in which participants in a strategic alliance function influence their structure, both indirectly by shaping motivations for participation and directly by imposing constraints on elements of structure?
C. How do the motivations and goals of members affect the way in which strategic alliances are structured?
D. How does the structure of strategic alliances affect the nature of the activities they undertake?
E. How does the structure of strategic alliances affect their performance, both indirectly through choice of activities, and directly by facilitating the carrying out of chosen activities?

in organizations. Under the assumption that this approach is reasonable, the dimensions of structure that we have proposed by no means exhaust the possibilities. There may be other dimensions, particularly from the area of organizational design, that should be considered in describing the structure of alliances. Or, alternative approaches to the conceptualization of structure might be more relevant in some cases. We believe that additional exploration of theoretical approaches to defining structure in alliances would be valuable and, in some cases, may be a necessary precursor to empirical research.

Whatever dimensions of structure are adopted in future empirical analyses, it will be important to develop appropriate measures for these concepts. Inadequate measures will make it difficult for researchers to discover and understand important relationships between different dimensions of structure. For example, our measures of complexity/

homogeneity of structure related to rural hospital networks were crude; the crudeness of these measures made it difficult to investigate relationships between homogeneity and other structural dimensions of rural hospital networks. Also, it will be important to develop better measures of structure related to dominance. The measure we used—percent of all acute care beds in a rural hospital network that were managed by the largest network participant—was not adequate because its construction assured that it would be correlated with other dimensions of structure.

## Environment/Structure Relationships

One avenue of future research views structure as the dependent variable in the analysis. Using this approach, empirical studies would focus on developing and testing theories that would explain differences in structure observed in a cross-section of alliances of the same type. For instance, what are the determinants of variation in the structure of rural hospital networks? What is the relative importance of these factors in explaining variation in structure? Based on our work with rural hospital networks, we hypothesize that the environments in which network participants function influence the different dimensions of structure directly and also indirectly through their influence on the motivation of participants for joining networks. For instance, consider rural hospitals located in a sparsely populated western state where the travel time between hospitals is great. A common environmental characteristic, the isolation of the rural communities, is likely to affect both the motivation for joining a network (e.g., to overcome isolation through the sharing of management expertise) and the structure of the network (includes a relatively small number of participants since the costs of participation in terms of travel time and expense preclude distant hospitals from attending regular meetings in which management expertise is shared on a formal or informal basis.) The elements of the environment, broadly defined, that affect structure may not always be easy to measure, and in many cases this will pose a challenge for empirical research. For instance, the culture of "independence" and "rugged individualism" that is found in many rural areas in the west may contribute to the adoption of a relatively informal governance structure for rural hospital networks and may make it less likely that such networks contain a dominant participant.

## Motivation/Structure Relationships

The motivations of participants in forming, or joining, an alliance may play an important role, independent of environment, in determining the dimensions of structure. As discussed previously, we hypothesize that the structure of alliances is the result of conscious decisions made by their participants. Structure will therefore be shaped by what the participants hope to accomplish through their participation. For example, if rural hospital administrators primarily see network participation as a means to increase the political power of rural hospitals in the state legislature, they may seek participation from a large number of geographically dispersed hospitals that are homogeneous with respect to their legislative interests, although heterogeneous in many other respects. A major research issue in establishing linkages between motivation and structure is how to best collect information on the motivation and goals of network participants. Presumably, surveys of executives in participating firms would yield this information, but there may not be agreement within a firm about the motivations for its participation. Also, in our study of rural hospital networks, we observed a very high rate of turnover among administrators of rural hospitals. This presumably would weaken any empirical link between observed structure and the motivations for network participation reported by a survey of administrators of hospitals participating in networks.

## Structure/Activities Relationships

A second approach to research on the structure of alliances would focus on dimensions of structure as independent variables in empirical analyses of the activities undertaken by alliances and/or the success of alliances in achieving their goals. We hypothesize that the structure of an alliance, once in place, is costly to alter. Therefore, while the activities that an alliance decides to pursue could influence structure, particularly in the case of new alliances, we would expect that the direction of causation would be predominantly from structure to activities, particularly for existing alliances. This assumption is supported by the observation that alliances may pursue several activities simultaneously (as was the case for the rural hospital networks in our study) and therefore that the structure of an alliance cannot easily be reconfigured to support each individual activity.

As part of our analysis of rural hospital networks, we explored in a preliminary way bivariate relationships between dimensions of structure and the activities undertaken by networks. We found several significant relationships. For example, we found that joint quality assurance programming and credentialing was associated with having a paid director. It could be that, because of the sensitive nature of quality assurance data, a paid director played an essential role as a neutral "third party" in facilitating this activity. We also found a significant correlation between the presence of a physician or staff education program and the "standard distance" measure of structure; the greater the geographical dispersion of network members, the more likely the network was to offer shared educational programming. Staff in rural hospitals in isolation from each other may have limited opportunities to access education programs through other means. While these provide examples of the sorts of individual linkages that could be uncovered through empirical research, they need to be interpreted within an overall theory of the relationship between structure and activities. Without such a theory, it will be extremely difficult to interpret the overall pattern of relationships present, particularly when there are multiple dimensions of structure and multiple activities being carried out by an alliance.

### Structure/Performance Relationships

We hypothesize that the structure of an alliance will be related to its performance indirectly through its influence on the activities that the alliance undertakes and directly through its influence on the effectiveness of those activities. As we argued above, the structural characteristics of an alliance are not likely to be a perfect fit to all of the activities it implements. Some structures will facilitate to a greater degree than others the ability of the activity to move the alliance closer to the achievement of a particular goal or goals. In assessing the performance of alliances it will be important to measure and control for variation in structural characteristics that could affect performance. Not only is the relationship between structure and performance of interest in itself, but it is essential to control for differences in structure when estimating relationships between programs and alliance performance. A failure to do so could result in an overestimation or underestimation of program effects.

## Conclusions

The topics we have proposed as deserving of future research have been described under the assumption that the data set consists of similar strategic alliances (e.g., rural hospital networks). There is, however, a different set of research issues that could be addressed through comparisons of different types of alliances. For instance, how do the relevant dimensions of structure vary depending on whether the alliance among health care organizations is vertical or horizontal in nature? How do the dimensions of structure for alliances in the health care industry differ from those of alliances in other industries? What accounts for the differences? While a broader discussion of such research issues is beyond our scope here, that does not mean that these issues are less interesting or important than the ones we have chosen to address.

Finally, while we have not explicitly addressed the statistical modeling issues that are likely to arise in conducting the sorts of research studies that we have suggested, we do not wish to minimize their importance. The relationships depicted in Figure 4.1 are multidimensional in nature. There are likely to be multiple indicators of constructs such as motivations, structure, and performance, as well as reciprocal relationships not depicted in the diagram. Based on previous work (Moscovice et al. 1991), we expect that it will be necessary to employ confirmatory factor analysis techniques, or some similar method of analysis, to uncover the complexities in the empirical relationships. Confirmatory factor analysis permits both random and systematic measurement errors in the data and yields an assessment of how well a given model, based on theoretically meaningful but unobservable constructs, captures the pattern of relationships that exist in a data set.

Whatever modeling approach is adopted, it seems likely that data limitations will continue to hamper the development of cross-sectional and, particularly, longitudinal studies relating to the structure of alliances. There are many interesting research questions relating to structure that require repeated observations over time. For instance, are observed changes in the structure of alliances consistent with life-cycle theories of organizational development (D'Aunno and Zuckerman 1987; Zuckerman and D'Aunno 1990)? The data needed to address these questions can only be collected as part of a long-term research effort involving funding for sequential surveys since, in general, no organized "associations" collect and disseminate annual data on relatively informal organizations such as alliances.

# References

Borys, B. and D. Jemison. 1989. "Hybrid Arrangements as Strategic Alliances: Theoretical Issues in Organizational Combinations." *Academy of Management Review* 14 (2): 234–49.

D'Aunno, T., and H. Zuckerman. 1987a. "The Emergence of Hospital Federations: An Integration of Perspectives from Organizational Theory." *Medical Care Review* 44 (2): 323–43.

D'Aunno, T., and H. Zuckerman. 1987b. "A Life-Cycle Model of Organizational Federations: The Case of Hospitals." *Academy of Management Review* 12 (3): 534–45.

Jarillo, J. 1988. "On Strategic Networks." *Strategic Management Journal* 9: 31–41.

Kaluzny, A., L. Lacey, R. Warnecke, D. Hynes, J. Morrissey, L. Ford, and E. Sondik. 1993. "Predicting the Performance of a Strategic Alliance: An Analysis of the Community Clinical Oncology Program." *Health Services Research* 28 (2): 159–82.

Kaluzny, A., and H. Zuckerman. 1992. "Strategic Alliances: Two Perspectives for Understanding Their Effects on Health Services." *Hospital & Health Services Administration* 37 (Winter): 477–90.

Kimberly, J., P. Leatt, and S. Shortell. 1983. "Organization Design." In *Health Care Management*, edited by S. Shortell and A. Kaluzny, 291–332. New York: John Wiley and Sons.

Longest, B. 1990. "Inter-organizational Linkages in the Health Care Sector." *Health Care Management Review* 15 (Winter): 17–28.

Luke, R., J. Begun, and D. Pointer. 1989. "Quasi-Firms: Strategic Interorganizational Forms in the Health Care Industry." *Academy of Management Review* 14 (1): 9–19.

Moscovice, I., J. Johnson, M. Finch, C. Grogan, and J. Kralewski. 1991. "The Structure and Characteristics of Rural Hospital Consortia." *Journal of Rural Health* 7 (Fall): 575–88.

Oliver, C. 1990. "Determinants of Interorganizational Relationships: Integration and Future Directions." *Academy of Management Review* 15 (April): 241–65.

Pfeffer, J. 1978. *Organization Design.* Arlington Heights, IL: AHM Publishing.

Powell, W. 1990. "Neither Market Nor Hierarchy: Network Forms of Organization." In *Research in Organization Behavior* vol. 12, 295–336. JAI Press.

Provan, K. 1983. "The Federation as an Interorganizational Linkage Network." *Academy of Management Review* 8: 79–89.

Shortell, S., E. Morrison, and B. Freidman. 1992. *Strategic Choices for America's Hospitals: Managing in Turbulent Times.* San Francisco: Jossey-Bass Publishers.

Size, T. 1993. "Managing Partnerships: The Perspective of a Rural Hospital Cooperative." *Health Care Management Review* 18 (Winter): 31–41.

Thompson, J. 1967. *Organizations in Action.* New York: McGraw–Hill.

Williamson, O. 1975. *Markets and Hierarchies: Analysis and Anti-trust Implications.* New York: Free Press.

Zuckerman, H., and T. D'Aunno. 1990. "Hospital Alliances: Cooperative Strategy in a Competitive Environment." *Health Care Management Review* 15 (Spring): 21–30.

# The Commentaries: A Summary

Christianson and his colleagues have identified components of structure that are important in at least one type of a strategic alliance—a rural hospital network. Commentary provides further examples and explication of the role that structure plays in the operations and performance of various types of alliance arrangements. ROBERT BAKER accepts the framework provided by Christianson et al., and attempts to illustrate and apply aspects of their structural framework and definitions. He describes the University Hospital Consortium (UHC) as a voluntary organization that links a group of academic medical centers to accomplish the group's objectives while allowing members to retain their autonomy and remain separate distinct legal entities. He discusses the motivation for its formation, the influence of change agents, and considers various dimensions of structure important to its operations including size, complexity, geographic relationships, and homogeneity.

Using SunHealth Alliance as an example, BEN LATIMER further analyzes the implications of structure—in fact suggesting that "We have successfully treated it (structure) as a strategy, that is, as a way to reach our goals. He goes on to state that we have selected various structures on the basis of what we thought was their correlation with successful results, outcomes, and performance. Two points are given extensive attention. First, the idea that alliances may be interim or temporary forms succeeded or was replaced over time. Experience from SunHealth suggests that this alliance (with almost 300 hospitals/health systems as participants, over 500 employees and over 500 million dollars in annual revenues) is permanent but in fact has undergone considerable transformation through structural change over its 24 years of existence. Secondly, attention is given to the location of alliance structures along a continuum of organizational forms ranging from hierarchy on one end of the continuum to market on the other. Latimer suggests that on the continuum a strategic alliance may be a hybrid with a tremendous capacity to change over time both in terms of structure and purpose given environmental changes.

Alliances involve more than just providers—they involve insurers and a major insurer in alliance formation in health care is Blue Cross/Blue Shield. STEPHEN WOOD reviews the definition of alliances, the motivation for alliance formation between insurers and providers, key success factors involving governance issues and expectations for the future from the perspective of Blue Cross/Blue Shield.

Finally, while recognizing the importance of structure, EDWARD ZAJAC emphasizes the role of political dynamics between alliance members and the alliance per se. He points to different strategies (i.e., win-win versus win-lose) as well as different structures focusing on resource flows within the alliance. Given the two dimensions of resource flows and performance, different strategies emerge which affect the very fundamental operations of the alliance structure.

# Robert J. Baker

Christianson, Moscovice, and Wellever present a conceptual framework for understanding the structure of alliances and of using that framework to analyze a specific type of hospital alliance were admirably achieved. By providing an example of one successful hospital alliance, that of the University Hospital Consortium (UHC), I will attempt to illustrate and apply aspects of their structural framework and definitions. It is my hope that this analysis will provide additional perspective on the relevance of various structural elements in differentiating such alliances and explaining their behaviors and performance.

## UHC: The Academic Medical Center Alliance

UHC is one of several strategic alliances that, as defined by the authors, can be described as an intermediate organizational form bounded by the free market at one pole and the hierarchical organization form at the other. UHC is a voluntary organization that links a group of academic medical centers (AMCs) to accomplish the group's objectives while allowing members to retain their autonomy and remain separate, distinct

---

Robert J. Baker is president of University Hospital Consortium.

legal entities. This form creates a relationship among UHC members that permits them to take advantage of opportunities without redefining and forming a new structure with each new situation. It creates "stable context for the functioning of the organization . . ."

The authors hypothesize that "a key element in understanding the structure of an alliance is the motivation for its formation . . ." and that the alliance is "the outcome of an attempt by managers of one or more of the participating organizations to manage the organization's environment more effectively." This is certainly true in the case of UHC.

## Motivation for Alliance Formation

The shared motivation of formation and the clarity of purpose are important dimensions of structure. UHC was originally formed by eight chief executive officers who were concerned with the lack of national support for the unique needs of university hospitals. In 1980, the group, then called the Consortium for the Study of University Hospitals, began researching the unique issues facing these institutions. By 1984, the group had grown to 23 institutions and the name was changed to the University Hospital Consortium. Along with that name change came an expanded purpose: to develop a wide array of services normally associated with large multihospital systems, without sacrificing the individuality that is essential for excellence in academic medicine. UHC functions as a business entity designed purely to assist its membership in competing more effectively in their respective markets. Freed from an advocacy or policy formulation role, UHC's enabling charter and values placed great importance on its functioning as a business support entity at the national level. UHC's ability to rely on its sister institutions, the Association of American Medical Colleges and the Association of Academic Health Centers, to support its members' needs in advocacy and policy formulation has allowed it to flourish by focusing on programs important to the management of the complex clinical enterprise.

## Influence of Change Agents

Since its formulation, UHC has enjoyed slow and steady growth, and currently comprises 62 of the nation's leading AMCs. Throughout its growth and development, UHC's mission and purpose have remained constant. The managers, or as the authors refer to them, "change agents," of UHC member institutions use UHC to accomplish goals as a group that are not readily attainable by individual hospitals, including influencing the health care environment to position AMCs to compete successfully in their local marketplaces. Participation in UHC allows members to capitalize on economies of scale and avoid making unnecessary monetary, staffing, and other resource commitments, since they are able to use the resources of the alliance to accomplish some of their goals. Examples include UHC's annual research project that defined the types of markets in which members find themselves, developed the models that explained and projected the markets' maturation, and identified effective strategies members could use to position themselves and compete effectively in these evolving markets.

*Rational versus political model.* During the early days of the alliance, there was a level of camaraderie and collective commitment that was important to the early success of the organization. With the growth in membership and the frequent turnover of members' senior management staff, commitment to the organization is balanced between collegiality and commitment to collective action and the significant value that members perceive they are deriving from participation in the alliance.

To ensure that UHC continues to provide its membership with significant value, the alliance has taken steps to secure its functioning under a *rational* model of behavior rather than a *political* model. In a rational model, alliance participants recognize that cooperation is in their best interest as long as they have some expectation of securing benefits from (that) cooperation over the long term. An example of this model is UHC's pharmaceutical purchasing program. In order to secure optimal pricing and obtain the greatest savings for the group, participating members commit to purchase their pharmaceuticals through UHC's purchase agreement. While some members may not save as much as others on specific line items, their commitment allows UHC to negotiate the overall agreement that best benefits all participants.

UHC avoids the political model of behavior in which participants cannot view the alliance from a global perspective. UHC evenly distributes "political" power by giving each UHC institution one representative on UHC's Board of Directors. This representative is usually the chief executive officer of the member institution. This equalizes the power among members and ensures that UHC's resources are directed to optimize value for the membership as a whole.

UHC is based on much more than short-term cost minimization or cost avoidance. It provides a stable structure in which members have access to critical resources, expertise, and information that cannot be as efficiently or effectively secured on an individual member basis. While the value of these assets is difficult to qualify, UHC's services in the areas of clinical and operational benchmarking, managed care, peer networking, and strategy development are a few examples of longer-term benefits of this alliance.

Although UHC initially focused on the direct reduction of transactional costs through its group purchasing programs, the organization had increasingly extended its services to encompass the collection, analysis, and dissemination of comparative information and the development of strategies necessary to compete effectively in the transformed health care delivery system. UHC now refers to itself as an information company and has placed great emphasis on drawing information from its members to assist in benchmarking best practices, not only as they relate to the effective management of the organization, but also to the effective management of clinical and technological resources in clinical practice. Finally, the organization has assisted its members in understanding the ever-changing health care delivery market, its rate of maturation, and where the individual members fit in the maturing marketplace, and developing unique strategies to be effective in the transformed, price-sensitive health care marketplace. This assistance has been seen as a tremendous value to the membership.

### Dimension of Structure in the Alliance

*Size.* Size is an important dimension of structure, and has been a critical factor in the success of UHC. The fact that UHC membership is composed of a small number of very large hospitals has enabled the alliance to obtain adequate financial support to develop a wide range of programmatic offerings and to maximize the potential of this type of organizational form.

*Conditions of membership.* The conditions of membership are also a critical dimension of structure. When UHC was formed, its purpose was to serve the unique needs of the major teaching hospitals of this country. While well over 1,000 hospitals call themselves teaching hospitals, the universe of potential UHC members is less than 130 institutions, composed of only those that are either university-owned or where the medical school departmental chairpersons either function as, or appoint, the hospitals' clinical chiefs of service. These conditions of membership permit UHC to focus its agenda around the unique requirements of this universe.

*Geographical relationship.* The geographical dispersion of members is an important dimension of the structure of alliances. Whereas a number of alliances function effectively at the local and/or regional level, others function equally effectively at the national level.

Another important characteristic of geographical dispersion is the extent to which competition among the membership is minimized. One of the values of UHC is to minimize market overlap and, with the exception of multiple memberships in Chicago and Philadelphia, the members generally perceive that their competitors are not represented within the alliance. The market overlap policy, designed to manage the degree of competition among participating members, is considered an important condition of membership and has been used to determine those organizations eligible to participate in the consortium.

*Complexity.* While the authors combine the structural dimensions of complexity and homogeneity, I believe that each of these dimensions is critical in differentiating the various alliances. UHC members are part of the broader academic environment and are responsible for providing, at least in part, an environment supportive not only of clinical service, but also of education and research. In addition, these organizations are typically owned and governed by large private or public universities that provide unique governance and organizational challenges. Even those university hospitals independent of university and public ownership are challenged by the broad tripartite mission and the need for decentralized organizational structures to effectively fulfill their complex mission. The complexity of UHC's members is a stimulus to greater participation in the alliance to the extent that the individual members believe they can gain insight through collaboration with their peers regarding the complex issues facing the AMC clinical enterprise.

*Homogeneity.* The sharing of a common academic mission and the values inherent in the learning environment are important differentiating dimensions of structure. This homogeneity brings UHC members together as a consolidated entity. Members frequently mention that the greatest value they derive from their membership occurs through interactions with their peers. Members' representatives comment that they do not need to explain the subtle dimensions of issues they confront when among UHC members. There is a broad recognition of the subtleties of managing the clinical enterprise within the AMC, and this characteristic is held in extremely high regard by the participating membership.

## Enhancing Members' Welfare

In focusing on the effective management of the clinical enterprise, it has been important for UHC to carefully select those activities it chooses to develop. As one might expect in this business, the alliance functions as a clearinghouse for consultants, manufacturers, and suppliers, and a day does not go by without someone bringing an "exciting opportunity" to the attention of UHC. In evaluating its agenda, the organization has tried to insist that all of its activities meet the following tests:

- The opportunity is unique to the academic clinical enterprise
- The opportunity can best be developed at the national level, as opposed to a regional or local level
- The opportunity requires the involvement of multiple institutions in order to contribute incremental value to the individual participating member.

By extending these tests to virtually every idea that is introduced either by the membership or by outside interests, it has been possible for the organization to stay focused on those factors that motivated UHC's formation.

Effecting change within AMCs is extremely complex. These organizations have been characterized as huge, ocean-going vessels, which are either rudderless or, at best, very difficult to maneuver, especially in the current, turbulent delivery system. Through UHC, members have been able to bring market perspective and strategic vision to the diffused, decentralized power structure of the organization, and perhaps, because the vision and strategies have been developed through the collective efforts of all the membership, they are perceived as having great credibility and influence in redirecting the course of the AMC.

Finally, UHC is perceived as a national representative and/or broker of the interests of the academic center. This role allows UHC to match the interests and needs of members with organizational entities structured to specifically address the membership needs. To the extent that UHC were to become a broad provider of service, it would compromise its representational role to its members. Examples would include the development of its own national supply distribution company or its own mail order pharmacy. Once the organization were to develop these capabilities, it would simply become yet another vendor selling services to its members along with a myriad of other competitors. By carefully limiting its agenda to those programs and services the members believe bring value to the clinical enterprise and by respecting its representational responsibility to its membership, the organization has been able to enjoy continued strong support and commitment from its membership.

# Ben W. Latimer

Intuitively, we know that alliance structure has a bearing on how well an alliance performs. In describing markets, economists who "juggle the three balls" of structure, conduct, and performance do not agree that structure and conduct are equal in influencing performance, but few if any would put structure last. Further, economics (exact science that it is) has identified the major elements of structure in markets. Research over time has given us some ways to identify the extent to which structural elements of markets (such as seller concentration and production differentiation) really do affect the performance of markets in reaching social goals such as the efficient allocation of resources.

I believe we know *intuitively* that the structure of a strategic alliance has a bearing on performance. Over the past 24 years, the SunHealth Alliance has adjusted, changed, and modified many times what we have thought of as structure, such as the number of participants and opportunities for others to take part, geographic constraints, the size of partner organizations, decision-making mechanisms and rules, tax status and its legal implications, and corporate shields to protect participants from liability. We believe structure is important, but we have essentially treated it as a *strategy*, that is, as a way to reach our goals. And we have selected various structures on the basis of what we thought was their correlation with successful results, outcomes, and performance. I have difficulty thinking of structure, or analyzing it, except in the context of that impact, and I am concerned that we will not be able to effectively evaluate structure until we have good measures of performance.

But on our intuitive assumption that structure is significant to the performance of alliances, all of us involved with alliances should be interested in (1) identifying the dimensions of alliance structure that we will describe and measure; and (2) determining which are the "critical few."

A good start is the work by Christianson, Moscovice, and Wellever of the Institute for Health Services Research of the University of Minnesota's School of Public Health. In particular, the research agenda they lay out is timely, relevant, and needed. Alliances do not fit any of our organizational molds. The answers to the research questions posed would be useful not only to those forming alliances or evaluating participation in them but to those of us involved in leading them as well. After more than two decades of alliances in health care, we each quite likely

---

Ben W. Latimer is president and CEO of SunHealth Alliance.

would describe our organizations differently, while agreeing they are not established structures such as hierarchies and markets.

Two things initially gave me some pause. The first was the report in the paper that some thought alliances were interim or temporary forms, possibly to be succeeded or replaced over time. My biased response obviously rose from having spent 24 years managing an alliance which (with almost 300 hospital/health systems as participants, over 500 employees, and about $50 million in annual revenues) looks quite "permanent" to me. Upon reflection, though, it is true that SunHealth has "reinvented" itself many times in response to environmental change and our partners' needs. Perhaps the choices are not just "remain as is" or "be replaced," but also "be renewed" or transformed through structural change.

I also spent considerable time deciding whether I agreed that a alliance is "an intermediate organizational form that falls between the hierarchical organization on one extreme and the market at the other extreme." It seemed to me that going from a hierarchy on one end of the continuum to a market on the other required some kind of metamorphosis in the middle. Not being an economist and able to make butterflies out of caterpillars, I found it easier to consider the nature of the transactions or exchange involved in the continuum. It looks like "make or buy" to me, with a hierarchy the way to "make" and the market the way to "buy." On the continuum, then, an alliance might be a hybrid way to make and/or buy.

The authors have done us a service by showing how elements of structure from both hierarchies and markets may be combined to describe alliances, falling somewhere in the middle. Overall, my experience says the structural elements selected are among those that are significant. The only additional element I would add (under the "hierarchy" side) is *legal form*. Alliances operate under various corporate, tax, and securities laws, and deal with issues from amassing capital to directing earnings back to participants. Legal form clearly circumscribes activities and strategies and, I would argue, thereby affects performance.

Assuming the "hybrid" place for alliances between hierarchy and market, I wondered if our perspective in choosing elements of structure might be clearer if we expanded the continuum to four points instead of three (Figure 4.1). In other words, we could see an alliance as either a mutant form of "make" (or a quasi hierarchy) or a mutant form of "buy" (or a quasi market). Whether an alliance is more one than the other might give us better pointers as to the significant elements of structure—what to draw from the structure of hierarchies and what to draw from the structure of markets.

The paper gives us clues that the differentiation between quasi hierarchies and quasi markets could be important. The fact that most studies

**Figure 4.1**   Continuum of Organization Structures

| Hierarchy | Quasi Hierarchy | Quasi Market | Market |
|-----------|-----------------|--------------|--------|
| Make | Jointly Make | Jointly Buy | Buy |

└──── Alliance ────┘

of alliance structure to date have focused on quasi firms such as joint ventures hints that many consider alliances complex ways to "make." The disparate views about the motivations of managers in forming alliances present another clue: although minimizing production costs as a motive points to "make," guaranteeing access to critical resources argues "buy." Further, the authors themselves give motivation (what the alliance is for) high significance in understanding alliance structure, conduct, and performance.

It seems to me that the structure of alliances that are formed primarily to "make" products, functions, or services (for example, a shared laundry service) is best compared to hierarchies or firms. And that important elements of the structure of "the quasi firm" are its size as a surrogate for scale, its legal form and control through governance and management, and its type of activities or purpose. I am not sure that the homogeneity of alliance members is as important as the integration of alliance activities into the operation of the member hospital organization. This is my "virtual reality" measure: how closely does the alliance activity emulate the same activity operated entirely within the hierarchical organization, without the inefficiencies?

In regard to alliances that seem to be quasi markets, my first thought was that organizations forming such an alliance are creating a private marketplace for themselves in which to buy or obtain needed resources—a friendlier, dedicated market whose conduct might include such features as favorable pricing and assured access to resources.

When I look at some alliances in this way (as quasi markets) I am not sure if the alliance fits in the category of supplier or buyer. Consequently, I am not certain how to apply some elements of market structure such as market concentration (usually defined in terms of the number and size of the sellers. If the alliance is seen as a *supplier* of resources serving its members as a group of *buyers*, then in terms of concentration there is essentially one seller—the alliance. The members make up another market structure feature—a concentration of buyers.

Viewed in this light, it seems to me that other recognized elements of market structure such as product differentiation and barriers to the entry of new firms take on different characteristics as well. Product differentiation, as I mentioned, might include favorable price and highly desired features not available elsewhere in the market, and barriers to entry might include the commitments of members to purchase or use alliance services to the exclusion of others. Market size (the number of member-customers) and market geography take on more traditional aspects in regard to the potential demand for service and type of services that can be fielded.

None of my comments address the likelihood that many alliances in health care are indeed hybrids between my mutants—organizations that are concerned with "making" and "buying" (which I suggest that SunHealth is). That leads us back to the research questions posed by the paper, and my encouragement of continuing study and research addressed toward them.

One formidable obstacle to our research is the large variety of alliances being formed today, with few as similar and simple as the rural hospital networks for which some research data fortunately were available. Another obstacle in regard to alliances in health care is the speed with which our industry is being transformed, with new consolidations, organizational forms, and alliances among different kinds of providers accelerating. Forward, backward, and vertical integration strategies are making not only strange bedfellows but also new organizational forms. Some examples are medical services foundations melding corporations with physician practice professional groups, and provider contracting organizations that are the equivalent of joint marketing firms for the providers involved. The organizational functions that are being "out-sourced" or joint ventured or partnered go far beyond our shared laundries, educational programs, and data systems of years ago.

I am not certain whether it is pride or experience that leads me to caution against the assumption that alliances are voluntary, loosely coupled organizations that are somewhat interim steps to some better solution. Not to be overlooked is the capacity of alliances themselves to change over time, both in structure and purpose, as environments change. For example, SunHealth today is a different alliance from the shared services organization it started as in 1969. Further, we should not overlook the capacity of alliances to serve as frameworks or platforms for superior structures over time—for example, integrated health services networks.

It seems appropriate to reiterate the importance of purpose or motivation in the formation of alliances, not only as a base for measuring performance over time but also in evaluating the significance of the various elements of structure. For example, the geographical size of an alliance or market would seem to be significant only if the service or activity had some permanent relationship to geography. I would say geography was highly relevant to an alliance building local health care systems but perhaps not relevant to educational programming that could be delivered by satellite or information highways.

Further, we should all look forward to building on this research effort and applying it to different kinds of alliances, perhaps with more complex purposes and composition than the set of rural hospitals studied. We may need to take caution in extrapolating these early results, since rural hospitals are unique in many characteristics. We expect that some will become parts of integrated health systems over time, which is an "alliance" of a different kind.

Obviously, performance matters most. Our studies of structure are relevant, because we believe structures affect performance and may be a predictor of performance. I am eager for our research to reach the stage when we have measures of performance to match our elements of structure.

# Stephen Wood

Thank you for the opportunity to speak with you today to relate our experiences with alliance formation in the health care industry. The Blue Cross/Blue Shield system, of course, is very active in studying and forming alliances with health care providers. One might say the Blue Cross/Blue Shield system itself is a strategic alliance among insurers developed in the '30s and '40s, but that's a whole other discussion.

I am going to share with you our current thinking regarding the definition of alliances, the motivations for alliance formation between insurers and providers, key success factors from governance issues, and our expectations for the future. We agree with Christianson and his colleagues that the study of alliance formation and operation merits further research. However, alliances forming between the health care financing and delivery organizations today tend to be much more highly structured or vertical than the types of alliances that the authors present. Market and reform forces in the health care industry may necessitate more highly structured approaches to organizing and financing delivery

Stephen Wood is manager of business services at the Blue Cross and Blue Shield Association.

than the loosely coupled intraorganizational relationships that the authors describe. I would like to share with you some of the motivating forces behind why we see alliances happening.

Exhibit 4.1 represents our ideas of fundamental principles of building alliances. Alliances and integrated delivery system definitions are fluid. Our operating definition of a vertically integrated organization is significantly different than traditional contractual relationship that health insurers have had with providers for a long time. For instance, I would not include PPOs or capitated arrangements between HMOs and providers in the categories of alliances. The alliances that we are talking about are characterized by long-term relationships—by long-term, we mean somewhere in the order of 10 to 15 years. There are clearly shared objectives, redefined responsibilities, and shared accountability for results. Most often what this means is equity positions among the insurer or the carriers and the providers. That's really what drives these organizations and makes them distinct from a health insurer just contracting with a hospital or medical group, even on a capitated basis.

There are some examples of long-term contracts that have been signed by Blue's plans and some other health insurance carriers and these things may fall into a category of alliances but what we're really focusing on here is a structure that provides some stability over the long-term.

One other distinguishing feature that we see in integrated delivery systems versus horizontal configurations of 15 or 16 hospitals, is that the alliances that we are talking about have far fewer players in them. We aren't talking 15 to 16 players. We're talking more on the order of five or less. Figure 4.2 provides some examples of possible alliance structures. And you can see the various configurations, either by examples there, or as many as you can think of, in how these things are structured. But it gives you an idea of how health care financing and delivery is no longer the clean operation it once was where the insurer pays claims, the provider provides the service, and the employer or individual pays the premium. We're seeing all sorts of different configurations and this is one simple example.

**Exhibit 4.1**   Building Alliances: Principles

- Long-term
- Shared objectives
- Redefined responsibilities
- Shared accountability for results

**Figure 4.2**  Integrated Managed Care: Experimentation with Partnerships

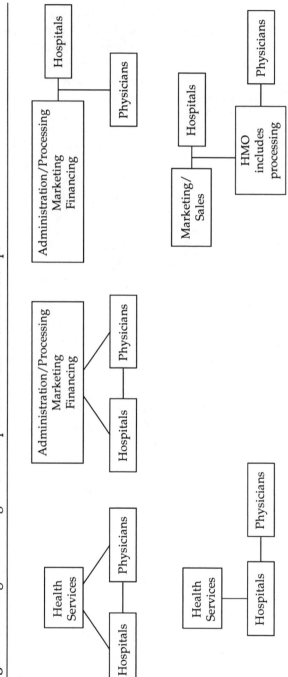

One of my tasks at the Blue Cross/Blue Shield system is consulting to Blue Cross/Blue Shield plans that are contemplating alliances with provider partners. Interestingly the providers often take the initiative in developing alliances. Plan senior management are seeking ways to appropriately respond. Our job is to assist them in thinking through what an appropriate response is and creating a win-win situation for the providers and the insurers.

Figure 4.3 is a synopsis of how we approach alliances in a strategic fashion and I think it summarizes a lot of what we heard so far today in terms of selecting partners, structure and relationships, and implementation. It focuses on, for instance, goal statements and structuring relationships, risk sharing, open communications, and creating a trust. The trust relationship must be built on something more fundamental than just an academic trust. We are talking about equity positions, equity relationships, or very long-term contractual relationships where the organizations are coming together as a vertically integrated provider and financier of care.

One version of the 1990s market that we have been thinking about is the position of insurers as risk managers. What this implies is that the role of a financing entity may be to evaluate price, select package, and forecast the sources of risk for the bearers of risk. The bearers of risk might well be an insurance company as well. In vertically integrated

**Figure 4.3**   Structuring for Effectiveness: Internal Organization

**Provider Alliances**

| Selecting Partners | Structuring Relationship | Implementation |
|---|---|---|
| • Goals | • Goal statement | • Team building |
| • Select strategic position | • Risk sharing | • Communication to constituents |
| • Identify provider candidates to match | • Open communications | • Reengineering |
| • Evaluate opportunity cost | • Division of authority | • Quality management |
| • Evaluate market/ access match | • Reduce duplication | • Measurement planning |
| • Develop negotiating approach | • Identify key shared activities | • Focus on results |
| • Evaluate | | |

alliance structures, however, you are looking at providers, employers in self-insured world. The core role of the insurer in this scenario is definitely to act as the risk manager and inform all what the costs and benefits are of an alliance.

I found Christianson's paper a useful construct for understanding these organizations and alliances. It really informed me as to how different our understanding of an alliance is from some of you folks in terms of horizontally organized programs. When you hear Blue Cross/Blue Shield plans and insurers, in general, talking alliances, I think you can be safely assured that we are talking about vertically integrated organizations. We are not talking about horizontal organizations. We're talking about combining the sources of the providers of care with the payers of care and the insurance mechanism as the intermediary or the risk-bearer between them.

# Edward J. Zajac

I am the last discussant and I have been trying to think of how I could be distinctive from all the other discussants who have preceded me. Perhaps it's the fact I don't have a nice witty anecdote to start off my discussion with other than something like: Rural networks, I thought we were talking about neural networks? Actually, the only distinction I really have right now is that I am an academic talking about another academic's writing. Thus, I could veer into the purely academic domain and say things like, I wish you'd use the Herfindahl Index, what about the endogeneity of market structure, and other traditional questions like that? But I won't bore this diverse audience with those kind of details.

Perhaps my contribution is as the academic here, to provide some perspective by stepping back a bit from the immediate issues of alliance structure and performance and talking about how do we locate alliances theoretically. I was particularly impressed with Ben Latimer's discussion about alliance motivation. It is important that we achieve a fundamental understanding before we start talking about specific alliance structures. My comments will focus on two figures; Figure 4.4 presents levels of analysis and illustrates that any such discussion of alliances involves a

Edward J. Zajac is the James F. Beré Professor of Organization Behavior at J. L. Kellogg Graduate School of Management, Northwestern University.

continuum. We usually present continua as horizontal but I prefer to show this as a vertical continuum to help avoid looking at one or the other end.

Alliances are located somewhere between a single organization and some other large collective. For example, earlier this morning we were talking about the role of government and how it affects alliances, and the role of industry and even societal constraints and how they affect alliances. That's one way to think about alliances. But some people focus on alliances per se. For example, in their analysis of rural alliances, our colleagues from Minnesota are trying to look at alliances per se and producing structural and performance measures of alliances.

However, I would also like to argue that we can take a level of analysis perspective that focuses on the relationship between alliances and individual alliance members. We can look at alliance failure in this way. What is an alliance failure? Well, you might say that an alliance failure is one where it breaks up. But let me ask you this: from the perspective of the individual players, is that necessarily a failure? I'd argue that in some cases, the breakup of an alliance is, in fact, quite advantageous to one player, maybe not so advantageous to the other, possibly advantageous to both; but, in any event, it requires you to consider multiple levels of analysis. Stated differently, one needs to think back down to the other level of analysis in Figure 4.4 to the individual organization level.

Given these distinctions, I'd like to focus my attention on the political dynamics between the alliance member and the alliance per se. I think a lot of the discussion that we've heard thus far has really been trying to get at this issue—what are alliances anyway? While a highly specific definition is not essential, it is possible to think of alliances in terms of ultimate performance aims. Why focus on alliance motivation? Because I define alliances in quite simple motivational terms, consider

**Figure 4.4**    Levels of Analysis

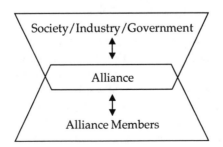

the following examples of alliances. The first one would be win-win. This is a truly rational strategy and, not surprisingly, much of the discussion of the alliances that we've heard today has implicitly been on win-win alliances. It is natural that both sides want something to work well. "You can benefit. I can benefit. We can benefit together." This sounds very nice but certainly doesn't address other possible (or even likely) alliance examples.

Consider the win-lose situation: this situation can be both rational or nonrational depending on the level of analysis. Christianson talked about how economic and political issues impact alliances and I'd like to push this a bit more in the political direction and say that there are some alliances that are dominated by "WIIFMs." This is a term I recently heard when I began teaching in some executive education programs at Northwestern. People would always talk about WIIFMs, which means, What's In It For Me? Academics would call this sub-goal pursuits. This issue of WIIFMs in alliances refers to what benefit accrues to the individual organization. Those of you active in alliances I would also suspect have a lot of WIIFM experience. Nevertheless, like the pursuit of world peace, the win-win strategy is an idea to which we all aspire. The reality, however, is that we need to deal with both types of alliances. If you are faced with a situation where you are thinking cooperative and your partner is thinking more competitively, it makes you realize that a strategic alliance is just a shell through which one can drive either a cooperative win-win strategy, or the exploitation of an partner. I hate to say this, but this means that in win-lose alliances, you are either the exploiter or the sucker.

Finally, consider the lose-lose alliance situation. The lose-lose alliance says to us that there are alliances out there that basically don't make sense, either because the strategic concept is flawed or the incentives are not aligned. In other words, the answer to the WIIFM question is "nothing" or worse for both sides. I am certainly not trying to argue that this is an exhaustive list of ways in which alliances fail, but rather that these are different types of failures.

In addition to considering alliances in terms of their ultimate performance aims, it is also important to look at them in terms of their resource flows. Alliances may take many forms such as a joint venture, a consortium, or other forms. We can step back, however, and consider more fundamental distinctions. One of them is what I call a *pooling* alliance. A pooling alliance involves two or more organizations combining similar resources. Now you might say that sounds rather obvious, but I also want to contrast this type with the *trading* alliance, which involves two or more organizations exchanging dissimilar resources. In other words, the pooling alliance involves similar resource combinations, while the trading alliance involves different or complementary resource exchanges. The reason I think about it in this way is that I often hear people claim that organizations should always create alliances with partners who have complementary skills. I always ask what that means. They say that it means that the people with whom you should ally are different from you. This means, however, that you would never have an alliance with someone with similar skills. Obviously you would. It's just a different kind of alliance. For example, some of the alliances we've talked about here, such as the joint-buy and joint-make alliances, would both fit into the pooling alliances category. The Johnson & Johnson–Merck alliance is a classic trading alliance. One party has very good marketing skills and the other has the product pipeline. You are supposed to get some synergy from that combination. The important point here is that the structure of alliance arrangements might be very different, depending on these basic underlying motivations.

Just to prove that I am an academic, I have another figure which is a 2 × 2 matrix. As Henry Mintzberg once told me, at McGill University, where he teaches, they have these actually painted on the blackboard so you can just erase the dimensions and fill in your own. Given our two dimensions of resource flows and performance, four quadrants emerge in Figure 4.5. This figure highlights both the political dynamics and the potential gains that can be found in an alliance. In the first quadrant you have a win-win alliance pooling alliance, in which you achieve some sharing of common risks or costs. And clearly that's something we recognize in the health care industry as descriptive of much of the current alliance activity. We also see it in other industries, such as offshore drilling in the Antarctic, where oil firms are combining similar resources to exploit the win-win potential.

Let's look at the potential dark side of these kinds of alliances. This is what some people call the "free rider problem," which I rephrase as "riding for free." In pooling alliances, what happens is that often there are more than just two players. You have, perhaps, an average of 15.7 as in the paper just presented, or an even larger number in some networks I have described. In this case, there are often questions about unequal contributions and the possibility that one party can basically free ride off the actions of others. For example, lobbying alliances, if you are part of the industry that's getting that benefit, then that benefit is basically yours to have whether you contribute to the alliance or not.

On the trading side the ideal win-win trading alliance is one that creates value from complementary distinctive competencies. And by this I mean simply that someone has something you would like, and you have something someone else would like. Through that trade, which is, if you think about it, the fundamental basis for a lot of economic exchange

**Figure 4.5**    Gaming Strategies for Alliance Members

|  | | **Alliance Performance Aims** | |
|  | | Win-Win | Win-Lose |
|---|---|---|---|
| **Alliance Resource Flows** | Pooling | Sharing of common risks or costs | Riding for free |
| | Trading | Creating value from complementary distinctive competencies | Racing to learn/absorb |

advantage is gained on both sides. That fills an obvious quadrant in Figure 4.5.

The last quadrant represents what I will call "racing to learn or absorb." Some people who claim that the purpose of an alliance is to learn as much as you can about the other guy so that when an alliance finally explodes, you have learned something about an ex-competitor who again becomes a competitor. That does not sound like a win-win situation to me. That sounds like a win-lose and I assign it to the lower right quadrant. This quadrant suggests that as you think about potential alliance partners, one issue is whether they have the same values as you have; if not, you may soon be facing a win-lose alliance. Whether this is advantageous to you as an individual organization will depend on which side of the win-lose you find yourself.

A final comment concerns trust. We've heard that trust is very important in all alliances. It seems to me that this may not be true in every case. However, I would note that the contingency framework in Figure 4.5 shows, in fact, with respect to win-lose alliances, trust is not a major factor. Not every alliance is the same if you look at it this way. I also don't think we'd want to go to the other extreme where we'd say that every alliance is unique; if this were true then we could never generalize or learn anything from experience. Rather, a contingency framework focused on more general terms like resource flow or ultimate performance objectives can get at the fundamentals of alliances formation, and ultimately help sort out useful distinctions across alliances. In this way, we will not lose sight of the fact that alliances are a many-leveled things.

# 5

# Strategic Alliances as a Structure for Integrated Delivery Systems

## William L. Dowling

At the risk of taking too narrow a perspective for some, this chapter focuses on strategic alliances as an organizational approach for structuring vertically integrated delivery systems. Forming integrated delivery systems is "job number one" for health professionals. Today's "nonsystem" of almost totally independent physicians, hospitals, and insurers, each acting in accordance with different aims and different incentives, requires complete reform. The pieces need to be reassembled into organized delivery systems capable of accepting responsibility for the health of an enrolled population, managing care across the full spectrum of services, and doing this within fixed financial limits determined largely by purchasers. Putting such systems together is extremely difficult. It is not even clear who will be the chief architect—insurers, managed care plans, hospitals, medical groups, communities, or public agencies. But it does seem clear that such systems will be built largely through alliances among providers and in some cases between providers and insurers.

The concept of the vertically integrated delivery system is an idea whose time has come, although examples of the idea fully implemented are few. Almost all proposals for health care reform give center stage to some type of organization that can assume responsibility for managing the continuum of preventive and treatment services for a defined population within fixed dollar limits. Most would also integrate financing with delivery through contracts or common ownership.

William L. Dowling is vice president of planning and policy development, Sisters of Providence Health System.

- President Clinton's proposal envisions "accountable health plans"—networks of insurance companies, doctors, and hospitals that would contract with "health alliances" to provide a standard federally defined benefit package to all who apply within a capitated premium.
- The American Hospital Association (AHA) has advanced the concept of "community care networks"—sets of providers which provide patients with an integrated continuum of care organized at the community level; networks are paid on a capitated basis.
- The Catholic Health Association (CHA) proposes "integrated delivery networks"—sets of providers organized to take financial risk for providing a coordinated continuum of health care services (including preventive care, primary care, and long-term care) to an enrolled population.

## Purposes

The purposes of this paper are to examine the movement toward vertical integration in the delivery of health care services. Alliances are almost always a central feature of the structure of integration. Attention is given to rationale for and types of alliances, the benefits or performance of integrated delivery systems, and on the relationship between structure and performance. Finally, some observations about factors that seem to help or hinder the formation or success of integrated systems are presented. All of this is somewhat speculative, based mostly on personal experience and descriptive reports in the trade journals; little empirical evidence about the performance of systems is available.

## Pressures for Vertical Integration

The pressures to transform today's fragmented financing and delivery structures into rationally designed, integrated health care systems come from the growth of managed care and the movement toward health reform. These forces are giving rise to two stark realities: (1) increasingly aggressive purchasers are going to curtail their spending to the point that the flow of dollars into health care will not sustain the delivery system as it exists today, and (2) as capitation-based payment ends the separate flow of payments to each category of provider and puts providers at financial risk, it will become obvious that today's "nonsystem" is not able to manage care within fixed dollar limits or deploy resources more rationally. Incentives will need to be aligned and structures changed to enable care to be truly managed. In short, as the financial incentives change, structures must change.

Another pressure is dissatisfaction with the present system from every quarter: consumers, purchasers, government, and providers themselves. CHA has said it well in its proposal for health care reform, *Setting Relationships Right*:

> The CHA proposal begins with *delivery reform*, in contrast to other proposals that focus primarily on financing. The current delivery system is deficient primarily because it is fragmented and too costly. Financial incentives too often encourage providers to function in isolation from one another with little integration among primary care, acute care, and long-term care settings. Some important services are excluded while others are duplicated. Health promotion and preventive care are often uncovered. The current system also lacks internal economic discipline, forcing purchasers to use costly and demoralizing external controls on physicians and health care facilities. Finally, access to the current delivery system is often restricted. This is especially true for the millions of individuals who have no insurance but also for many persons with insurance. (Catholic Health Association 1993)

## Definition: Vertically Integrated Delivery System

Vertical integration refers to coordinating, linking or incorporating within a single organization activities or entities at different stages of a production process—in health care the processes of producing and delivering patient care (Conrad and Dowling 1990). These activities or entities would otherwise be completely independent, or would interact through arm's-length transactions. Vertical integration can be *forward* toward an organization's consumers (e.g., patients, physicians, and increasingly enrollees and purchasers) or *backward* toward the inputs to production. Taking the perspective of the hospital, forward integration might include linkages with physician practices, ambulatory care facilities, nursing homes, and home care agencies, since these are the sources of the hospital's patients and/or where patients go following hospitalization. Backward integration might include ownership of a durable medical equipment company, laboratory, or group purchasing organization, or affiliation with a nursing school or medical residency program, since these are the sources of the personnel, equipment, and services used in producing patient care.

An extreme form of forward integration intended to capture patients at the source (i.e., when they choose a health insurance plan) is integration of delivery with the financing or insurance function. A number of delivery organizations are starting up health plans or contracting with a plan to be the plan's exclusive or preferred provider network. At the same time, a number of insurers and health plans are approaching this from the other direction and assembling their own provider networks through selective contracting.

Although there is no standard use of these terms, "delivery system" refers to a system that has integrated a range of facilities, services, and providers (including physicians), and "health care system" refers to a system that also incorporates the insurance or health plan function.

The above comments relate mostly to the anatomy of integrated delivery systems. The purpose of the delivery system is to be able to contract with purchasers to provide (or arrange for) and coordinate a continuum of health care services for a defined population, and accept financial risk for managing the health care of this population within fixed payment limits.

Another way to define vertical integration is in terms of its generic elements:

1. *A broad range of facilities and services*—prevention, primary care, inpatient care, long-term care, and home care—under a single organizational umbrella. This facilitates coordination and continuity of care and use of the appropriate site of treatment

2. *A group or network of primary care physicians* committed to the delivery system. The primary care physicians must be organized to manage care. Ideally, they should be geographically dispersed to provide access to the delivery system from throughout the region served. The economic incentives and organizational loyalties of the primary care physicians must be aligned with the rest of the delivery system, so that responsibility for costs and outcomes is shared.

3. *Relationships with specialists* and other providers willing to work with the delivery system to achieve cost-effective, quality care.

4. *Mechanisms for coordinating/integrating care* across the entire spectrum of services to produce cost-effective treatment and reduce fragmentation and duplication. Examples include primary care physicians acting as care managers, formal case management systems, inpatient and outpatient critical paths/treatment protocols, an integrated data system, a single medical record, and discharge coordinators/social workers in both inpatient and outpatient settings.

5. *Information systems* that enable monitoring, improving, and publicly reporting on cost-effectiveness, quality, and outcomes. Information systems should be able to track enrollees/patients over time and across providers/sites, and integrate data from all settings. Information systems must be able to support the management of patient care

as well as the management of financial risk. Information should enable the profiling of both providers and treatment patterns to identify cost-effective providers and to highlight the most effective treatment regimens.

6. *Integrated planning, resource allocation, and assessment of system performance* facilitated by management and organization structures.

7. *Unified strategy formulation, marketing, and contracting* such that the delivery system is able to approach the market as a single entity.

8. *Integration of financing and delivery through ownership* and/or exclusive or preferred relationships with health plans.

**Definition: Alliances**

Zuckerman and D'Aunno (1990) have defined alliances (or federations) as three or more organizations that pool their resources to achieve stated objectives. The participants do not give up corporate ownership, but give a management group or organization the authority to coordinate or direct certain of the participants' activities or to perform certain activities on their behalf. According to D'Aunno and Zuckerman, alliances are more than trade associations in that they set and adhere to criteria for membership. They are differentiated from mergers because more than two organizations are involved, and because the participants don't give up independent ownership. But they go beyond coalitions in establishing a management group or organization to carry out alliance activities.

Multihospital alliances such as AmHS, Premier, SunHealth, and VHA fit this definition well. Hospital alliances have been in existence for a decade or more. They initially focused on giving members access to management expertise, gaining economies of scale through group purchasing and insurance and providing a forum for sharing. In recent years, they have broadened their role to help their members cope with the changing health care marketplace.

Although the elements of this definition are pertinent, it is framed mainly in terms of hospital alliances. The term alliance used here ascribes a broader meaning to include any type of organizational arrangement that links elements or parties in a way that contributes to integrated delivery. My definition encompasses any form of association or joining together for mutual benefit that contributes to this end and gives "mutual benefit" a broader meaning than "common objective." The different parties may be seeking quite different benefits from the relationship, and may not even see themselves pursuing the goal of integrated delivery, although this may result from their working together.

The nature of the relationships among parties can arrange from loose and informal to tight and formal, from narrow in scope in relation to the participants' activities to encompassing all of their activities, from allowing participants to retain almost complete autonomy to requiring them to subordinate their interests to the organizational arrangement. Nonbinding agreements to work together and complete consolidations into a single organization (perhaps through acquisition, merger, or employment) are examples of "strategic alliances."

## Alliances and Vertical Integration

Why pursue vertical integration through strategic alliances rather than internal development or some other organizational arrangement? In general, because:

- Each party brings something to the relationship the others need
- This "something" can be acquired more cheaply, more surely, or at less risk through an alliance than by developing it internally
- Many forms of alliance permit the parties to benefit from the relationship without giving up too much autonomy or independence
- An alliance may be a politically acceptable step when the parties are not willing to go further
- An alliance may achieve the critical mass or market presence required to produce benefits for the participating parties more quickly or surely than they could on their own
- An alliance may give rise to synergies or intangibles whereby the whole is greater than the sum of its parts
- It is often impossible for any one party to respond to the great variety of needs in a community or demands in a marketplace.

The key to success is creating a balanced relationship among the participants featuring collaboration rather than control of one party by another. The goal is a "win-win" relationship in which all participants benefit.

The rationale for alliances can be looked at from a more theoretical perspective. For example, D'Aunno and Zuckerman (1987) have proposed three general hypotheses to explain the formation of alliances:

*Resource dependence.* Organizations attempt to reduce their dependence on external parties or other organizations for important resources (e.g., for physician support, information, access to facilities for the transfer of patients, access to managed care contracts, technology, regulatory approval, etc.), especially when withdrawal of these resources is perceived to be a threat. Dependence reducing strategies include mergers, joint ventures, or entering into alliances, either with the supplier of the needed resource, or with others who are similarly dependent to increase collective leverage with the supplier. Alliances increase the members' market power vis-a-vis suppliers of needed resources as a result of their collective size or visibility.

*Transaction costs.* Alliances occupy a middle ground between markets and organizational hierarchies in mediating the transaction costs associated with interorganizational activities such as exchange of information or transfer of patients.

*Organization-environment relations.* Alliances can enhance their members' legitimacy and hence support from the environment by helping them meet external norms or expectations regarding their behavior (e.g., that hospitals should cooperate rather than compete). Alliances may also influence which hospitals survive in a demanding and selective environment, not only by the benefits and legitimacy they provide, but also because they select and then give greater strength and visibility to hospitals that are efficient and effective in the first place.

## Types of Strategic Alliances

It is helpful to think of vertically integrated health care systems as comprising three distinct components:

- Integration of the various providers, facilities, and programs that supply the array of services which make up the full continuum of care—primary care, acute care, long-term care, health education, prevention, community-based services, and social and support services.
- Integration of physicians
- Integration of the financing/insurance function.

Having a full spectrum of services under a single organizational umbrella enables a delivery system to accept responsibility for the entire continuum of care, to coordinate care, and to place patients in the most appropriate setting. Having the full spectrum also enables resources to be allocated more rationally internally to expand or downsize services in accordance with the needs of the population served, and it minimizes transaction costs across settings. Collaboration with community-based and public health services allows a delivery system to go beyond just health care to impact other factors that affect the community's health. To serve a large geographic area, it may also be necessary for a delivery system to include a number of hospitals in addition to other types of providers.

Physician participation, especially by primary care physicians, is essential for a delivery system to assume risk for managing care within fixed dollar limits and for it to accept responsibility for quality. Alignment of physician and system incentives is probably the most important single determinant of delivery system success, since costs are driven largely by the physician's pen. And an adequate base of primary care physicians distributed throughout the geographic area served is important in providing access to the system.

The growth of managed care has made integration of financing and delivery important. Previously, insurers paid claims to whatever providers individuals chose to go to. Few providers were excluded. But with the advent of HMOs, PPOs, and selective contracting, insurers/health plans began to contract only with selected providers and to discourage their enrollees from using others. Hence, health plans became the providers' link to consumers. Under the managed competition approach to health care reform this role is formally assigned to "accountable health plans." Integration of finance and delivery also enables the delivery system to (1) align incentives, (2) rationally deploy resources internally (which is almost impossible if insurers are paying each provider independently and often in a contradictory manner), and (3) benefit financially from being efficient.

Linkages with providers enable insurers/health plans to offer purchasers a complete package under one organizational umbrella, and should increase their influence with the ever larger purchasing entities of the future. More important, alignment with a delivery system enables a plan to work directly with providers to achieve cost-effective delivery vs. relying on discounts and utilization controls to contain costs.

## Benefits of Integrating Finance and Delivery

A number of benefits could accrue to providers, especially if organized into integrated delivery systems, by the additional step of integrating the financing/insurance function. Integration could be by contractual participation in one or more health plans, a strategic alliance, or ownership of a health plan. Consider the following benefits:

- Providers become a direct participant in the design of the interfaces between themselves (as sellers) and employers and other purchasers (as buyers). They are able to shape critical decisions about product development and marketing strategy and are directly involved in contract negotiations. And, they may have greater influence with the huge purchasing alliances envisioned under health care reform.

- Providers are able to direct marketing and contracting strategies in ways that further their mission. A delivery system may be committed to serving the elderly or poor, for example. At the same time, as a matter of public policy, HCFA is encouraging Medicare beneficiaries to enroll in managed care plans, and a number of states are requiring Medicaid recipients to do the same. In pursuing its mission, the system would want to participate in the managed care plans serving these populations. The surest way to be certain to have this opportunity would be to align with these plans.

- Alignment of physician and hospital financial incentives and the rational deployment of resources within a delivery system are greatly facilitated by a close relationship with the financing/insurance element. Otherwise, separate and often contradictory forms of payment to the different categories of providers are likely to continue.

- Replacement of external often highly intrusive utilization controls with internal self-regulation, ideally through internally developed treatment protocols and care management systems, is possible when payor and provider are integrated.

- Cost savings can be achieved by simplifying and streamlining the interactions between purchasers, payers, and providers. Today these interactions generate huge transaction costs.

- Finally, linkages with insurers/health plans position providers to be a part of multiple-plan offerings which have become increasingly attractive in the marketplace.

Nerenz (1992), commenting on the essentials of system integration, suggests that: "An additional feature of system integration is the integration of finance and delivery . . . The ability of an organization to arrange financial incentives . . . to support key delivery system goals is a clear advantage. For example, a system capable of creating financial incentives for conservative care would be in a better position to eliminate unnecessary testing than a system trying to manage utilization (under) fee-for-service. A system's ability to control both financing and delivery becomes a third 'test' of systemness."

Although control of both finance and delivery appears to be an extremely important feature of a fully mature integrated health care system, control does not need to extend to ownership of the insurance or health plan entity. The key is the ability to control the payment of providers. For example, a delivery system might not have its own health plan, and so would not act as the insurer vis a vis employers or other purchasers. Rather it would contract to assume the financial risk for the care of the enrollees of health plans operated by others. The critical elements are that the delivery system be at risk and be in the position to control the methods and levels of payment to its providers. It needs to be able to "manage the capitation dollars." Not only does this enable the delivery system to align provider incentives with system utilization goals or treatment protocols, but also to allocate resources internally in support of care management and cost-effective delivery. Care management may call for investment in the development of treatment protocols, information systems, uniform multisetting medical records, case management systems, and discharge coordinators and other support personnel. And cost-effectiveness may be enhanced by employing nurse practitioners to assume functions that would otherwise be done by physicians; or by investing in (or contracting for) long-term care beds or home care capabilities as a substitute for hospital beds; or by investing in prevention, occupational health, and primary care to reduce the incidence of more advanced conditions.

Examples of attempts to integrate financing and delivery through alliances abound. Blue Cross-Blue Shield (BC-BS) of Iowa, Iowa Methodist in Des Moines, and two multispecialty groups are joining together to create a managed care delivery system called Iowa Health Partners. All parties will share the financial risks and rewards (alignment of incentives) of a new managed care insurance plan to be called CommUnity Choice. BC-BS of Michigan has entered into a similar relationship with Henry Ford Health System and Mercy Health Services in the Detroit market. An alliance has been formed between Mutual of Omaha, two major hospitals in Omaha, and one in Council Bluffs, across the Mississippi in Iowa. The goal is to position the parties to be an accountable health plan under reform.

## Horizontal Integration of Hospitals

Although this paper focuses on vertical integration and its three key components—integration of facilities and services, integration of physicians, and integration of financing—it is important to recognize briefly the importance of two other types of integration: horizontal integration of hospitals and the newest phenomenon, horizontal integration of medical groups.

The growth of horizontally integrated hospital systems began in earnest in the mid-1960s, spurred by the entry and rapid development of investor-owned systems. Not-for-profit system growth picked up in the mid-1970s. Today 300 systems own, lease, or manage about half of the nation's hospitals. Early system growth was motivated by opportunities for economies of scale, sharing of management expertise and support services, and greater political clout. More recently, hospital acquisitions, mergers, and affiliations have aimed at better positioning the participants to compete for market share. Since most markets are local or metropolitanwide in nature, local systems have gained in importance, and large multistate systems have tended to plan their strategies and investments on a market-by-market basis, even divesting themselves of hospitals in markets where they don't have much presence. Luke (1992) has explored the "local hospital system" phenomenon and reports that over 1,000 (25 percent) of the nation's hospitals belong to one of 400 urban-centered local systems.

For the purposes of this paper, the key point to be made about horizontally integrated hospital systems, and especially "local systems" (or the local subsystems of larger systems) is that they often represent the first step toward vertical integration. Shortell (1988) has predicted that "Horizontal growth will set the stage for subsequent vertical growth as hospitals in an area or within a system see opportunities to expand outside of acute inpatient care. All of the forces in the environment will be pushing in this direction. . . ." In most circumstances, a horizontally integrated system's resources, whether capital, management expertise, contracts with purchasers, or market dominance, should give it a leg up on nonsystem facilities in deploying internal resources and establishing external linkages in the pursuit of vertical integration.

Years earlier Starkweather (1972) proposed that "in many communities there must be a concentration of resources along horizontal lines in order to create the 'critical mass' necessary to achieve . . . expansion along vertical lines." Starkweather saw horizontal integration by hospitals as aimed at efficiency (although he argued that this was the legitimating reason for system formation, the real motive being institutional survival or expansion) and vertical integration of an array of health services as aimed at effectiveness in extending more comprehensive, coordinated care to the population served. This early observation anticipated today's view of the central purpose of vertical integration as enhancing coordination of the full continuum of care, although we now believe that cost savings can be achieved as well.

The observation that horizontally integrated systems tend to diversify from acute care toward a broader range of services was given early support by Ermann and Gabel's (1984) review of the status and performance of multihospital systems. In 1982, over half of the nation's hospital systems operated health promotion programs, ambulatory care facilities, nursing homes, and physician office buildings. Ermann and Gabel give no comparative data from nonsystem hospitals, however. Today broad diversification of services by hospitals is commonplace.

That systems are ahead of independent hospitals in moving toward integrated delivery is supported by a 1993 survey by Witt/Keiffer, Ford, Hadelman, and Lloyd (Health Progress 1993). Of the 137 hospitals responding to the survey, 8 percent reported having an integrated delivery system in place, and 48.9 percent said a system would be implemented within 12 months. Multihospital systems were found to be more active in seeking integrated delivery arrangements: 14.3 percent of 56 respondents were already part of an integrated system and 73.9 percent indicated they would be within 12 months. Even for those hospitals and multihospital systems with no immediate implementation plans, almost all reported having discussions about the possibility of forming or joining an integrated delivery system.

Medical group practices responding to the survey were somewhat less likely to be aligned with an integrated delivery system. Although 15.6 percent of the 135 responding group practices were part of a system (a higher percentage than either hospitals or multihospital systems), 14.8 percent reported they were not considering integrated delivery. Nonetheless, a significant portion (45.2 percent) of the medical groups indicated they would be part of a system within a year.

All the organizations surveyed reported making large investments in developing systems (on average, $471,268 for hospitals, $1,420,675 for systems, and $691,141 for group practices). Of the factors prompting integrated delivery systems, the two most frequently cited were the prospect of health care reform and providers' need to position themselves for managed care contracting.

## Horizontal Integration of Physicians

Horizontal integration of medical groups into "supergroups" is the most recent type of alliance. A good example is Mullikin Medical Center in Artesia, California. Mullikin is a for-profit, physician-owned, Southern-Californiawide network of medical groups and independent practitioners that competes for contracts with health plans and other purchasers as a unified delivery system. Mullikin can accept capitated risk for physician services or for both physician and hospital care.

Mullikin is one of the nation's largest supergroups, consisting of 400 physicians, practicing out of over 40 offices. The physician groups are heavily oriented toward primary care. Mullikin holds contracts with 22 HMOs for 300,000 lives. The organization owns one hospital and subcontracts with others. Mullikin is structured as a management service organization (MSO) that acquires and manages groups and acts as their agent in the marketplace. Physicians see Mullikin as giving them appeal and market power in bargaining with health plans as a result of the large number of groups involved, their geographic distribution, and their ability to assume risk. (deLafuente 1993)

Just as horizontal integration of hospitals has led to vertical integration, physician supergroups are likely to move toward alignment with other elements of delivery. Integration of a medical group with one or more hospitals would enable the group to offer a more comprehensive range of services, closely integrate tertiary services, provide a respected image in the community, and could give access to capital. Mullikin recently entered into an affiliation agreement with the six-hospital Daughters of Charity Health System–West region in San Francisco to jointly move toward a statewide integrated delivery system. To this alliance, Mullikin brings expertise and a proven track record in acquiring and establishing medical groups, and in contracting, assuming risk, and managing care. The Daughters of Charity bring capital, hospitals, and a strong Northern California presence.

Key success factors for the emerging physician-driven mega-groups are:

- Having the right number and mix of physicians, especially primary care physicians
- An ability to assume risk
- Geographic coverage
- Reputation
- Determining which ancillary services to offer
- An ability to demonstrate appropriate utilization and good outcomes.

Another recently reported example of the "supergroup" model is the coming together of Portland's 50-physician Metropolitan Clinic, 35-physician Portland Clinic, and 20-physician Suburban Clinic to form a jointly owned entity called Coordinated Healthcare Network (CHN). Eighty percent of the network's physicians are primary-care physicians. They practice out of 11 sites throughout the Portland metropolitan area. CHN will compete for contracts with insurers and health plans. CHN plans to arrange for after-hours care, establish a physician referral service, and initiate educational programs for physicians and management staff. An expressed purpose of the alliance is to enable the sponsoring medical groups to control their own business dealings and maintain their independence from hospitals and insurers. It is expected that the alliance will

give the participating medical groups economies of scale and leverage
in the marketplace they would not have on their own.

## Tightness of Alliance Relationships

For each type of integration a variety of organizational arrangements may
be used to link the parties. These may be thought of as ranging along a
continuum of "tightness" from informal, loose, nonbinding agreements,
to contractual agreements, to joint ventures, and finally to complete
amalgamation into a single organization. That is, alliances can range
from a handshake to a merger, along a continuum from cooperation,
through collaboration, to consolidation.

Three important dimensions of alliance relationships are: (1) the
breadth of the relationship in relation to the activities of the participants,
(2) the degree of commitment or exclusivity, and (3) the extent of the
alliance's authority to act on behalf of its participants, such as in contracting. Using the physician-hospital organization (PHO) to illustrate,
with regard to "breadth," does the PHO offer just a menu of practice
management services for physicians to choose from, or does it acquire
and assume full management responsibility for their practices, or does
it also negotiate contracts on their behalf? With regard to "degree of
commitment," are the participating parties allowed to contract outside
of (and perhaps in competition with) the PHO, or does the PHO act
as the exclusive marketing arm of the participants? An intermediate
degree of commitment would be a right of first refusal agreement under
which the PHO gets first crack at contracts but allows participants to
contract directly when a given opportunity does not meet its criteria or
is otherwise unacceptable.

It is logical to assume that the comprehensiveness and exclusivity
of the relationship between the parties to an integrated delivery system
would affect its performance, although these relationships have not received any rigorous tests of this hypothesis.

Baker (1990), from a survey of 13 physician-hospital organizations,
identified the following continuum of legal arrangements:

- Affiliation: "voluntary joint activity based on implicit or formal
  agreement."
- Contract: "a legal agreement."
- General or limited partnership: "the parties co-own a business
  activity. The assets and other resources of the activity are jointly
  managed and profits shared, but only for the particular business
  of the partnership; the parties do not consolidate their activities
  or interests in other areas."

- Parent corporation: "a new corporation created entirely separate from the sponsoring parties themselves."
- Vertical integration: also "a separate legal entity created apart from its shareholders," but "usually involving a merger or consolidation of the entities."

Baker posits that affiliations and contractual agreements involve little legal or management commitment; no new legal entity is created; and such arrangements are easy to establish or discontinue. As a result there is little "stress" on the parties since their autonomy is maintained. On the other hand, Baker sees the potential rewards of such arrangements to be low, since an affiliation or contractual agreement is generally not sufficient to enable the participants to make significant commitments, such as to accept contracted risk. In addition, these arrangements often have no clear image in the marketplace and are often not taken seriously by purchasers.

Tighter forms of integration align the interests of the parties more completely, but the parties give up more autonomy. Baker observes that tighter arrangements are administratively and legally more complex, entail substantial costs, and require considerable management expertise to establish and maintain. A high degree of commitment on the part of the parties is required to put together fully integrated delivery systems and to make them successful. Especially important is leadership to deal with the inevitable conflicts that arise. But such structures increasingly appeal to the marketplace because they can assume risk, act to eliminate duplication, change patterns of delivery, and rationalize the internal flow of resources. Fully integrated structures provide a rational basis for long-term investment of capital in infrastructure development, and they hold substantial promise for success.

McManis and Stewart (1992), among others, note that many physician-hospital arrangements have yielded mixed results because they do not go far enough in terms of real economic integration. Practice management support through a management services organization, for example, may build good relations, but in and of itself is not a close enough relationship to align financial incentives or enable the parties to assume risk together.

## The "Tightness" of Physician-Hospital Relationships

The continuum of tightness can be illustrated using different types of physician-hospital relationships. Least binding are the various "bonding" activities offered by hospitals to members of their medical staffs to engender greater loyalty. Next is the *management services organization* (MSO) where a hospital or an entity jointly owned by the hospital and physicians offers a menu of practice enhancement and management services to the medical staff. The expectation is that physicians receiving services from the MSO will feel greater loyalty to the hospital and use it more, although they are not formally required to do so. Further along the continuum, some MSOs offer complete practice management services, and a few acquire the physical assets of physician practices and take over all management. Also, a few MSOs have begun to take on the role of negotiating contracts on behalf of participating physicians and hospitals, but that is more characteristic of *physician-hospital organizations* (PHOs).

The term PHO has been applied to almost any arrangement between a hospital and physicians, but the defining features of a PHO are:

- A jointly owned entity, often 50–50, formed to undertake cooperative business initiatives
- Sharing of risk and rewards
- Physician participants may be individual physicians or a physician cooperative, medical group(s), or IPA(s)
- PHOs often do not involve all members of the medical staff.

Typically PHOs are formed to seek contracts with managed care plans, although some sponsor day surgery centers, MRIs, or other business ventures. A defining feature of a PHO is whether or not it is open to all members of the medical staff. Conventional wisdom has it that only physicians who share the delivery system's vision and who are committed to accepting risk for cost-effective care should be invited to join if the PHO is to be successful. A PHO enables the parties to take advantage of the particular contributions of each for the benefit of all. Physicians benefit from the expertise, capital, management resources, and name recognition of the hospital, and gain the opportunity to participate in decision making and the pursuit of contracts and other sources of revenue. The hospital gains a physician base and is able to diversify its services without competing with its physicians.

The strength of intermediate degrees of tightness is also a weakness; what is easy to get into is also easy to get out of. Hence, PHOs are inherently somewhat fragile and unreliable. They depend upon the goodwill of participants. Participation rarely requires an exclusive commitment, so the physicians are often free to pursue contracts in competition with the PHO. And 50–50 control may confound decision making. On the other hand, intermediate forms of structure tend to lead to a greater awareness of the interdependencies among the parties. This may lead to greater trust which in turn may lead to the evolution toward more tightly structured arrangements.

A *foundation* is an infrequently used but highly visible organizational form for structuring a high degree of integration between physicians and a hospital or hospital system. Most foundations are not-for-profit corporations established by a hospital or system to provide medical services, education, and research. The foundation purchases the non-physical assets of the practices of physicians or medical groups and provides all marketing and management services to support the practices from that point on. The physicians typically form a professional services corporation, which contracts exclusively with the foundation to provide physician services. The foundation negotiates and manages contracts with purchasers for the delivery of physician and hospital services.

And finally, the tightest form of physician-hospital relationship is *employment* of physicians by the hospital or system (generally following acquisition of their practices). The hospital or system in this model is fully responsible for clinical care and costs.

## Structural Characteristics

Zuckerman and D'Aunno (1990) have identified several additional organizational characteristics or dimensions which can be used to describe some of the key features of alliances devoted to vertical integration:

- Purposes of the alliance
- Basis of organization—such as geography, type of ownership, types of institutions, common interests, and common dependencies. Any or all of these could be important foundations for vertical integration
- Structural forms—ranging from loosely coupled consortia, to joint ventures, to umbrella holding companies
- Membership criteria—such as mission, operating philosophy, size, finances, management capabilities, market position, reputation, or range of services. Again, these and other criteria could be important in forming integrated delivery systems
- Cost of membership
- Governance and management structures
- Programs and services—most pertinent to integrated delivery systems might be diversification into a broad range of services, development or affiliation with managed care plans, market positioning, brand name promotion, or regional networking.

# Assessing the Performance of
# Integrated Delivery Systems

The performance of integrated delivery systems must ultimately be judged on how well they address societal, community, purchaser, and consumer needs. Do systems contribute to improvement of the health of the communities they serve? Do they respond to purchaser demands for affordability and responsiveness? Are those who use them satisfied with the access, provider choice, and quality of service they offer? Do they achieve good clinical outcomes, and are they able to deliver a defined benefits package to an enrolled population within fixed dollar limits?

Granted accomplishments toward goals such as these are difficult to measure. And measuring the contributions of a delivery system is complicated by the fact that many other factors affect health status, costs, and satisfaction. Nonetheless we must "keep our eye on the ball" of ultimate social-purpose goals or values in designing and managing the next generation of delivery systems.

Performance measurement may be made easier by the next generation of information collection and reporting. President Clinton's health care reform proposal, for example, would establish a National Quality Management Program to develop quality and performance measures, conduct consumer surveys, and determine the data health plans would have to report to regional data centers. Annual reports on the comparative performance of health alliances and accountable health plans would be made public. Clinton's proposal calls for development of up to 50 measures of access, appropriateness, outcomes, health promotion, disease prevention, satisfaction, and costs/premiums. Drawing on these data health alliances would provide "report cards" to consumers giving cost and quality comparisons, physician and hospital performance, and patient satisfaction.

A second perspective on performance is to focus on how well a delivery system achieves its own goals. Typically the core goals are to compete successfully, to gain market share, and to be financially viable. To achieve these goals, a delivery system must be able to put together the essential building blocks of integrated delivery, secure needed resources, and satisfy the expectations of internal participants. Hence, performance indicators reflecting this perspective look at the delivery system's ability to develop the infrastructure and internal processes required to attract enrollees, manage care, and achieve good outcomes.

In contrast to looking at performance from the perspective of the delivery system as a whole, a third perspective reflects the expectations and needs (or hopes) of the system's participants—physicians, hospitals, other providers, and affiliated or owned health plans. Is the delivery system bringing physicians more patients? Is it helping them cope with managed care? Is it lowering practice costs? Is it increasing incomes? Some of these indicators reflect strategic and political concerns. Does the alliance deter participating physicians from forming independent entities or contracting with competing health plans? Does it enhance the participants' bargaining power with purchasers?

A helpful source of ideas and suggested indicators for measuring the performance of integrated delivery systems is the Consortium Research on Indicators of System Performance (CRISP) project of Henry Ford Health System's Center for Health System Studies. CRISP is a joint undertaking of 23 health systems and group practices to develop ways of measuring the performance of vertically integrated health care systems. System-level performance is differentiated from the performance of the individual participants in its focus on the health of the population served versus individual patients, and its focus on entire episodes of care versus individual services. The health care system's goal is assumed to be to maximize health outcomes and minimize the resources used in complete episodes of care.

## The Constituencies Served Perspective

A delivery system's ultimate purpose is to meet the needs and expectations of four constituencies:

- The community/region served by the system
- Purchasers—employers, insurers, health care plans, Medicare, Medicaid
- The enrollees of the insurers/health plans that use the system (which may include enrollees of the system's own plan)
- Individual patients.

In general, the delivery system seeks to meet the needs of these constituencies by:

- Improving the overall health of the community and providing other community benefits. (It may target particular population segments of the community)
- Providing convenient access to care
- Keeping costs down by being efficient and cost-effective
- Providing quality care and good service.

Borrowing on CRISP, examples of performance measures that reflect the "constituencies served" perspective might include:

- Community health/benefits
  - Communitywide health status indicators
  - Communitywide immunization and screening rates
  - Communitywide prevalence of behavioral/lifestyle risk factors
  - Charity care provided.
- Access
  - Enrollment in affiliated or owned health plans
    The delivery system may be interested in the enrollment of targeted population segments or in whether enrollment matches communitywide demographics.
  - Percent of enrollees who make one or more primary care visits
  - Number and geographic distribution of primary care physicians.
- Costs—efficiency, effectiveness
  - Cost per member per month
  - Annual PMPM cost increase in relation to CPI
  - Administrative costs as percent of total costs
  - Units of service per enrolled population per year (e.g., hospital days/10,000 population)
  - Units of service per episode of care for defined conditions (e.g., average length of stay for DRG xyz)
  - Frequency and costs of specific high-cost procedures
  - Capacity and nonduplication of facilities in relation to the population served.
- Quality
  - Immunization and screening rates
  - Low birth weight incidence
  - Condition-specific outcomes
  - Compliance with treatment protocols
  - Readmission rates.
- Service
  - Enrollee and patient satisfaction
  - Reenrollment rate
  - Waiting times.

CRISP has helpfully differentiated between "members" (persons enrolled in a delivery system's managed care plan[s]), "users" (persons connected to the system via use of one or more of its services), and "episode users" (persons who used the system for a specific type of episode of care or procedure). Definitions of these categories of persons served are being developed and tested.

CRISP focuses on the *delivery system* as the unit of analysis for performance measures. Another important initiative—Health Plan Employer Data and Information Set (HEDIS)—focuses on the *health plan*. Note that a given health plan may offer a number of products and use a variety of delivery systems and/or providers. Alternatively, a given delivery system may participate in a number of health plans. Hence, HEDIS's perspective is different from CRISP's, although there can be considerable overlap, especially where a delivery system operates its own health plan or is aligned exclusively with a separately owned plan from which it gets the bulk of its volume. As finance and delivery become increasingly integrated, plans and systems will become more and more synonymous. HEDIS is currently testing about 50 indicators covering access, quality, member satisfaction, membership, utilization, and financial performance. Many HEDIS indicators are similar to those developed by CRISP, although CRISP is more oriented toward outcome vs. process measures.

An important prerequisite for maximizing a system's contribution to community health would be for it to define the geographic area or population it seeks to serve. This would provide a basis for assessing community needs, taking an epidemiological or population-based approach to planning, identifying which community organizations and providers to collaborate with, judging the accessibility of the points of entry to the system, deciding where to locate facilities, and so forth. The question of who should decide the geography or population to be served by a system will undoubtedly need to be addressed in health care reform. Left to their own, accountable health plans might try to avoid high risk areas or populations, by, for example, not locating providers in these areas. Presumably whatever regulatory structure is put in place to "manage" managed competition will have to monitor or even assign geographic areas to accountable health plans.

## Studies of System Performance

A scan of the last 2–3 years of professional journals suggests that there is little hard evidence of the effectiveness of vertically integrated delivery systems. This despite a widespread belief in their superiority. Evidence or not, the AHA, CHA, and others are advocating such systems as the centerpiece of health care reform, and an amazing amount of consolidating, diversifying, integrating, and networking is going on as providers rush to join systems. Perhaps this phenomenon is too new for there to have been time for formal evaluation studies. Clearly system leaders feel they must act quickly to adapt to the changing marketplace, data or no. And certainly, as a nation, we underinvest in health services research. But whatever the reasons, conventional wisdom and antidotal evidence of the benefits of integration, not empirical proof, dominate the literature.

An important exception to the above is Shortell's (1988) seminal review of the evidence on the performance of hospital systems. Based on the handful of then available studies and comparative data from nearly 1,000 systems and freestanding hospitals, Shortell concluded that "there is little support for any of the alleged advantages of system hospitals relative to their nonsystem counterparts . . . Little if any economic or service 'value added' appears to be present." Areas of performance looked at by Shortell included the following:

- Costs, economies of scale, efficiency, productivity
- Prices
- Financial performance, profitability
- Access to capital
- Charity care provided
- Services offered
- Managed care involvement
- Quality, patient care outcomes.

Shortell hypothesized that the unimpressive performance of systems was due largely to the fact that systems had come together mainly as a defensive reaction to the increasingly hostile health care environment. Systems were seeking security rather than lower costs or greater community health benefits. Nor did most systems really behave like systems in the sense of "operating as an organic whole with a strategic intent." Shortell's findings may also be due to the fact that many systems were then in the formative stages, and most undoubtedly viewed themselves as horizontally integrated hospital systems, not as vertically integrated delivery systems. Nonetheless, evidence of beneficial system performance was and continues to be sparse.

Shortell and his colleagues at Northwestern University, in collaboration with KPMG Peat Marwick, are continuing to study system performance focusing on the relationship between integration (of clinical services, administrative and support functions, and physicians) and financial and marketplace success. Their current study (HSIS) draws on data from nine participating multiunit systems (Gillies et al. 1993).

Shortell's 1988 findings are consistent with conclusions reached earlier by Zuckerman (1979) in his examination of the "promise and performance" of multi-institutional systems. Zuckerman conceptualized the potential benefits of systems as *economic* (e.g., economies of scale, lower capital costs), *manpower* (e.g., ability to recruit and retain clinical and management personnel), and *organizational* (e.g., growth, survival, political power) and noted that these benefits could accrue either to the community, to the system, or to both. He concluded from an extensive review of the available evidence that support for economic benefits at the institutional level was mixed, and evidence of lower prices at the community level lacking. Systems did seem advantaged in their ability to recruit and retain personnel. And, system hospitals experienced greater growth than nonsystem institutions and generally offered a broader range of services. Empirical support for these conclusions was quite spotty, however, and in general systems fell far short of the expectations ascribed to them.

Again, it should be noted that the systems existing in the early 1970s were mostly horizontally integrated hospital systems. These systems were probably not consciously pursuing many of the goals we now ascribe to systems. Certainly, the financial incentives prevailing at the time (i.e., cost reimbursement) did not encourage aggressive efforts to contain costs. Nor were the structures of these systems (horizontal integration) particularly suited to the pursuit of the types of benefits we seek today from vertical integration. And physician integration was almost nonexistent at the time.

Looking at the 1978–81 period, Ermann and Gabel's (1984) review of system studies found that multihospital systems enjoyed better bond ratings than freestanding institutions. Systems were able to attract quality personnel to rural facilities, although this advantage was not demonstrated in urban areas. For-profit system hospitals used fewer personnel per unit of output than not-for-profits. No other efficiencies or economies of scale were found, and even the lower cost of capital and personnel efficiencies did not translate into lower costs. A review of 18 empirical studies that had looked at costs indicated that system hospital costs were higher than nonsystem hospitals, apparently because of the costs of mergers, capital investments in increased services, newer facilities, and greater mark-ups in pricing. No significant differences were found on a number of access and quality measures.

## The Delivery System Perspective

All organizations seek to satisfy the requisites for their own success or survival. For delivery systems, success boils down to maintaining or increasing market share and remaining financially viable. To be successful, the delivery system needs to:

- Attract needed resources including contracts with purchasers and the participation of physicians and other providers
- Put together the internal infrastructure, processes, and incentives for managing and marketing the system, managing care within fixed dollar limits, achieving good outcomes, and allocating resources
- Provide meaningful information to internal participants and to external entities on costs, quality, outcomes, and enrollee and patient satisfaction.

Griffith (1987) has argued that market share may be "the single most important measure of performance for not-for-profit hospitals, although it must be judged in the light of long-term financial stability . . . Under conditions of free choice, market share is an important, realistic test of consumer opinions . . . The basic measure of [the extent to which community wants have been satisfied] is the willingness of doctors and patients to use the institution at a price that recovers the full economic costs of service" (Griffith 1987). The same argument holds for delivery systems.

Conceptually market share and financial status as measures of system performance are straightforward. However, many practical problems confound the actual use of these measures, especially the system as the unit of analysis, and nonavailability of data. Data on hospital activity is usually available, but data on out-of-hospital activity by physicians and other system providers is usually not. In addition, as CRISP is addressing, systems serve several different categories of customers. Measuring market share requires data on competitors' volumes as well as one's own, but this data is often not available.

In addition to evaluating market share and financial status, it is meaningful to evaluate delivery system performance in terms of how well systems do the essential tasks of building the internal structures and processes that support an integrated or unified system. There is almost no hard data on how systems go about these tasks. Even carefully done case studies are rare. Trade journals and professional meetings, however, are filled with exhortations by consultants and practitioners as to the importance of these tasks and descriptions of how they are doing them, presumably successfully. Consider the following key system structures, processes, behaviors, and resulting managerial challenges:

1. Unify strategic decision making
2. Approach the market as a single entity in aligning or contracting with insurers/health plans and in dealing with purchasers

3. Integrate the delivery of physician, hospital, and other services

4. Align the incentives of participating providers, and rationally allocate resources internally

5. Assume and manage risk for the cost-effectiveness of care and for the health of an enrolled population over time

6. Assume responsibility for quality, outcomes, and patient satisfaction across the entire spectrum of services

7. Replace external utilization controls with internal self-regulation; reduce paperwork

8. Develop the infrastructure to support integrated delivery and management of care

9. Achieve efficiencies and economies of scale

10. Attract capital for system growth and development

11. Monitor public policy, regulatory and payment initiatives.

## Unify Strategic Decision Making

The complex, uncertain, rapidly changing, increasingly demanding environment of health care makes the management of delivery systems extraordinarily difficult. Health care managers frequently face situations where no decision will satisfy all relevant parties. The key players are typically independent and act in response to different and often conflicting incentives. This is aggravated by the fact that payers typically interact with each category of provider separately, and what may optimize the situation of a payer vis a vis one party is often contrary to the interests of others. Examples of conflicts abound, and the conflicts have become even more intense in recent years as competition has intensified. Specialists compete with each other and with primary care physicians for patients, hospitals compete with physicians for outpatient services, providers compete with each other for contracts with health plans, and so on.

A critical step in integration, then, is to unify strategic decision making among the key parties—physicians, a hospital or hospital system, other providers, and insurers/health plans. The "easier said than done" goal is to create governance and management structures wherein the parties share decision-making authority and share responsibility for the success of the organization. A good understanding of health care trends and candor in communicating the perspectives of the different parties are essential to create a "felt need to change" and acceptance of the advantages of working together. Hopefully, working together leads to trust. Most observers advocate a collaborative decision-making style. It is important that each party recognize both the needs and the expertise of the others.

It is also important that organization leaders "put on the table" the critical issues of cost, quality and outcomes, market share and financial viability, what parties to align with, what physicians to invite to join, how much risk to take, how to divide up the capitation dollar, and so on.

In responding to questions about how the hospitals, nursing homes, home care agencies, and other services operated by HealthOne function together, Wegmiller (1992) commented:

> These activities are organized and managed in our Diversified Services Division. . . . the senior managers of that Division (are) linked in and share in capital and strategic decision making with the people who run the Acute Care Division. That's our structure . . . We have physicians managing clinics and other medical programs in our Medical Affairs Division. These senior physicians also participate in our strategic decision-making process. All of these executives meet on the budget and determine the priorities on who gets how much capital.

Everyone agrees that physician participation in system governance and management is essential. In fact, there is evidence of successful physician-hospital integration without strong physician leadership. Early findings from the HSIS study indicate that physician involvement in system governance and top management is positively associated with other aspects of physician integration. Another interesting finding is that systems with greater physician integration feel less threatened by the changing health care environment.

## Unify Approach to the Market

With all the essential elements aligned under a single organizational umbrella, an integrated delivery system is able to approach the market as a single entity. Together, market research can be undertaken, new products designed, the geographic placement of clinics planned, marketing strategies developed, and contracting criteria agreed upon. Together, providers can increase their bargaining power with purchasers, leveraging strengths to offset weaknesses.

A system may be strong enough to prohibit independent actions by its participating providers, capturing their commitment by providing sufficient benefits to hold their loyalty and by formal agreements under which all parties agree to act only under the aegis of the system.

Increasingly, purchasers seek to deal with a single entity that can deliver a full spectrum of services for an agreed to capitation amount. This trend will undoubtedly intensify under health reform as accountable health plans assemble provider networks in order to counterbalance the purchasing power consolidated in health alliances. Clearly, by joining together, providers will be in a better position to respond to these market pressures.

## Integrate the Delivery of Physician, Hospital, and Other Services

It is ultimately the integration of physician, hospital, and other health care services that permits care to be managed across the entire spectrum of services not only over the course of the illness of an individual patient, but over the long-run period that enrollees as a group are with a health plan. Because health plans and delivery systems will be required to accept risk for the overall health of enrolled populations, the range of pertinent services is broad, including health education and lifestyle improvement at one end of the spectrum and the management of chronic care and delivery of support services at the other end. Clearly, the coordination of such a broad range of services involving different providers, different settings, and even different philosophies (e.g., the "social" versus the "medical" model of long-term care) is beyond the capacity of today's fragmented "nonsystem." This failure underlies the growing call by health care reformers for fundamental restructuring. Integration is the central concept underlying the AHA's "community care network," the CHA's "integrated delivery network," and President Clinton's "accountable health plan." What is missing in health care today is a clear locus of responsibility for the health of each and every individual over time. Only an organization can accept such responsibility, and the more the organization has control of the full range of services, the better able it will be to fulfill this responsibility.

The HSIS study has articulated this argument very clearly in introducing the fundamental hypothesis underling the study:

> We believe the potential payoff of systems is not in their financial performance alone but also in their clinical performance; that is, the extent to which they can provide an integrated continuum of coordinated services to meet patient needs. This will require a transition from a focus on acute hospital care to coordinating care across the health care continuum. We hypothesize that the key variable in this transition will be the ability to integrate various functions and activities across operating units (hospitals, nursing homes, multispecialty group practices, home health care agencies). In this context integration is not seen as an end in itself but as a means for improving the performance of a system in its marketplace, especially as health care increasingly centers on managed care. (Gillies et al. 1993)

## Align the Incentives of Participating Providers

Almost every commentator on what is needed to reform health care argues for an end of fee-for-service payment, and for aligning the incentives of the various parties so they are not acting at cross purposes.

Capitation is generally cited as the answer and, in my opinion, it is, at the purchaser-delivery system (or health alliance–accountable health plan) interface. Capitation payment of the delivery system is also appropriate where the system is not integrated with a health plan but contracts with health plans as a distinct entity.

It is important to recognize, however, that from its capitation dollar, the delivery system can compensate its participating providers in various ways and still align their goals with those of the overall organization. Capitating primary care groups for primary care or for primary and specialty care; salaried employment with rewards built in for helping the delivery system grow, practicing in a cost-effective manner, achieving good outcomes, maintaining patient satisfaction, and being productive; fee-for-service payment with significant withholds to be shared if financial and other goals are met, and other payment methods have all been used successfully. A few health plans and delivery systems are beginning to allocate a predetermined portion of their premium revenue to a fund for each specialty. The physicians in that specialty decide how they will be paid out of their fund, but the total dollars are fixed.

**Assume Risk and Responsibility for Outcomes**

With clinical and administrative management unified, the provider elements integrated, and incentives aligned, the delivery system is in a position to accept risk for the cost of what it does and assume responsibility for the quality of what it produces, because it controls the array of activities that determine costs and quality. For example, an integrated system can develop treatment protocols and/or critical paths that go beyond just acute inpatient care to all the settings that comprise the continuum of care. Joint assumption of risk motivates the parties to work together. Linking hospital and physician payment funds, for example, encourages collaborative efforts to reduce length of stay which might otherwise be seen as just the hospital's problem.

**Internal Self-Regulation**

As delivery systems demonstrate their ability to manage care within fixed financial limits, purchasers, themselves protected from risk by capitation, should be willing to discontinue the plethora of intrusive utilization controls they now administer to protect themselves from overutilization— prior approval for costly procedures, preadmission certification, length of stay limits, required referrals to case management, required use of certain providers for certain procedures, etc. These controls are costly, demoralizing, subject to abuse in both directions, and not always in the best interests of patients. In short, an effectively integrated system may be able to substitute "care management" for "cost management," and internal self-regulation for external controls.

## Develop the Infrastructure

The greater a system's size and resources and the greater the commitment of its participants, the better positioned it is to invest in the structures, systems, and technology needed to integrate the delivery of care. This infrastructure consists of: (1) information systems capable of integrating data from different providers/settings to enable costs, utilization, and outcomes to be looked at across patients, episodes of care, and providers, (2) care management technologies such as critical paths, treatment protocols, formal case management programs, health education and lifestyle improvement modules, expanded roles for personnel, a single electronic medical record, etc., and (3) integration of the physician component of the system including criteria for selecting physicians, practice acquisition, the formation of medical groups, practice management, the established MSOs, PHOs, IPAs, or other linking structures.

Nerenz has suggested that the "real essence of systemness" in health care may reside in two significant relationships among the participating parties—information integration and control.

> Through one mechanism or another, the component parts of a system must be connected for purposes of information exchange. Test results, discharge plans, consultant reports, and other forms of patient information must . . . move across system entities and be useful in multiple locations. Absent that information flow, a 'system' . . . is not very system-like from the patient perspective. At a more aggregate level, information relevant to strategic planning, personnel management, and resource allocation must have a way to move among system entities. Control (or at least, coordination) . . . implies some mechanism for determining what methods or protocols (for tests and procedures) should be used and ensuring their use. Likewise, the broader issues of strategic planning, capital allocation, and credentialing of providers imply some mechanism for deciding that certain directions will be taken and others will not. (Nerenz 1992)

The HSIS study is finding all of its study systems to be struggling with learning how to manage care, and most reported basic building blocks such as information systems, patient care management systems, a base of primary care physicians, links with medical groups, etc. not in place. The HSIS study has developed measures of "clinical integration" such as the existence of common clinical protocols and uniform medical records to look at the state of infrastructures that support care management. The study systems clearly have a long way to go. The systems average only three treatment protocols per facility. Only 10 percent have information systems capable of integrating data across different facilities. Little sharing of clinical or ancillary services goes on among facilities. Since most of the systems' facilities are hospitals, we can assume even less integration of infrastructure elements between hospitals and ambulatory care, long-term care, and other delivery settings. Overall, the highest reported extent of integration is in administrative and support areas like financial management and human resources; the lowest integration is in the areas of clinical integration, information systems, and physician integration. Importantly, system respondents perceive a positive relationship between degree of integration and effectiveness.

Two-thirds of the study systems own or are involved in HMOs; 88 percent are involved with PPOs; half have one or more hospitals with PHOs. Seventeen percent operate physician practice support services. Thirty percent of the active medical staffs practice in system hospital sponsored medical office buildings.

### Efficiencies, Economies of Scale, and Access to Capital

Systems would seem to be advantageously positioned to introduce management and operational efficiencies, to share expertise and services, and to eliminate unnecessary duplication. Facilities and services can be sized to meet the needs of defined enrollee populations. Patients can be channeled to fewer service sites, especially for high-cost tertiary services.

As noted, the HSIS study is finding perceived integration to be associated with perceived effectiveness. And perceived integration appears to be positively associated with the comparative performance of study hospitals vis a vis competing hospitals in their markets. There is also some indication that the degree of physician integration is positively associated with some measures of financial performance (Shortell, Gillies, and Anderson 1994).

We will have to wait, however, for more compelling evidence from this or other studies that integrated delivery systems really do take advantage of the potential efficiencies and economies of scale ascribed to them, and that they pass these cost savings on to purchasers. Determining this will be complicated by the fact that purchasers will be comparing the cost performance of systems with the costs of heavily discounted fee-for-service arrangements involving less organized but more intimidated nonsystem providers.

# The Participating Parties' Perspective

Physicians, hospitals, and others align into systems because they feel a system can meet their needs or serve their interests better than other options can. Hence, we can look at the performance of systems in terms of how well they satisfy participants' needs (or hopes). This perspective may not be altruistic, but it is pragmatic. Those who would design and manage systems must find ways to offer benefits to potential participants of enough value to attract and hold their participation. Expectations of the key parties frequently mentioned in the literature include:

- Physicians
    - Education: help keeping up with the changing health care scene
    - Involvement in planning to meet future challenges
    - Help with marketing, contract negotiations, and contract management
    - Added patient volume through participation in capitated contracts
    - Specialists gain volume via access to a primary care referral base
    - Bargaining power with purchasers
    - Lower practice costs
    - Management expertise
    - Help recruiting
    - Help complying with the requirements of scores of managed care contracts.
- Hospitals
    - Market share
    - Greater ancillary and outpatient volumes from aligned physician base
    - Expanded primary care base
    - Opportunity to negotiate reimbursement within the system
    - More certain physician relationships.

That integration can benefit sponsoring hospitals is supported by one of the few empirical studies to look at this question, a major study of hospital-affiliated primary care group practices (Wheeler, Wickizer, and Shortell 1984). The study found that such practices, when jointly developed and sponsored by hospitals and physicians, did increase the hospital's market share of inpatient services as a result of increased referrals from participating physicians.

- Insurers/health plans
  - — Access to a committed provider network
  - — Economies in network acquisition and management
  - — Access to discounts or at-risk payment arrangements
  - — Differentiation of their health plan based on the delivery system offered
  - — Protection against a diminished role under health care reform.

## Which Party Will Be the Central Force in Integrated Delivery System Development?

Many observers see the hospital- or hospital system–sponsored integrated delivery system as the ideal organizational form and inevitable end point toward which health care delivery is transitioning. After all, most hospitals are nonprofit or public institutions with deep roots in their communities. They have capital, community ties, and management leadership, and most have already diversified vertically into a broad range of services. Some enjoy dominant market positions.

Hurley (1993) has recently challenged this "conventional wisdom" in an insightful and thought-provoking analysis. Hurley highlights a number of a obstacles to provider leadership of delivery reform, many of which are rooted in the reality that "provider-sponsored integration proposals are inherently self-serving." And he notes that neither communities nor purchasers seem inclined to trust providers to redeploy the resources they have historically controlled to convert from hospital-centered to continuum of care–centered systems. Clearly, a basic conflict exists between the desire of purchasers to spend less and providers' insatiable appetite for more. Medical staff politics which often stymie change is another major impediment.

Competition for the central role in reorganizing delivery is coming from increasingly aggressive purchasers. As meaningful information on costs, efficacy, and customer satisfaction becomes more readily available, and as markets, restructured around the principles of "managed competition," assure purchasers alternative providers to choose from, purchasers will be in a position to selectively contract with whatever providers they believe give them the most value. In short, purchasers will be able to put together their own provider networks.

Between the provider-sponsored and purchaser-sponsored models, Hurley defines a third model—a long-term, bilateral contract between a single provider entity or small number of providers and an intermediary who plays the role of exclusive distributor of the providers' health benefits product to one or more purchasers. A group model HMO marketed by a single insurer or health plan approaches this model. Typically, the intermediary is in the driver's seat in this model.

A fourth candidate for the central role in integrating the delivery of care and controlling the flow of dollars is the conglomerate of medical groups. Such supergroups can pursue contracts on behalf of the participating physicians and accept financial risk, often for hospital as well as physician services.

## Critical Success Factors

System executives, consultants, and others involved in putting together alliances or managing integrated delivery systems offer fairly similar observations when queried about the key determinants of success. These observations are based on experience, often hard won. The HSIS study, in contrast, is one of the first to formally test the "voice of experience" and to build on the observations of practitioners through the systematic formulation of conceptual models (Shortell et al. 1993). The HSIS study comes none too soon, as a better understanding of what works and what does not is sorely needed at this point in time to provide a sounder basis for the massive restructuring of the nation's health care system that is under way.

What have practitioners learned from the "school of hard knocks"? There is considerable agreement about the following points:

- Commitment and leadership by the board, CEO, top management, and key physicians are essential to champion and manage the great amount of change required to move from today's structures to true integration. The HSIS study is finding that physician leadership is especially critical. Leadership qualities identified as particularly important include the ability to articulate a compelling vision of the future, to inspire, to empower and support others, to build teamwork, and to manage conflict and change. The American Hospital Association's Hospital Research and Education Trust (1993) recently published the proceedings of a forum on the role of trustees in the integration of community health care emphasizing the importance of board leadership.

- The importance of decision making and control being shared among the key participants is almost always cited as a key success factor. The old adage, "to gain power, one must be willing to give up power," appears to be a critical factor in forming mutually satisfactory, "win-win" relationships upon which to build integrated delivery systems. Especially important is making physicians "coowners" of the delivery system vision and partners in delivery system success. Many observers warn, however, that change leaders should expect initial skepticism, distrust, and even outright hostility from physicians to proposed organizational arrangements, especially those which reduce autonomy or impose risk.

- Education is a critical tool for strengthening organizational leadership. Education should encompass both the changes going on in health care and the skills needed to manage change. It is generally believed that a good understanding of the implications of market and payment trends, managed care, health reform, etc. leads to a "felt need to change" which in turn engenders "ownership" of the changes to be made. The HSIS study identified "an inability to overcome the hospital paradigm" and "failure to understand the new core business" as major deterrents to integration. Education can also build trust as the participants come to have a better understanding of each other's perspectives. Trust, which is frequently cited by practitioners as critical to success, comes not only from a better understanding of the environment and of participants' perspectives, but also from open communication, respect for others' views, and a willingness to share power.

- Selectivity in choosing physicians for leadership roles is important. The most respected physician opinion leaders, for example, may not be the elected officers of the medical staff. The goal is to find or develop physicians who are open to change and enthusiastic about improving the delivery of care. Once identified, it is critical that physician leaders participate fully in decision making and develop commitment to and a sense of responsibility for delivery system goals, directions, and success. Although difficult to organize, "closed" PHOs or IPAs that are selective in choosing physician participants are more likely to succeed than entities that are open to all.

- One of the advantages of alliances is that they consist of different parties, each of whom brings needed expertise and resources. Although a sharing of goals across participants is critical, it is also important that differences be respected. Affirmation of the physician's autonomy in clinical decision making is especially important. In addition, practitioners emphasize over and over that physicians are more open to new ideas that come from other physicians than from nonphysicians. And a number of observers have noted that when physicians have the job of selecting physicians to join a PHO or IPA, they tend to be more selective than nonphysicians.

- Decisions about the size and scope of the delivery system and about the inter-relationships among its elements should be based on the population to be served and on the logic of the continuum of care. Epidemiological and population-based planning methods should be used to determine which services to offer, and treatment protocols/critical paths should define the movement of patients through the continuum to the most appropriate care settings. A critical watershed in the development of integrated delivery systems seems to be when a system recognizes that the population it seeks to serve will not need all existing beds or specialists, and deliberately begins to downsize resources to fit the population.

- A clear vision of the future that spells out the delivery system's commitment to the health of the community and population served and to cost-effective, quality care should drive change. The vision must be compelling both in its commitment to inherently important, socially valued ends and convincing as a road map to organizational success. The vision must be explainable, but even more important, it must be "felt." An important complement to the vision is a firm belief within the organization of its ability to shape its own future.

- Organizational roles, strategies, structures, management systems, and incentives should flow from and be aligned with the vision. Considerable ambiguity, uncertainty, conflict, and stress inevitably accompany major change, but clear direction, agreed to measures of success, and focused retraining and support all help. One of the key roles leaders play in managing change is to validate the acceptability of new ideas and endorse deviations from old ways. The HSIS study found that top leadership must often act to counter the traditional autonomy of the system's "cash cows" and "flagships" in moving toward a truly integrated system. The HSIS study also found that change is impeded more often by an inability to execute new strategies than by a lack of vision as to where the organization should be going. This suggests that change implementation skills should be emphasized.

- Managers throughout the organizational must be helped to acquire new attitudes and skills through education and training. Major change is a big job, and almost all who have attempted it note the need for adequate management resources and a range of expertise in areas like antitrust, legal, tax, and information systems that most systems do not initially have.

- It is important to keep the goals of better serving the community, enrollees, and patients out front. Discussions of physician-delivery system alignment too often focus on economic versus patient care issues. The focus must shift to continuous improvement in patient care management. Participants who see the benefits of integration to the community, to enrollees, and to patients, as well as to themselves, are more likely to support the delivery system when "the going gets tough."

- An important aspect of vision is an openness to the needs and expectations of the constituencies served and to the demands of purchasers. Providers must become more market-driven and truly open to respond to the demands of consumers and purchasers. Some organizations are forming partnerships with employers or other purchasers, and bringing external consumers in to the system design process.

- Finally, almost all observers note that the transformation to integrated delivery requires fundamental changes in organizational culture. New cultures must embrace change, endorse innovation, and accept risk. The need to break away from the acute hospital paradigm and see integrated delivery as the new "core business" is cited as a key determinant of success by the HSIS study. The goal of optimizing the health of the population served within fixed financial limits must be internalized within the organization's culture. There must be a fit between the environment, the delivery system's vision, and its strategies and structures. Culture is central to achieving this alignment, and some argue that alignment is impossible without a supportive culture.

# References

Baker, G. 1990. "Hospital Physician Organizations." *Group Practice Journal* September/October.

Catholic Health Association. 1993. *Setting Relationships Right: A Proposal for Systemic Healthcare Reform.* St. Louis: The Association, p. xi.

Conrad, D. A., and W. L. Dowling. 1990. "Vertical Integration in Health Services: Theory and Managerial Implications." *Health Care Management Review* 15 (Fall): 9–22.

D'Aunno, T., and H. Zuckerman. 1987. "The Emergence of Hospital Federations: an Integration of Perspectives from Organizational Theory." *Medical Care Review* 44 (Fall): 323–44.

deLafuente, D. 1993. "California Groups Join for Survival." *Modern Healthcare* 23 (21 June): 24–26.

Ermann, D., and J. Gabel. 1984. "Multi-hospital Systems: Issues and Empirical Findings." *Health Affairs* (Spring): 51–64.

Gillies, R. R., S. M. Shortell, D. A. Anderson, J. B. Mitchell, and K. L. Morgan. 1993. "Conceptualizing and Measuring Integration: Findings from the Health Systems Integration Study." *Hospital & Health Services Administration* 38 (Winter): 467–89.

Griffith, J. 1987. *The Well-Managed Community Hospital.* Ann Arbor, MI: Health Administration Press, pp. 185, 219, 222.

*Health Progress.* 1993. "Integrated Delivery: Gearing Up for Reform." November: 11.

Hospital Research and Education Trust. 1993. Forum proceedings. Chicago: AHA.

Hurley, R. 1993. "The Purchaser-Driven Reformation in Health Care: Alternative Approaches to Leveling Our Cathedrals." *Frontiers of Health Services Management* 9 (Summer): 5–35.

Luke, R. 1992. "Local Hospital Systems: Forerunners of Regional Systems?" *Frontiers of Health Services Management* 9 (Winter): 3–51.

McManis, G., and T. Stewart. 1992. "Hospital-Physician Alliances." *Healthcare Executive* (March–April): 15–21.

Nerenz, D. 1992. "What Are the Essentials of System Integration?" *Frontiers of Health Services Management* 9 (Winter): 59.

Shortell, S. 1988. "The Evolution of Hospital Systems: Unfulfilled Promises and Self-fulfilling Prophesies." *Medical Care Review* 45 (Fall): 177–214.

Shortell, S., R. Gillies, and D. Anderson. 1994. "New World of Managed Care: Creating Organized Delivery Systems." *Health Affairs* Winter: 46–64.

Shortell, S. M., R. R. Gillies, D. A. Anderson, S. D. Mitchell, and K. L. Morgan. 1993. "Creating Organized Delivery Systems: the Barriers and Facilitators." *Hospital & Health Services Administration* 38 (Winter): 447–66.

Starkweather, D. 1972. "Beyond the Semantics of Multihospital Aggregations." *Health Services Research* 7 (Spring): 58–61.

*Trustees and the Integration of Community Health Care.* AHA, Hospital Research and Education Trust, Chicago, 1993.

Wegmiller, D. C. 1992. CEO Interview: "Consolidation Benefits Community." *Healthcare Strategic Management* January.

Wheeler, J., T. Wickizer, and S. Shortell. 1984. "Vertical Integration of Hospital and Physician Care: The Effects of Primary Care Group Practices on Hospital Utilization." *Hospital and Health Services Administration* 31 (3): 67–81.

Zuckerman, H., and T. D'Aunno. 1990. "Hospital Alliances: Cooperative Strategy in a Competitive Environment." *Healthcare Management Review* 15 (Spring): 21–30.

Zuckerman, H. S. 1979. "Multi-institutional Systems: Their Promise and Performance." In *Multi-institutional Systems*, edited by L. E. Weeks. Hospital Research and Educational Trust, Chicago.

# The Commentaries: A Summary

Four papers address the issues presented by Dowling. MICHAEL BICE, using his experience in the actual development of alliance networks, identifies a number of issues associated with network building including the very definition of system, functions of the corporate office, and the role of physicians in the development of networks. He concludes by sharing lessons learned in the building of health care networks. The other three commentaries take a more conceptual perspective complementing the reality of on-site alliance management.

DAVID BERRY notes the potential importance of strategic alliances as an organizational strategy for rural America, suggesting, however, that the barriers to their development may be quite different than in urban areas. Distinguishing between a "competitive health care market strategy" and a "community necessity strategy," Berry sees the latter as particularly applicable in rural settings. Alliances will be sorely tested as they seek to manage the intersection of rural and urban environments, and to address the complex and growing health care problems—notably AIDS, the aged, and drugs—in rural communities.

STEPHEN SHORTELL suggests that there are six major challenges that alliances need to deal with if they are to have a significant impact. These include an overemphasis on acute care, shortage of primary care physicians, lack of sufficient physician leadership, need to develop clinical outcomes data that can be used for both internal quality improvement and external accountability, obsolete management and governance structures, and lack of appropriate incentives. Performance, however, is the bottom line and, in the short run, the primary measures of alliance effectiveness should be focused on the extent to which they are helping to promote integrated systems of care in local communities and regions. In the long run, he suggests that "one needs to examine such indicators as the number of enrolled lives, clinical outcomes of care for prevalent conditions, achievement of widely agreed upon preventive service measures, and population-based measures of the health status of enrolled populations." The commentary ends with a series of example hypotheses toward which future research is required.

JERALD HAGE's commentary addresses not only the issues raised by Dowling, but also the challenges outlined by Nurkin in his discussion of the creation of an alliance as well as Christianson and his colleagues in their discussion of structure. Hage emphasizes that there is a considerable variety of strategic alliances and these should not be confused. Perhaps one of the most immediate tasks is to carefully delineate the various kinds of horizontal and vertical strategic alliances. Secondly, he suggests that a taxonomy is a necessary but not sufficient step. The crux of the issue is the lack of coordination of health services, resulting in a gross misallocation of scarce resources. The critical indicator of any alliance would be its capacity to alleviate these coordination problems. The commentary concludes with several political principles in attempting to construct the ideal type vertical network for health care delivery.

# Michael O. Bice

Over the past year, the amount of integrated delivery network building has increased exponentially, due to federal and state reform initiatives, and in Florida, to the merger of Columbia Health Corporation and HCA. This combination will control 20 percent of the beds in Florida at the outset, and will quickly move to enhance their position as the dominant system in the state. Nonprofit providers are scrambling to form competing networks to avoid being overwhelmed by Columbia/HCA.

For example, The Franciscan Sisters of Allegany began their health care ministry in 1883 at St. Elizabeth's Hospital in Brighton, Massachusetts. For 100 years, each sponsored hospital functioned independently. The Allegany Health System (AHS) was formed in 1982, and now includes health providers in New York, New Jersey, and Florida. Our corporate offices are in Tampa, Florida. We have an asset base of $1 billion, are relatively strong financially, and have leading market positions in four major metropolitan areas.

In Tampa Bay and southern New Jersey, we have formed networks with 5–6 other nonprofit providers, and will market a PPO product. In Palm Beach County, we have chosen to strengthen our base of operations

---

Michael O. Bice is president and CEO of Allegany Health System.

via acquisition and/or merger. We presently have an equity interest in a PPO covering 150,000 lives in Palm Beach County, and intend to aggressively grow this business.

Heretofore, our corporate strategy was facility focused, and this is rapidly migrating to a network focus. Our relative position in a network is key, as is the need to concentrate resources in the local market. We also see ourselves moving from an emphasis on operational control to an emphasis on having significant influence in a network where we are a minority shareholder. These trends have caused us to examine who we are, and how we conduct our business. This activity is both invigorating and unsettling!

There appear to be a number of issues associated with network building. The more vexing ones follow:

1. **What is a health care system?**

   Nonprofit systems control their member facilities by the legal device called the corporate member (equivalent to a 100 percent shareholder in the business world) and an architecture of governance called reserved powers. In our system, there are five powers reserved to the congregation and 18 powers reserved to the system. Examples of such powers are control over mission, major transaction approvals, and the selection and removal of trustees and CEOs. They represent the "Holy Writ" of system governance. Normally, we are loath to change a period or comma of these reserved powers. In current merger discussions, we are being asked to share reserved powers, and to permit the merger partner to erode our powers of selection and removal. For example, we have been asked to accept the other party's CEO as the joint venture leader, have a 50–50 board even though AHS is liable for 100 percent of the debt, and have super majorities govern selection and removal. How can we concede to these demands and still have a system?

2. **What are the duties of the corporate office?**

   For example, our annual tax on the member facilities should result in "value added" services. What does "value added" mean today? It seems that the current portfolio of corporate services will fall short of facility needs. We have to help the facilities achieve critical mass in their markets. This means we should be developing networks and creating facility growth opportunities, rather than counting FTEs and worrying about the days in accounts receivable. We also have to weigh whether we should move corporate resources into the regions, rather than build up the corporate office. I see a current need for market managers, who are assigned to our major markets, and who reside in the community and build networks.

3. **What is the future of Catholic health care?**
This topic far transcends this paper, but we need to acknowledge this as a significant unanswered question. We are in a minority status in Florida communities, and worry about our influence on benefit packages, care for the poor, and network governance.

4. **How to give physicians a meaningful role in the network?**
We all agree that physician involvement in integrated delivery networks is essential. Most of our physicians are in solo practice. The specialists call the shots, income streams are relatively assured, and they prize their independence and entrepreneurial options. Please tell me how I can put the doctors at risk, move them into multispeciality group practices, and turn the power structure on its head, giving control to the primary practitioners!

I envision AHS as a "learning" organization, committed to experimentation and risk taking, as pathways to organizational growth. Growth, if it occurs, is painful, and we have made our share of mistakes. We have also hit some home runs! Let me try to share some lessons we've learned from network building.

1. The three critical success factors of network development are:
   • Costs under control, lower than the competition, and growing at or near inflation.
   • Doctors are active partners in the enterprise.
   • Information systems in place and producing useful management information.
2. Our core competence as an organization is changing from inpatient care to accepting and managing risk for populations.
3. You need to exhibit patience, persistence, and a sense of humor. Negotiating skills are critical!
4. Network building proceeds from a base of trust, through nonclinical sharing, clinical sharing, and then to governance. Leapfrogging these developmental stages leads to fragile enterprises.
5. Beware of culture clash! Most merger failures ("the merger from hell") are caused by clashing cultures. Successful mergers place equal emphasis on software (people, styles, values) and hardware (legal, financial, and strategic matters).
6. Be flexible! Everitt Dirksen, a childhood idol, used to say "You need to know that I am a man of principle, and my first principle is flexibility."

7. Keep administrative overhead to an absolute minimum. The fewer people in the corporate office, the better. Aim to have 99 percent of system net revenues remain in the community.

8. As the late Tip O'Neil used to say, "All politics is local." All health care delivery is local, too.

9. Manage the politics of the transaction. Remember that powerful vested interests are involved. See through sound bites and posturing. Stay focused. Keep your expectations in check. Look for the middle ground. Use community benefit as the ultimate decision criteria as system interests don't always align with community interests.

10. Finally, learn by doing. There is no advantage staying on the sidelines these days. You must enter fully into the fray, take your lumps, and learn the business of managed care.

Thank you, and I wish all of you well in your own network building endeavors.

# David Berry

Dowling has presented an excellent overview of vertically integrated health care delivery systems. Such organizational forms offer considerable hope for the future. Unfortunately such vertically integrated alliances are limited in rural areas; much more common are horizontal alliances.

Dowling has also linked vertical alliances to some of the major themes emerging in health care reform. He notes that "a central locus of responsibility for the health of each and every individual" is one of the most significant ingredients missing in our health care delivery system. Specifically, he is concerned with geographic responsibility for health care services and notes that on their own high risk areas or populations will be avoided by many health care providers.

My perspective is primarily rural. Previous research that I have participated and am currently participating in reinforces Dowling's concern, since many parts of rural America are not especially attractive from a

David Berry is a professor and chair of the department of health administration at University of Nevada–Las Vegas.

financial perspective. Previous work has focused on small rural hospitals and current work focuses on the emerging AIDS epidemic.

In a national study of 311 independent self-managed hospitals, 144 independent systems managed, and 235 systems—owned and managed hospitals—we compared occupancy levels and select secondary measures of performance (Berry, Tucker, and Seavey 1987). While a few indicators favorable to systems were found at the aggregate level, a closer look at environments was revealing. In supportive environments all three forms of ownership and management had very similar results; systems tended to avoid the less supportive environments.

In addition to questioning systems, the role of management and the influence of ecology on performance were strongly reinforced by this research experience. Recent work explored these two theoretical perspectives in relation to small rural hospitals with less than 50 beds, the most rapidly closing group of health care facilities in rural America (Seavey, Berry, and Bogue 1992). This research began with a classification of all rural hospitals by their environment, a regression analysis suggested several factors that were linked to "being in the black." They included degree of rurality (i.e., population per square mile and income) an inverse relationship. All hospitals were placed in one of twelve environments.

While environment was very useful in explaining success at the aggregate level, a series of case studies were conducted and the findings were somewhat different. Hospitals were selected among the top performers in their environment. While the aggregate patterns of high performance associated with a supportive environment were found among some hospitals, in others where the environment was supportive, low performance followed and for others where the support was not extremely supportive, high performance had resulted. Good management as well as a supportive environment are thus both very important.

Vertically integrated alliances for health service delivery as described by Dowling are a very important potential organizational strategy for consideration in rural America. The barriers to their development may be somewhat different from rural to urban areas.

Two strategies were utilized among the rural hospitals we studied. First is a "competitive health care market strategy" that hospitals attempted to survive in, based on patient revenues, and sought to become a "mini medical center" with an extensive range of medical services and excluding a small number of tertiary services (e.g., open heart surgery) focused on family practice and ambulatory care with select involvement of urban specialists from multiple urban groups and facilities.

A second strategy, "a community necessity strategy," emphasized services less extensive than the "mini medical center," but clearly essential to the community. For example, hospitals in some rural areas with less than 100 beds may be as much as three hours or more from a hospital with 100 beds, an especially common pattern in Western frontier areas. Hospital survival is dependent on local government affiliation to protect it from closing during bad financial periods for the local economy.

Linkage with physicians is a concern of many hospitals which also extends to alliances and is described by Dowling in his paper. To my knowledge no research on physician alliance relationships has been conducted in rural areas. A study by Morrisey, Alexander, and Ohsfeldt (1990) that compares physician integration in urban and rural hospitals is however, of interest. They specifically looked at attempts to involve physicians through board membership, expanded roles for physicians on administrative committees, and salaried positions and the impact of these strategies on the production function that impacted output including case mix adjusted discharges. All of the measures of physician integration studied except for salaried physicians impacted on output in rural hospitals and none did in urban areas.

Rural hospitals are not just small versions of urban hospitals. We observed very common goals between hospitals and physicians in successful rural hospitals with each sacrificing some of their own goals for the mutual benefit of the community. Most relationships with urban areas were attempts to work with multiple urban groups in a competitive way rather than strong linkage to a single group.

Finally, I am especially concerned with and recognize the significance of Dowling's comments related to the voluntary acceptance of responsibility for health services to select population groups. Few alliances seek to affiliate with hospitals that are in settings that require them to utilize a "community necessity strategy." Furthermore, the growing health problems of rural America are especially difficult to address. Among these, three of the most significant are the needs of the aged, AIDS, and drugs.

While most are familiar with the needs of the aged, most do not recognize the growth of AIDS or rural drug problems. Last year the prevalence of AIDS in rural America grew by 9.4 percent compared to large urban areas including the epicenters where the growth was 3.1 percent and urban areas of 50,000 to 500,000 where the growth was 3.3 percent (Centers for Disease Control 1993). Total numbers of rural AIDS still remain relatively small compared to urban, about 6 percent, however, the rate of growth is of considerable concern.

Drugs and substance abuse in rural America have expanded beyond the traditional abuse of alcohol to similar problems found in urban areas. This is especially evident along interstate highways. The epidemics of AIDS and substance abuse are overlapping and presenting many rural areas with some of society's most complex health and social problems (Steel, Fleming, and Needle 1993; Steel and Haverkos 1992).

Health care reform will potentially include the rural populations impacted by AIDS and drugs among those to be served in a geographic location. Such populations will undoubtedly wish to be heard in the decision making process. They may frequently bring diverse cultural backgrounds poorly integrated in traditional decision making including blacks, Hispanics, gays and lesbians, and others.

Will the challenges be more than the promises of vertically integrated health care alliances can deliver?

An international perspective of how Chile addressed its rural problems suggests another option (Gandolfo-Giaconi, Belmar, Montesinos, et al. 1988). In the mid-1970s, Chile found that health status indicators at the national level compared favorably or better with countries such as the United States and many industrialized countries. However, their rural health indicators looked more like underdeveloped areas of Latin America and other parts of the world. Urban health matters were left to a competitive "market-like" approach. Rural health services were removed from the market and placed in the public sector.

The health needs of rural America require attention. Their growing complexity including overlap with other sectors of society will require the best that vertically integrated health care alliances have to offer. Dowling has done an excellent job of bringing to our attention the present and potential role such alliances could play in this process.

# References

Berry, D. E., T. Tucker, and J. Seavey. 1987. "Distress and Efficacy of Systems Linkage for Small Rural Hospitals in Multiple Environments." *The Journal of Rural Health* 3 (July): 61–75.

Centers for Disease Control. 1993. *HIV/AIDS Surveillance: Year End Edition.* Atlanta, Georgia: CDC.

Gandolfo-Giaconi, B., N. Montesinos, and A. Villalobos-Schalchii. 1988. "Rural Health Care in Chile." *The Journal of Rural Health* 4 (1): 71–86.

Morrisey, M., J. A. Alexander, and R. L. Ohsfeldt. 1990. "Physician Integration Strategies and Hospital Output: A Comparison of Rural and Urban Institutions." *Medical Care* 28 (July): 586–602.

Seavey, J., D. Berry, and T. Bogue. 1992. *The Strategies and Environments of America's Small, Rural Hospitals.* Chicago: American Hospital Association, Hospital Research and Educational Trust.

Steel, E., P. Fleming, and R. Needle. 1993. "The HIV Rates of Injection Drug Users in Less Populated Areas." Letter to the Editor. *American Journal of Public Health* 783 (2): 286–87.

Steel, E., and H. Haverkos. 1992. "AIDS and Drug Abuse in Rural America." *The Journal of Rural Health* 8 (1): 70–73.

# Stephen M. Shortell

Dowling's chapter on "Strategic Alliances as a Structure for Integrated Delivery Systems" is a comprehensive and cogent review of the current state of knowledge regarding the impact of these organizational arrangements. The paper is particularly useful because it takes a broad view of what constitutes a strategic alliance, while at the same time focusing its analysis on the contributions that alliances make to forming more vertically integrated delivery systems. In other words, while some may find alliance formation of interest in and of itself, the payoff for practitioners and policy makers is to learn about the contribution that alliances can make to the formation of delivery systems that can manage population-based health care in a cost-effective fashion.

The paper also highlights some of the major aspects or dimensions of alliance activity including the following:

1. *Strategic intent.* That is, the goals or objectives of the parties involved. These can be arrayed on a continuum from similar to dissimilar.
2. The *scope of activities* undertaken by the alliance partners. These can be arrayed on a continuum from broad to narrow.
3. The *degree of control* over alliance activities. This can be measured in terms of the degree of centralization or tightness of control versus decentralization or looseness of control.

These are important dimensions and worthy of further investigation. For example, I would expect that other things being equal strategic alliances that have similar expectations and common goals and objectives will outperform those that do not; that alliances which match their scope of activities (whether broad or narrow) to the breadth of their objectives (whether broad or narrow) will perform better than those that do not; and that alliances that match their degree of control (whether tight or loose) to the capabilities of alliance members and to the demands of the goals and objectives will outperform those that do not.

I also believe that if the ultimate goal of alliance relationships is the formation of more integrated delivery systems that can assume risk for delivering cost-effective care to defined populations, then alliances with more similar goals, a wider scope of activities, and tighter forms of control will in the long run outperform those with more dissimilar goals, a narrower scope of activities, and looser forms of control.

Stephen M. Shortell is the A. C. Bueller Distinguished Professor of Health Services Management, J. L. Kellogg Graduate School of Management, at Northwestern University.

But I also want to suggest that issues of intent, scope, and control are really not the crux of the issue, except insofar as they influence the *accomplishment of cooperative activities*. For it is the accomplishment of cooperative activities that will determine the relative success or failure of strategic alliances, whether in health care or in other industries. (Noble, Stafford, and Reger 1993) It is in this area that I would like to focus my comments and observations. Most of these are based on three years of ongoing research examining nine different organized delivery systems across the United States (Shortell, Gillies, Anderson, et al. 1993).[1] In this work, we have identified a number of major barriers and challenges to alliance formation in the development of more integrated delivery systems. In addition to environmental constraints, these primarily involve issues of culture, capabilities, structure, and incentives. I will briefly highlight six of these challenges below.

## 1.  An Overemphasis on the Acute Care Hospital Paradigm

Until relatively recently, the "core business" of American health care was acute inpatient care represented by the hospital. While hospitals will remain important, the new "core business" of American health care is primary care. Financial, technological, and social forces have all given rise to the tremendous increase in outpatient and primary care services across the country. Each of the systems that we are studying is in the process of making the transition from the hospital paradigm to the primary care paradigm. In the process, many are struggling with overcoming the entrenched interests of certain hospitals within the system—particularly the "cash cow" hospital that has contributed much of the system revenue over the years and has been the central focus for much of the alliance building activity within the system. Behavioral indicators include the fact that strategic planning is frequently still centered on the core hospital or hospitals of the system. Further, even though many understand the need for expanding the primary care network, some of them see this simply as a strategy for increasing admissions to the hospital as opposed to managing population based wellness in a capitated environment. In brief, there is a need to transform the role of the acute care hospital within the newly emerging alliances and systems. In the process, these hospitals will be asked to give up services that are better placed elsewhere in the alliance or system and, at the same time, will be asked to take on services that, if left to their own initiative, would not be undertaken.

## 2.  A Shortage of Primary Care Physicians and Associated Challenges in Developing Multispecialty Group Practices

This is both an external environmental constraint and an internal leadership challenge. The external constraint is, of course, represented by the fact that in most areas of the country there is a severe shortage of primary care physicians with little hope in the short run that medical schools will be producing more primary care physicians. Thus, there are likely to be significant "holes" in many systems strategies for developing integrated continuums of care. Some systems are attempting to fill these "holes" by recruiting and expanding the responsibilities of nurse practitioners and physician assistants, by retraining specialists to become primary care physicians, and by more aggressively recruiting the relatively small number of primary care physicians produced by nearby medical schools.

### 3. Lack of a Sufficient Base of Physician Leadership

While we would all agree that leadership is a key factor in putting together successful alliances and systems, our research suggests that *physician leadership* is particularly important. The new alliance building in health care will not occur until a sufficient base of physician leadership emerges to work with nursing and nonclinical managerial leadership to address the challenges identified in this conference. As Dowling has noted, a key finding from the Health Systems Integration Study (HSIS) has been that the greater the degree to which physicians are involved as members of the top management team of the system and the greater the degree of active physician participation in system management and governance, the greater the degree of physician system integration and the greater the degree of clinical integration achieved. Since the beginning of the study, nearly every one of the study systems has initiated formal physician education/leadership development programs; often in conjunction with local graduate schools of management or public health. The result has been much more informed discussion and debate centered around data and facts relative to alternatives facing physicians and the system at large. These programs have generally been credited with helping speed up decision making and helping the physician community to begin to adjust to the requirements of change.

### 4. Formation System Deficiencies Particularly in Regard to Development of Clinical Outcome Data that Can Be Used for Both Internal Quality Improvement and External Accountability

This challenge, of course, is not a surprise to anyone. The need for information that can link providers and patients throughout the continuum of care in a real time fashion and that can also produce outcome data to meet the demands of purchasers is a major challenge. In fact, a key litmus test to predict the likely success of a given alliance might well be the extent to which it has common information system goals and needs, and can agree upon a common platform and associated software. To give some indication of the magnitude of this challenge, the HSIS participants have committed between $35 million and $85 million over the next three years to their information system needs.

## 5. Outmoded Management and Governance Structures

If one takes alliance building and systems building activities seriously, then one must face up to the realization that people no longer manage institutions or organizations or departments or units. Rather, they are managing networks, coalitions, relationships, spaces between boundaries and across boundaries. The same can be said for governance. As a result, many of the study systems are reorganizing their management and governance structures to bring them into better alignment with the realities of delivering population based health care in local regions. Examples include the elimination of the position of hospital administrator, the development of systemwide regional market managers, the development of systemwide managers of clinical service lines, and the elimination of policy making boards at the individual operating unit level which are replaced by regional governance bodies. In other words, if one is going to ask physicians and nurses to deliver medical care differently—that is to truly manage patient care across episodes of illness and pathways of wellness—then shouldn't one demand similar changes in the management and governance infrastructure that supports the clinical activity?

At the center of the new management and governance structures will be the ability to *effectively manage boundary spanning personnel*. This has been an important ingredient of effective strategic alliances in other industries as well. As health care professionals talk about the "seamless continuum of care" it might be instructive to view these as a series of strategic alliances involving key boundary spanning personnel. It is particularly important that alliance activity be well coordinated at the patient care hand-off points. For example, the surgeon and the surgical nurse transferring the patient from the operating room to the ICU are involved in an internal alliance; similarly, the ICU nurse about to move the patient out of the ICU to the floor is operationalizing an alliance; the patient's physician and floor nurse about to discharge the patient must work with the discharge planner involving another alliance; and the discharge planner and the patient's physician in planning for follow-up care with the home health care agency are involved in a still further alliance. Thus, a series of internal and external alliances are involved comprising many boundary spanning personnel forming a network of integrated care delivery for individual patients.

## 6.  Lack of Appropriate Incentives

At the macro level, there is great need to align economic incentives of payers, physicians, hospitals, and all components of the system. But there is also a need for internal incentives that reward behavior which contributes to the overall success of the alliance or system and to maintaining the health of an enrolled population as opposed to incentives that reward individual unit operating performance or other forms of suboptimization. Most of the HSIS systems have developed performance appraisal and compensation systems in which a majority of merit pay is based on how well the system or overall alliance performs as opposed to the individual operating unit. However, these criteria have not yet been pushed down to the middle management level and below where most implementation activity occurs. Further, budgeting is frequently still done on a departmental or individual unit basis as opposed to a cross unit service line basis such as cardiology, oncology, or behavioral medicine. Dowling's review of the past literature and our own emerging research suggest that these barriers are formidable. It is extremely difficult and challenging work because it is terribly disruptive of the existing order of things. Alliances represent major *intrusions* into each partner's traditional way of behaving and of doing business. They are, of course, undertaken when the parties involved perceive that the benefits will outweigh the cost. But the great challenge in health care lies in the realization that most of the benefits have a long run rather than short run time horizon. The issue, therefore, becomes not one of "holding the gain" but rather "tolerating the pain." It seems to me that a major job of alliance and system leaders is to try to shorten the period of pain but therein lies an important paradox—namely, attempting to shorten the period of pain usually means being willing to inflict greater pain by directly confronting the issues and, thereby risk making matters worse—again in the short run. Could it be that the reason there are so many half-way alliances and incompletely developed systems is the reluctance of leaders to "turn up the heat?"

The alliances that will be most difficult to put together and that will face the greatest obstacles to success are also those that are most likely to have the greatest impact on community health status. These are alliances that involve fundamental changes in the way in which patient care is delivered or what we have called clinical integration of services in local markets. In our judgment this is where the payoff lies; not in administrative economies of scope or scale. This shift in emphasis from administrative to clinical is the major difference between the systems we studied in the '80s and the ones we are studying today. Further, our research suggests that integrating the physician component into the alliance is the strongest correlate of achieving a greater degree of clinical integration. Systems that are willing to entertain a variety of alliance relationships with physicians—ranging from group practices without walls to physician-hospital organizations (PHOs), to management service organizations (MSOs), to foundation models, to staff models—achieve greater progress than those that tend to favor a single approach. I believe this leads to an important point: Most organizations are involved in *multiple alliance relationships* at a given point in time and that the success of these alliance relationships largely determines the success of the focal organization. This means that in a world of limited resources, focal organizations face real problems of *choice* in regard to allocating time, people, and dollars across alliance partners. Perhaps most importantly the challenge lies in aligning alliance relationships or achieving a coherent alliance strategy that is consistent with the organization's overall objectives. Henry Ford Health System in Detroit, a HSIS participant, serves as a useful example. Gail Warden is fond of noting that Henry Ford Health System cannot possibly achieve its objectives with its own resources and capital. In order to do what it needs to do to serve its community in Southeastern Michigan, it needs to enter into and manage a variety of alliance relationships over time. In addition to its HMO activity, Henry Ford has a medical school affiliation with Case Western Reserve in Cleveland, a financing alliance with Blue Cross/Blue Shield of Southeastern Michigan; and a delivery system alliance with the Mercy Health System of Farmington Hills, Michigan. Henry Ford has found that maintaining and articulating these alliance relationships with each other is a formidable challenge resulting in a strategically complex agenda. As Warden notes: "Trying to develop an integrated health system which has a large managed care base and a large teaching and research commitment is unique in this country. In the long run, if managed care is to be the delivery model, organizations will have to use it as a platform for teaching and research. Henry Ford Health System has taken on this complex agenda."

## Summary

In the short run, the primary measures of alliance effectiveness should be focused on the extent to which they are helping to promote integrated systems of care in local communities and regions. In the long run one needs to examine such indicators as the number of enrolled lives, clinical outcomes of care for prevalent conditions, achievement of widely agreed upon preventive services measures, and population based measures of the health status of enrolled populations. To do well on these kinds of performance criteria will require meeting the challenges of cooperative activity outlined above. I will end my comments by providing examples of hypotheses that could be tested in this regard.

- H1: Alliances between two or more different partners will be more difficult to implement and will fare worse using short run measures but may provide greater long run value to the community.

- H2: Alliances between organizations that have largely developed internally rather than through mergers and acquisitions will be more difficult to implement *and* will have less long run value or impact. This is due to the entrenched interests of internal partners within each alliance.

- H3: Alliances of partners involved in different stages in the production process of delivering health care services (e.g., hospitals, physicians, and home health care agencies) will have greater impact than alliances among partners involved at the same stage of the production process (for example, hospital to hospital).

- H4: Alliance structures and networks dominated by primary care and community health interests will outperform those dominated by acute care hospital interests.

- H5: The greater the prevalence of managed care activities in a given market, the greater the likelihood that tighter, more integrated alliance structures will outperform looser, less-integrated structures.

The rationale for the above hypotheses has largely to do with the ability of the different intent, scope, and control mechanisms to successfully manage the implementation challenges of cooperative activity raised earlier. Not to address these issues may well result in fulfilling the following definition of a strategic alliance as, " . . . an arrangement by which two parties agree to share resources until the money runs out."

## Note

1. The nine participating systems are Baylor Health Care System, EHS Health Care, Fairview Hospital and Healthcare Services, Franciscan Health System, Henry Ford Health System, Sharp HealthCare, Sisters of Providence, Sutter Health, and UniHealth America.

# References

Noble, C. H., E. R. Stafford, and R. K. Reger. 1993. "A New Direction for Strategic Alliance Research: Organizational Cognition." Paper presented at the 1993 Strategic Management Society Meeting, 11 September. Chicago.

Shortell, S. M., R. R. Gillies, D. A. Anderson, J. B. Mitchell, and K. L. Morgan. 1993. "Creating Organized Delivery Systems: The Barriers and Facilitators." *Hospital & Health Services Administration* 38 (Winter): 447–66.

# Jerald T. Hage

Health care reform, at all levels of government and within the private sector, has called into question the viability of health care provision by stand-alones, whether these be primary care groups, HMOs, acute care hospitals, or nursing homes. Perhaps the best evidence for this assertion is the number of mergers that have occurred recently. And while horizontal strategic alliances for the objectives of joint purchase of services, shared advertising, and even management has become quite common for several decades (Zuckerman and Kaluzny 1991), only recently have alliances across the production chain of health care such as the one described in the paper by Harry Nurkin begun to appear.

The creation of vertical service integration as one kind of strategic alliance poses a number of specific conceptual issues that I would like to briefly comment upon. First, there is a considerable variety of alliances and these should not be confused. Therefore, one conceptual task is to carefully delineate between kinds of horizontal and vertical alliances. Second, health care reform is being advocated because of a number of coordination problems in the health care industry, most notably what might be labeled misallocations of resources. These need to be specified so that any particular kind of alliance or merger (and these are not the same) could be evaluated on its capacity to alleviate these coordination failures. Once the problems are specified, then the third task is to suggest what might be an ideal design for an alliance, which can serve as a normative model. Finally, I will consider briefly several political principles in attempting to construct the ideal typical vertical network of health

Jerald T. Hage is a professor of sociology and the director of the Center for Innovation at the University of Maryland.

care delivery. It is easy to propose a utopian vision of society and much more difficult to implement such a vision.

## A Typology of Strategic Alliances

Alliances can be defined as networks of organizations involving exchanges of various resources, the concerted action for some group goal, and even joint production or provision of services. This is consistent with the definition provided for by Bill Dowling (see Chapter 5) in his excellent review of the literature (D'Aunno and Zuckerman 1990) as well as the work of Barry Stein provided at the conference. Alliances are nonhierarchical collectives that are distinguished by joint decision making across organizational boundaries. Mergers as in chains for profit are not, therefore, the same as an alliance because there is one dominant hierarchy of decision making; mergers of health care organizations across the production chain are examples of vertical integration. What makes alliances both interesting and problematic is that they require cooperative behavior between groups that have approximately equal power. In fact, one group or organization might dominate and when it does, we find the alliance begins to behave more like a merger. But this is an empirical question. Furthermore, in the both the discussion of the ideal design of the alliance and political principles of implementation we return to this problem of power.

Recently Cathy Alter and I have published a book, *Organizations Working Together* (1993), where we suggest that there are three basic dimensions for describing the variety of alliances in both the public and private sectors. The most obvious dimension is the number of organizations or groups that are involved in the alliance. These can vary between three or four to a hundred or more. When there are only a few organizations, we prefer to label this as a linkage and when there are a sizable number of organizations, the term network seems more appropriate. The more the number of organizations the greater the difficulties of coordinating the exchanges, concerted actions, or provision of services.

The next dimension reflects the degree of cooperation between the organization, specifically the number of concrete kinds of exchanges and activities that are being coordinated. For example, the pooling and exchange of information (e.g., information networks in public health efforts at detecting high blood pressure) is common in many communities as are the joint purchase of various services. Another example of what would be considered limited cooperation is preferred referral of clients to highly specialized clinics or hospitals or nursing homes or the contracts between HMOs and hospitals. The next level of cooperation involves joint lobbying, fund raising, and research as in the Community Clinical Oncology Programs (Kaluzny, Morrissey, and McKinney 1990). At this level of cooperation there is a pooling of resources that affects the solidarity of the group (Hechter 1987). In the literature, these are referred to as promotional activities and the most common example involving large numbers of organizations are joint research efforts as in Sematech. The broadest form of cooperation is teamwork across organizational boundaries to provide quality health care in what might be called joint programs (Aiken and Hage 1968). This level of cooperation is much higher because it commits the organizations and groups involved relative to their main goal, rather than some ancillary one, and involves day-to-day coordination of health care services. Good examples of this kind of cooperation are seen in hospice services, services for the frail elderly, and treatment programs for the chronically mentally ill (for extended discussion of examples of this kinds of service delivery systems, see Alter and Hage 1993). Much more rare are networks that provide vertically integrated health care across a large number of acute illnesses as distinct from the highly specialized networks associated with, for example, long term disabilities. The greater the extent of cooperation, the more difficult is the task of coordination because organizational and occupational conflicts are more common and the divergent self-interests of the members in the network create tensions.

Finally, the third dimension is whether or not the organizations are competitors or have symbiotic relationships with each other. Cooperation between primary care groups and acute hospitals are easier than integrating primary care groups or integrating acute hospitals within the same geographical area, which leads to what is an implicit dimension, namely ecological spread.

One might add this as a fourth dimension, because it has been involved in a number of the examples of horizontal alliances, including the very fine study of rural hospitals by Jon Christianson et al. (see Chapter 4). Since rural hospitals exist in different ecological niches they are not directly competing against each other in the normal sense of the term. In contrast, within an urban area there would be much more direct competition (how much depends upon how specialized the services provided are).

Together, the first three dimensions create a typology of 12 distinct kinds of alliances. The addition of ecological spread would add even more (although not necessarily another 12). The objective, however, is to highlight two specific kinds of alliances, what Dowling refers to as integrated delivery systems. One kind includes only organizations and groups that are symbiotic or weakly competitive and another kind includes organizations and groups that are competitors. As we shall see, it is this latter form of vertical integration that speaks to most of the basic reasons for health care reform—specifically to resolve the misallocations of resources—while the former is relevant in discussions of managed care, namely the idea of having two or more vertically integrated delivery systems competing against each other in the same ecological area.

## The Concept of Coordination

Unfortunately, the naming of a phenomenon does not necessarily make apparent what should be done. In particular, the term "strategic alliance" is quite vague about the particular kinds of linkages and activities that should be involved. For me, the crux of the issue is the coordination of health care services, prices, medical personnel, and the like. The concept of coordination is itself quite complex, but at minimum (see Alter and Hage 1993, chapter 3) involves the elements of information, clients, resources, services and programs, and professionals and staff. As was suggested above, coordination can evolve from linkages involving the first two, to promotional activities which commit limited resources and/or staff to total involvement as in the joint provision of services. A well-coordinated system would involve comprehensiveness, accessibility, and compatibility. From an economist's perspective, coordination involves the allocation of scarce resources.

The campaign for health care reform has specifically focused on the lack of access and the skyrocketing costs of health care. But in addition there are the following misallocations of scarce resources:

1. Too many hospitals in some areas and not enough in others
2. Duplication of services across hospitals in many areas
3. Surplus of specialists and absence of family physicians
4. General absence of physician assistants
5. Imbalance of fees across specialty areas
6. Surplus of expensive equipment (CAT scan machines).

These might all be considered as market failures and they represent the kinds of problems that one would need to consider in the design of a vertically integrated delivery system of health care.

In a recently published book, *State Intervention in Health Care* (Hollingsworth, Hage, and Hanneman 1991), I contrasted the health care systems of Britain, France, Sweden, and the United States in 1890 and 1970 to understand why market failures occur in the health care area. Two specific examples are worth mentioning. The greater the number of physicians per 100,000 population and therefore the extent of competition, the *higher* the fees. Similarly, the greater the number of hospitals per 100,000 population and again the more extensive the competition, the *greater* the number of duplicated services per hospital. There are a number of reasons for these market failures but the most basic are the differential power of the physicians and the inability of the client or her representative to evaluate the necessity for certain kinds of medical intervention. This suggests that market coordination as implied in managed competition will not effectively deal with these misallocations. And this leads to the next question of how should the system be designed.

## An Ideally Designed System

One dimension of a vertically integrated delivery system is the representation of the four major groups that are involved in the provision of health care: professional groups, consumer groups, payer groups, and health care providing organizations (acute care, specialty care and mental health hospitals, nursing and half-way houses, HMOs, and other primary care groups). Specifically, each of these four types should have about one-fourth of the representation on the board. The professional groups would include not only the physicians but the physician assistants, nurses, laboratory technicians, and other health care professions. Rather than have citizens represent the consumers, they should be mobilized into the specific kinds of problematic areas including the elderly, the handicapped, AIDS victims, the mentally ill, cancer victims, etc. In other words, the key is representation of specific illnesses and disabilities that present unique problems for health care. Similarly, organizations include medical schools, HMOs, acute hospitals, nursing homes, mental hospitals, and other kinds of organizations providing health care would have to have their representation. Finally, the payer groups would include insurance companies, private for-profit, private nonprofit, and public (Medicaid and Medicare). The importance of this four-estate model of board representation is that it creates a context where more effective communication can occur between these groups, equalizing the power between them. Without representation of each group, there is likely to become a vertically integrated system that is dominated by a specific set of interests. As is apparent in this example, the diversity within consumers, professional groups, organizations, and payers is enormous. In practice, there would have to be intermediary boards for each of these groups to ensure adequate representation of the variety.

A second dimension that must be emphasized is the continuum of care that is represented within the vertically integrated system. Medical schools are one critical component, because how medical research is shaped and directed is influenced by how much contact exists between researchers and patients. Also, if interns and residents have the opportunities to rotate in a large variety of different kinds of health care organizations, including rural hospitals, their own education will be enhanced. Equally important is the inclusion of long-term care as well as acute care, mental health, and other kinds of disabilities that are not normally treated in a acute care hospital. There is too much emphasis on acute care and not enough on long-term care.

The third dimension is how much ecological spread there is. Given the importance of including medical schools and their associated hospitals, as well as rural areas—where there is an underprovision of services—the nature of this spread would be quite large and unusual. For example, Georgetown might include one-half of Washington, DC and the western part of Maryland, while George Washington would be involved in the service delivery system for the other half of Washington, DC and northern Virginia. In a similar way, the two medical schools in Baltimore would split the city and the surrounding countryside. This kind of an ecological arrangement is necessary because it speaks to the imbalance of resources across space.

The fourth dimension is the retention of choice. Since HMOs and primary health care groups, especially those located in urban areas, would cut across these service delivery systems, the patients would still have choice. They could select one or another kind of primary care provider to have access to the system. Providing choice and eliminating duplication of services are not the same thing.

## The Politics of Implementation

The proposed design is quite complex and politically problematic. Any proposal for reform must concern itself with the likely resistance to any kind of limitation on the autonomy of the various parties. Several of the design features speak to the fears that many health care providers and organizations are likely to have about any health care reform. Concerns about power and autonomy are addressed in several ways. First, each of the four estates—providers, consumers, payers, and organizations—are represented on the board. Second, each unit retains its autonomy but must bargain within the framework of the network of services. Third, the consumers are provided choice within these delivery systems.

Still another principle from organizational research is that significant reform is only possible when there is perceived to be some performance gap. Fortunately, there is widespread recognition of the health care crisis. Unfortunately, this crisis has been defined too much in terms of access and costs and not enough in terms of the various kinds of misallocations or market failures that were listed above.

Given the complexity of the proposed ideal health care delivery system, it seems wise to allow the creation of several systems within each ecological area defined on the basis of the medical school. Only so many health care providers, organizations, and consumers can be mobilized at a time. Therefore, even though it results in a duplication of services, the practical considerations of allowing smaller numbers to gradually develop trust and learn how to negotiate and solve their problems of duplication justify the existence of multiple delivery systems at first. Politically this would speak to the perceived value of competition, even though in practice it does not work as people assume it will (Hollingsworth, Hage, and Hanneman 1991).

# References

Aiken, M., and J. Hage. 1968. "Organizational Interdependence and Intra-organizational Structure." *American Sociological Review* 33 (6): 912–30.

Alter, C., and J. Hage. 1993. *Organizations Working Together.* Newbury Park, CA: Sage Publications.

Hechter, M. 1987. *Principles of Group Solidarity.* Berkeley: University of California Press.

Hollingsworth, J. R., J. Hage, and R. A. Hanneman. 1990. *State Intervention in Health Care: Consequences for Britain, France, Sweden and the United States.* Ithaca, NY: Cornell University Press.

Kaluzny, A. D., J. Morrissey, and M. McKinney. 1990. "Emerging Organizational Networks: The Case of Community Clinical Oncology Programs." *Innovations in the Organization of Health Care: New Insights into Organizational Theory,* edited by S. S. Mick and Associates. San Francisco: Jossey–Bass.

Zuckerman, H. S., and T. D'Aunno. 1990. "Hospital Alliances: Cooperative Strategy in a Competitive Environment." *Healthcare Management Review* 15 (Spring).

Zuckerman, H. S., and A. D. Kaluzny. 1991. "Strategic Alliances in Health Care: The Challenges of Cooperation." *Frontiers of Health Services Management* 7 (3): 3–23.

# 6

# Implications for Research

## Thomas C. Ricketts III, Arnold D. Kaluzny, Howard S. Zuckerman, and Geoffrey B. Walton

## A Managerial Perspective:

Let's evaluate the challenge in the minds of the research, policy and operational world. It's a very exciting time for shaping how we wish to define, how we wish to organize, how we wish to structure, how we wish to govern an organization responsible for the health of our communities.

*Ed Connors*, 1993

## A Research Perspective:

I have two basics from a research perspective. First, I realize that there are some who say "it doesn't matter what we call it—it's how the thing works." It *does* matter what we call it. If we don't have a clear definition of what we are going after in a research design, we are in big trouble.

Secondly, there are lessons to be learned and relearned—using what's already available in our arsenal of interorganizational theory and methods. These include the theoretical models of resource dependence, transaction cost analysis, institutional theory and population ecology. Also to be considered is network analysis and how we can use that to conceptualize and describe alliances as they form. Four key research challenges must be kept in mind as we develop research agendas; a clear definition of what an alliance is, agreement on the level of analysis we wish to focus on; understanding the role of time in the life cycle of alliances; and finally, an ability to articulate the underlying conceptual focus to be used in the analysis.

*Mary Fennell*, 1993

# A Policy Perspective:

I think the fundamental issue can be summed up by paraphrasing Hamlet: "To manage, or to be managed, that is the question." Well, this is how we're being managed by the team in blue: prior authorization, second opinion, utilization, review, diagnostic related groups, resource-based, relative value scales, therapeutic protocols. I call it the Lilliputian scenario. Why? Because I think that Jonathan Swift was prescient when he wrote *Gulliver's Travels* in 1726: Captain Lemuel Gulliver was the ship's surgeon on the *Swallow* when it was wrecked at sea, and he was washed ashore on the land of Lilliput. He awakened to find himself bound to the beach by an army of Lilliputians from HCFA, the Temple of Doom in Baltimore, using prior authorization, second opinion, utilization review, diagnostic related groups, resource-based relative value scales, therapeutic protocols. When I see that, contemplate it, I go over on the Penn campus and sit down on the bench with Ben Franklin, and say to myself, "I wonder what Ben might have done?" And then I can almost hear him speaking to his colleagues at the Second Continental Congress as they were about to sign the Declaration of Independence. He said: "Gentlemen, if we do not hang together, we most assuredly will hang separately." How do we hang together? In alliances within the health care system "hanging together" means collaboration and coordination in a supportive infrastructure.

*Bill Kissick, 1993*

While each perspective adds a new reality to the challenges facing strategic alliances, their ability to function effectively within the context of a changing health care system is less clear. Proponents (Kaluzny and Zuckerman 1992) and skeptics alike (Begun 1992) cite a range of advantages and disadvantages, yet all agree that alliances have evolved with no clearly defined policy and managerial guidance. This is especially relevant to rural health care organizations which are now being integrated into networks and alliances. The expansion in number and reach of alliances has occurred without a specific focus toward rural places, but rural communities are, when they become involved, likely to be affected more comprehensively by the changes alliance affiliation or network membership brings.

To truly meet the policy and managerial challenges of a changing health care system, alliances require guidance; however, their complexity and the uncertainty inherent in the future suggest that this can be achieved only through dialogue involving both the practice and research community. Managers of these new organizational forms are facing new challenges, are involved in decision making and policy without the benefit of insights and knowledge generated by health services research.

Moreover the health services research community, by not being involved with many of these developmental efforts, are not provided the opportunity to have their perspectives and methods challenged by the realities of the current health care environment. The research community provides the perspective and methodology, and the practice community the reality of operations. While these two groups have not always shared a common vision, they are not mutually exclusive. As described by Lawler (1985):

> Theory and practice are not competing mistresses. Indeed research that is useless to either the theoretician or the practitioner is suspect. If it is useful to the practitioner, but not the theoretician, then one must wonder whether it is a valid finding and whether it has addressed the correct issue. If it is useful to the theoretician but not to the practitioner, then one must wonder whether the research is capturing a critical issue. Indeed it can be argued that we should always ask two questions about research: Is it useful for practice, and does it contribute to the body of scientific knowledge that is relevant to theory? It if fails either of these tests, then serious questions should be raised. It is a rare research study that can inform practice but not theory or vice-versa (page 4).

The purpose of this chapter is to present a series of research hypotheses that correspond to the substantive areas of the conference—formulation, structure, process, and outcomes—and provide the basis for policy and managerial options. Using a nominal group process outlined in Appendix A, the conference participants identified a number of underlying concerns, methodological issues, and substantive research questions.

Figure 6.1 presents the relationship of the substantive areas of the conference to the concerns, methodological issues, and research questions generated by the discussion groups. The objective was to translate broad substantive areas into a set of variables relevant to a policy, management, and research perspective, that can be grouped into research questions and associated methodologies, all of which represent a working research agenda. That agenda is relevant to all strategic alliances but we emphasized questions that related to rural organizations and rural settings. Below we present the deliberations of that process—beginning with underlying concerns, followed by methodological issues, and finally the presentation of substantive research questions.

## Underlying Concerns

The interaction of the health services research community and those responsible for the management of existing alliances is at best an uneasy if almost nonexistent alliance. Each group has its perceptions of reality

**Figure 6.1**    Developing and Linking Research, Policy, and
Management Issues

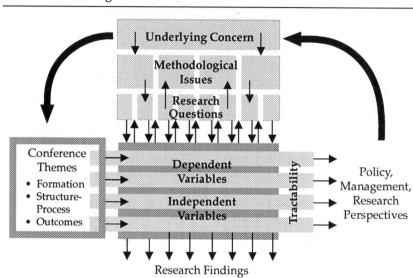

and the future, its own priorities as well as preconceptions of the future
of alliances and the fundamental challenges they face. Nevertheless, the
opportunity to engage in dialogue is of paramount importance. Through
this mechanism it is possible to promote what Argyris and Schon (1985)
have described as "single loop" and "double loop" learning. "Single
loop" learning means that both practitioners and researchers will acquire knowledge of basic definitions and parameters involved in the
organization and management of alliance structures. The ability of single
loop learning to predict the future is limited. "Double loop" learning,
however, means that both the researchers and practitioners will achieve
a fundamental understanding of the basic assumptions that underlie the
definitions and parameters. From this fundamental understanding, stable
and reliable predictions of future behavior and markets can be made.
Clearly both kinds of learning are needed; however, the latter is critical
if both groups are to make a contribution to the effective organization
and management of alliances within the context of health care reform.

The conference provided the opportunity for "double loop" learning among the participants. While a number of substantive and methodological issues were identified and these are addressed in subsequent
sections, the groups identified three fundamental concerns, two that
relate to strategic alliances in general and one that focuses on alliances
as they relate to rural areas.

- **A need for a shared vision about the future of alliances in a changing health care industry and in integrated systems.**

It is this need to anticipate the future that is paramount to both researchers and practitioners. While there will be alternative futures depending upon the way in which the details of the present are examined, we should explore the degree to which we can agree on the fundamental forces or theories which will guide the health care system. To agree on fundamentals can be very difficult when ideological differences arise, however, there is broad agreement that strategic alliances are favored given current and the most probable future policies.

While we look for the broad parameters that may guide the future we also must look to broadly applicable concepts that describe social structures including alliances. The degree to which centrality, cohesion, communication, goal-setting, and other key organizational concepts work in alliances are as important in future alliances as in bounded organizations of the past. It is only the way they are scaled or the degree to which they influence performance that may change.

- **A need to develop "organizational impact statements"—descriptions of how research can improve decision making and how decision making can help refine the identification of issues worthy of substantive research.**

While we need to agree about the broader issues, we also need to know how to cope with the future in regional and network environments. Impact statements are really the application of a general theoretical model at a less global level. In this approach the research processes that predict the general future provide the framework in which the particular conditions of a network or alliance can be used to develop plans for the immediate or the specific future. The process is predictive but it is also selective; there will be areas in which research can do better at predicting the future or providing stable advice for decision making than others. We must work together to understand the limits of research at the network and alliance level.

- **A need to consider how to properly involve rural communities and rural organizations that give high value to independence.**

This issue relates to the balance of control between potentially imperial urban systems that include rural organizations in their alliances and the sometimes fierce independence of rural communities who may not see the real benefits in affiliation. Size, for example, described a system that was in its conceptualization independent of urban control but relied heavily on the resources of urban based partners. Systems and alliances that involve rural partners need to know how to structure themselves to take into account this balancing process.

## Basic Methodological Questions

Strategic alliances, as an emerging reality, present some fundamental mutual challenges to the research, policy, and managerial communities.

### Definition of a "Strategic Alliance"—The Need for a Taxonomy

When we see new forms of organizations emerging how we cognitively describe them is important in itself. The process of naming social activity creates bounds and a context for understanding and expectations. As Scott (1993) suggests, "old dichotomies have failed" citing organization-environment and markets-hierarchies as the two that are most inappropriate in a world of alliances. We need to develop a more sensitive scale and determine if there are directional effects or multiple, organic systems that can explain and predict.

From the previous chapters it is easy to see that alliances can take on very different forms while adhering to a general concept. That general concept of independent organizations collaborating for common goals is too general to allow comparison with other forms of production. As the practitioners have described processes and structures, the theorists and researchers have interpreted them using common overarching concepts, describing existing alliances using scales that variously contrast: markets and hierarchies, degree of centralization, or interpreting them as following more of a rational than a political model. Shortell (1993), for example, has proposed a useful set of dimensions to describe alliances based on strategic intent, scope of activities, and degree of control. This set of three dimensions springs from a more conventional approach to the analysis of organizational forms. While it may not completely capture the nuance of alliance formation that finds optimal rather than maximal levels preferable, it is a useful beginning.

A taxonomy is key to understanding a system of structures, particularly as they change over time. New and old versions of an alliance are different from alternative types of alliance and maturing alliances may become another type. The naming of types reflects the differences we can see and represents the distillation of our assessment of an organization.

### Alliances Require Qualitative Research for Rapid Feedback and Mapping of Basic Parameters

Since this process of alliance formation is relatively new and since taxonomies have not been agreed upon, the research approach most appropriate to gathering information and systematizing data is essentially qualitative. Qualitative approaches can have more or less rigor and can be more or less useful depending upon the degree of conscious method used in a qualitative study. Since we are discussing strategic alliances in an era of fundamental change in the provision of health services, or at least rapid change, the demand for information on which to base decisions is intense and immediate. This condition also favors qualitative research methods since they can gather information more quickly using focus groups or observational studies with feedback built into the process.

### Indicators of Alliance Performance and Operations (across varying forms)

The first requirement is to understand the range and mix of outcomes of alliances and how they differ and are like outcomes from other organizational forms. We must be able to scale and quantify outcomes that are multiple and potentially conflicting. The papers made the point that there were conflicting goals of members of alliances as they entered networks or agreements and that the successful alliances began to develop a feeling of consensus over the outputs of the arrangements while those that failed could not agree. This process is important in and of itself, but the measurement of whatever is agreed to be the system output is the necessary condition for comparing and measuring the effectiveness of alliances. After we learn what constitutes outcomes we can move on to the substantive research issues outlined below.

## Substantive Research Issues

There are many specific questions that can be asked about alliances and these discrete questions can be collected into a general research agenda. However, to understand the process, structure, and outcomes of alliances in a truly systematic way we should show how these different individual questions are related to each other. In viewing this list, it is important to recognize that these questions must be prioritized for specific alliances and these priorities may vary among policy, management, and research perspectives. The priorities may also conflict due to scale and strategic versus tactical information needs of the various perspectives.

*Outcomes.* Alliance outcomes are of key interest because these describe the social goals of organizations, and their future depends on the quality and relevance of these outputs. Outcomes are the basis for measures of the effectiveness, efficiency, and productivity of alliances, and how we define outcome is crucial to the assessment of alliances.

- What alliance forms are most effective? For example, are the same forms which have proven useful for short-term, temporary alliances equally useful for longer term, permanent alliances? Similarly, are there differences among alliances organized informally or through contractual arrangements or equity positions? Clearly we must find the most efficient and effective forms to promote in policy and to guide practitioners toward implementation. This process rests heavily on the decisions we make about outcomes measurement.

- How can we integrate the needs of rural communities which may be able to achieve outcome measures which are "lower" than what can be achieved in urban or suburban systems?

- Can performance influence alliance structure? It is equally clear that the structures of alliances have evolved as a reaction to conditions that demand rationalization of effort and superior performance that may cause changes in rules that guide structure. How much of this happens and can happen is important to predict.

- What feedback loops are available? Alliances require significant investments in information transfer for the maintenance of the alliance itself and this maintenance burden may overwhelm any planning, review, and modification process.

- Does prior alliance experience or prior relationship among partners predict success in future alliances?

- What strategic alliance forms are most effective for implementation? Implementation is a necessary but not sufficient condition for effective performance. Are different alliance forms more easily implemented—yet have only marginal effect versus forms which are more difficult to implement but have more substantive effect. Consideration needs to be given to breadth of relationships among participants, degrees of commitment, exclusivity, and authority of alliances to act on behalf of members.

- Is there learning in alliances as in other institutions? For example, do alliances serve to shorten product development cycle? Do alliances reduce capital requirements in product development?

*Structure and process.* Alliance structure and process are of interest because they focus on the mechanics and activities and represent the potential leverage points for the development of policy and management options.

- What are the organizational and environmental predictors of alliance success and performance—legal, geographic, cultural experience, governance scale, and traditional network characteristics such as centrality and dominance? For example, cultural differences have been cited as barriers to effective alliance performance. Complementarity among participants has been suggested as a key variable. Degree of dependency may be another important factor associated with alliance success—supplementing and complementing, not substituting for, competencies. Degree of trust and commitment among parties are continuously referenced as factors related to success.

- How does the structure and size of a strategic alliance relate to the types of services and resources shared across the alliance? Are there negotiation process and conflict resolution strategies that are effective and under what conditions?

- How can we effectively create governance structures that take into consideration the needs of rural components who have relatively fewer resources to bring to an alliance but which demand equality of voice and influence?

- What information systems and transfer mechanisms can best cope with the demands for quality, sharing, and accountability? What mechanisms can be put into place to assure technology transfer among participating organizations and how does the alliance assume that existing information technology is used?

- How do alliances develop their products and services and get them to the market? Do alliances serve to shorten the product development cycle or reduce capital requirements?

- What are the antitrust issues alliances face? Specifically, do the cooperative structures which characterize alliance activities interfere with competition? For example, do alliances seek to engage in dividing up markets, fixing prices, limiting competition? This will be of particular concern where organizations in the same market seek to build an integrated system using alliance as a connecting mechanism. For alliances that involve rural components there may be different legal considerations as states and the U.S. Justice Department have attempted to immunize mergers that involve rural institutions from antitrust. The stability of this intention in actual case law is not clearly understood.

***Formulation.*** Alliances are not static but involve a dynamic interchange with a larger environment providing resources for their various activities.

These resources include funds, information, and personnel, all of which shape the way in which the alliance functions.

- What competencies are required in alliances that we do not have in adequate supply? This relates directly to observations made at the conference that we will need more boundary-spanning workers who can process paradoxical and conflicting organizational goals and who also understand the diverse needs of rural and urban members.
- What is the role of needs assessment in the allocation of resources? How does the approval differ with an alliance configuration? This is especially relevant when there are imbalances tied to geography.
- How do we develop a standard of effectiveness and quality that can be used for accreditation of alliances taking into consideration size and location? Perhaps more basic is whether the concept of accreditation is relevant to the alliance form.
- Are there transference skills that are effective in horizontal and not in vertical alliances and vice versa?
- How do you manage alliances in such a way as to accommodate political and policy influences? Many policy differences exist between urban and rural constituencies based on differences in their economies; these differences spill over into institutional arrangements and must be considered.
- What is the proper role of academic medical centers in alliances? Particular emphasis on vertical dimensions—what is the role of academic health centers in building integrated delivery systems? How well do academic health centers integrate into clinical teaching and research functions within such systems without adversely affecting overall cost structure of the system? How can academic health centers link with rural communities to provide access to technology as well as assure a systematic flow of patients?

## Summary

Clearly a strong working relationship between the health services research community as well as the practice community benefits all parties. By initiating the dialog, the participants at the National Invitational Conference on Strategic Alliances began to understand the concerns and the needs of the others. The practice community, concerned with the rapid and chaotic changes in the industry and their own markets, want to know what will work "on Tuesday," not in 1997. Many of these executives are entering into uncharted territory for their organizations. They are looking at financial incentives that have completely shifted, seeing former competitors as possible partners and are beginning to realize that their organizations may have to take on a radically different shape if they are to survive and fulfill their missions. They are desperate for some guidance, some history, and some indication that they are on the right track.

The research community is anxious to understand the changes that are taking place, the incentives that are driving them and what changes are successful. They need real world laboratories and input to make this research relevant and useful. This curiosity is born out of a wish to know what the future will bring. This desire to know what will happen is not unique to the research community, providers need to know what the future will be like in order to adjust in time and anticipate changes that can affect their ability to perform.

Rural communities and the rural policy constituency see the prospect of strategic alliances and network affiliations with mixed feelings. Although affiliations and closer organizational relationships can produce tangible benefits in efficiency of care giving and for organizational performance, they can also result in the loss of local resources and, sometimes more importantly, loss of local autonomy and identity. These points were stressed in the conference and their importance to the rural community reinforced. Research strategies that neglect these characteristics of geographically diverse alliances may miss key elements that predict success or failure in the formulation, process and the outcomes of new systems.

All too often the research and practice communities go forward with their own agendas without regard and perhaps distrust of each others' interests. The Conference attempted to provide an opportunity for mutual learning and sharing of information. What has been generated is the result of a strategic alliance between these two communities. It is a start, and a good one at that. Yet like so many problems and challenges we face:

> We clearly have not succeeded in answering all of our problems—indeed we have not completely answered any of them. The answers we have found have only served to raise a whole new set of questions. In some ways we feel we are as confused as ever, but we think we are confused on a much higher level about more important things.
>
> *Unknown*

# References

Argyris, C., and D. Schon. 1978. *Organizational Dynamics*. Reading, MA: Addison–Wesley.

Begun, J. 1992. In *Strategic Issues in Healthcare Management: Point and Counterpoint*, edited by W. J. Duncan, P. M. Ginter, and L. E. Swayne. Boston, MA: Kent Publishers.

Connors, E. 1993. Comments at the National Invitational Conference on Strategic Alliances, Chapel Hill, NC.

Fennell, M. 1993. Comments at the National Invitational Conference on Strategic Alliances, Chapel Hill, NC.

Kaluzny, A., and H. Zuckerman. 1992. In *Strategic Issues in Health Care Management: Point and Counterpoint*, edited by W. J. Duncan, P. M. Ginter, and L. E. Swayne. Boston, MA: Kent Publishers.

Kissick, W. 1993. Comments at the National Invitational Conference on Strategic Alliances, Chapel Hill, NC.

Lawler, E. E. III. 1985. "Changing Traditional Research Assumptions." In *Doing Research That Is Useful for Theory and Practice*, edited by E. E. Lawler III, and A. M. Mohrman Jr. San Francisco: Jossey–Bass.

# Appendix A

# A Method for Identifying Research Issues

Thomas A. D'Aunno

This chapter has a twofold purpose. The first is to describe key steps we followed to identify priorities for research at the National Invitational Conference on Strategic Alliances in Health Care. The second is to discuss the identified priorities and classify research issues into three groups. These groups are: (1) overarching questions about the future of strategic alliances, (2) basic research issues concerning alliance formation, processes, and performance, and (3) elaborations on these basic issues. Moreover, these issues are linked to the relevant literature on health care alliances. Finally, suggestions for next steps are offered.

## Setting Priorities Using the Nominal Group Technique

As discussed above, the overall purpose of the conference was to develop a set of priorities for research on alliances. Further, the conference was designed to represent multiple perspectives on alliances. That is, we wanted to know the views of policymakers, leaders of alliances, health service researchers, consultants with experience outside the health care field, and others. In addition, we had relatively little time (one and a half days) to achieve the goal of seeking consensus among 80–90 participants with diverse views. Given these circumstances, the conference organizers

Thomas A. D'Aunno is an associate professor at the University of Michigan School of Public Health.

211

elected to use nominal group technique (NGT) as a way to make decisions about research priorities (Delbecq, Van de Ven, and Gustafson 1975).

*NGT: A brief introduction.* For people who work in groups, it comes as no surprise that research on work groups shows that they often fail to meet their potential. For example, many studies show that, contrary to the old adage that "two heads are better than one," individuals can solve problems better than groups (Fried and Rundall 1994). The work of Janis (1972) on poor decisions made by policy groups (e.g., the Bay of Pigs fiasco) highlights some critical weaknesses with groups as tools for decision making. One such weakness is that when groups are making decisions, they often fail to take into account a range of alternatives.

Researchers developed NGT to combat such weaknesses in group decision making. In brief, NGT consists of four major steps. The first is that group members generate as many solutions to a problem (or answers to a question) as possible. They do so by taking several minutes to think about the problem and, then, each individual makes a list of his or her ideas. Next, each member of the group reports aloud (or "nominates") one item from her or his list. Items are recorded by a scribe on a blackboard or large piece of paper that is visible to all group members. The reporting of each member's ideas proceeds in a round-robin fashion until all ideas from every member's list are recorded.

No discussion is allowed during this time; ideas are simply listed and group members listen to each other. The above procedures are critical to the success of NGT. Their purpose is to force group members to generate and consider a wide range of alternatives, rather than focus on a few ideas that are promoted by vocal or powerful group members.

Third, there is a discussion period in which ideas are clarified, elaborated, critiqued, and, often, similarities or differences in ideas are noted. Sometimes, ideas are grouped into categories to simplify discussion. Finally, there is a silent, private vote in which each group member selects his or her preferred ideas (sometimes by ranking them). Votes are tallied, usually by a neutral party, typically the scribe who recorded ideas for the group.

The discussion period helps to identify strengths and weaknesses with various proposals. The silent, private vote protects confidentiality so that individuals have less fear about reprisals by powerful group members whose ideas are not supported. In sum, research results from several studies indicate that groups using NGT produce more high-quality decisions than groups that rely on discussion alone (Delbecq, Van de Ven, and Gustafson 1975).

*Application in this conference.* The conference began with four paper presentations and panel discussions of these papers. These papers, on which earlier chapters in this volume are based, examined a range of topics, including lessons on strategic alliances from other industries (Stein), processes in alliance formation (Nurkin), alliance structure and operations in a rural setting (Christianson, Moscovice, and Wellever), and finally, strategic alliances as integrated delivery systems (Dowling).

Following these presentations and discussion, we divided conference participants into four equal groups of about 20 members each. Each group was diverse with respect to members' backgrounds in policy, research, and practice. Each group had a moderator who was trained in the use of NGT. The groups were given almost two hours to address the question, "What are the most important issues for research on strategic alliances in health care?" The results of the groups' work are reported below.

## Priorities for Research on Strategic Alliances in Health Care

Participants discussed a relatively large number of issues that can be placed in three categories, beginning with the more general and moving to the more specific. These are: (1) overarching questions, that is, questions about health services research and the future of strategic alliances in health care, (2) basic issues in the definition, formation, structure, operations, and performance of alliances, and (3) specific questions that elaborate on these basic issues.

*Overarching questions.* Participants raised two overarching questions. First, can health services research keep pace with changes in alliances and conduct studies that contribute to practice as well as to theory? The issue of pace is clearly difficult. Alliances seem to be forming at a rapid rate and, moreover, they seem to be evolving and dying at a rapid rate as well. As a result, researchers need to be in the field as soon as possible. Further, researchers need to use longitudinal, as opposed to cross-sectional, designs to capture the changes in alliances and their processes. The issue of timing relates to the issue of contribution to practice: practitioners (either policymakers or alliance members/leaders) will benefit most from studies that address key problems in a timely manner.

Of course, the relationship of research to practice, with its implications for research design and timing, is an enduring concern (D'Aunno and Price 1983). Strategic alliances strain the practice-research relationship for two reasons. One is that alliances are relatively fragile compared to other organizational arrangements (e.g., multihospital systems). As a result, they may have a higher birth and death rate than other organizations. This, in turn, makes it important that research is timely enough to capture these changes. Second, alliances are at the heart of many proposals for health care reform. This means that we need to know as much about them as possible, as soon as possible.

Indeed, the second overarching question raised by participants was the role of alliances in a reformed health care system. Specifically, will policymakers cast alliances in a central role in the delivery of health care services? And, if so, can alliances achieve the benefits that their supporters envision, while minimizing the costs that their doubters foresee (Kaluzny and Zuckerman 1992b; Begun 1992)? Participants agree that this last question should be central to the health services research agenda.

*Basic issues.* The NGT approach produced a good deal of consensus on the need to address five basic issues. These are as follows:

1. *Definition:* What are strategic alliances, how are they distinctive from other organizational arrangements, and what are the types of alliances?

2. *Formation:* Under what conditions do organizations form alliances?

3. *Structure:* What are the various structures that mark alliances?

4. *Processes:* What are the mechanisms, routines, and programs by which alliances function?

5. *Performance:* What are the effects of strategic alliances for their members, communities, and other constituents, and what structures and processes lead to better results?

These priorities are consistent with two recent reviews of alliances in health care (Zajac and D'Aunno 1994; Kaluzny and Zuckerman 1992a). In other words, there is a consensus emerging, not only from this conference, but in the literature as well, about the major issues that need to be addressed. Nonetheless, perhaps more interesting than the consensus on the five major issues above, was the elaboration of these issues with specific questions.

*Elaborations on themes.* In the course of reaching consensus on the major issues listed above, participants discussed several specific questions. These questions are important because they refine the major issues and add depth to the research agenda. That is, studies that take these questions into account will be able to focus on a more precise set of issues. Under each major heading below, examples (rather than a complete list) of specific questions raised by participants are presented.

*Definitions.* One participant asked, What are the critical distinctions between strategic alliances, coalitions, multihospital systems, multidivisional corporations, and trade associations? In other words, it is important to distinguish alliances from other multiorganizational arrangements (Longest 1990). More importantly, what are the costs and benefits of alliances compared to these other arrangements? In addition, many participants indicated the need for an empirically based typology of alliances. For example, one important variable that should be included in such typologies is the extent to which alliances are intended for vertical versus horizontal integration (Zajac and D'Aunno 1994).

*Formation.* Under what conditions do organizations form strategic alliances? Participants suggested that alliance formation is affected by several factors, including characteristics of (1) organizational environments (e.g., regulatory constraints), (2) organizations themselves (e.g., mission), and (3) organizational leaders (e.g., propensity for risk-taking, previous experience in alliances).

Specific factors noted include: geographic proximity (or distance, especially distinguishing rural from urban organizations); antitrust laws or perceptions of such laws; organizational ownership (including religious sponsorship); number of potential members; the role of academic medical centers; prior experience of potential members in such arrangements; levels of trust and competition; symbolic versus rational reasons for alliance formation; similarity or dissimilarity of potential members in values, mission, and services provided; role of membership in multiple alliances.

Another important set of questions concerns organizations that are not selected for alliances, that choose not to join them, or that exit them. What happens to such organizations? Can the performance of alliances be attributed to selection effects at their formation? That is, do weak organizations tend to join alliances, thus depressing their performance? Or, conversely, do alliances tend to form among strong organizations that would have performed well on their own? What can we learn by comparisons to organizations that go it alone? In short, these are a set of questions about alliances that parallel questions asked about multihospital systems (Shortell 1988).

Finally, participants agreed that, because change is the order of the day, studies of alliance formation should be longitudinal, following members over time as they exit and enter alliances.

*Structure.* Important questions were raised about structures for governance, legal affairs (equity positions, contractual arrangements), and management (Zuckerman and D'Aunno 1990). Central concerns underlying these structural arrangements include: how do they protect the equality of alliance members? How can they encourage members' participation? How can they maintain the flexibility of the alliance and protect the autonomy of individual members?

It is widely agreed that the distinctiveness and potential benefits of alliances rest on their ability to pool members' resources while maintaining their freedom (Zuckerman and Kaluzny 1991). The question is, What structural arrangements best achieve these dual goals? Finally, as was the case with alliance formation, participants put a high value on studies of the evolution of alliance structure. That is, it is also widely agreed that alliances evolve and their structures change. Empirical models of such evolution are needed (conceptual models exist, but have not been tested, see D'Aunno and Zuckerman 1987).

*Processes.* The term "processes" refers broadly to activities and mechanisms involved in the operations of alliances. Several important questions emerged about alliance processes. One focuses on information systems and their role in managing alliances and their programs; what sorts of information systems do alliances have in place and what systems will be needed? How can information systems be used to coordinate alliance efforts?

Another set of questions concerns staffing and involvement of various groups in alliance management and governance. Central questions involve physicians and board members: what roles should they play in the management and governance of alliances? Further, what skills do alliance staff members need? How should they be motivated and rewarded?

A third set of questions involved linkage mechanisms or ways to coordinate members' efforts. Participants called for descriptive studies of such mechanisms: What are they? How do they work? Such mechanisms range from trust and informal communication (in meetings, via electronic networks) to committees, contracts, and equity ownership positions. Which mechanisms work best under what conditions? Do linkage mechanisms evolve as do alliance structures?

A fourth set of questions focused on alliance programs. That is, what are the programs that alliances engage in and under what conditions are they effective? What are the administrative versus clinical linkages in alliances? Do rural alliances help with physician recruitment? What are the characteristics of effective recruitment programs? Similarly, what are the characteristics of successful joint purchasing programs? In general, what alliance programs are in place to promote the quality, cost and access of their members' services? These could include, for example, educational programs, benchmarking efforts, and the development of clinical guidelines.

*Performance.* Perhaps the largest set of questions focused on the issue we know least about, alliance performance. The questions here fall in three broad categories. First, participants wanted to know whether alliances make a difference in terms of key performance measures such as cost, quality, access, and community health status. There were many variations on this theme. For example, do alliances help rural communities (Carman 1992)? Do they help special populations? Do alliances differentially affect various groups (e.g., employers)? Do alliances have community-level effects as well as benefits for members? Do alliances change service patterns (e.g., reduce unnecessary duplication)?

Second, what characteristics of alliances (formation, structure, processes) affect their performance? In other words, what are effective ways to begin and manage an alliance?

The third set of questions concerned research methods for assessing alliance performance. Specifically, participants pointed out the need to develop appropriate performance measures and to select appropriate comparison groups (e.g., communities without alliances).

## Suggestions for Next Steps

Both researchers and practitioners concerned with strategic alliances in health care now are faced with a difficult challenge. On the one hand, alliances of all types are forming at an increasing rate and policy-makers are considering them as a central component for organizing and delivering care in a reformed national system. This makes for exciting but dangerous times.

This is because, on the other hand, practice in this area is far outstripping research. We have relatively little data on which to base important decisions about how to form and manage effective alliances. How can we best produce information that quickly advances both practice and theory concerning strategic alliances? Perhaps this question is best addressed by heeding Voltaire's advice: The perfect is the enemy of the good. Translation: perhaps we ought to conduct small-scale, qualitative case studies as soon as possible so that we at least have descriptive information about the various aspects of alliances identified above. Given tight funding for health services research on organizations and management, and given the cost of a large-scale comparative study of alliances, it would be risky to wait for funds for a large-scale, quantitative, analytic study.

Indeed, we have so little data (compared to so many ideas) about how alliances work, we might be better served by conducting descriptive studies, even if funds were available for large-scale analytic work. Participants at the conference seem to agree. Many of them called for qualitative, descriptive, and longitudinal studies to begin immediately.

At the same time, work to design larger, comparative, and analytic studies could proceed in parallel. For example, work to develop measures of linkage mechanisms in strategic alliances and alliance effectiveness could begin, drawing from case studies. In short, there is no need to abandon traditional research designs; there is simply a need to conduct traditional health services research in tandem with less conventional (for health services research) case studies that describe alliances. If every researcher and practitioner who attended the conference agreed to work together to do one descriptive case study of an alliance (even without any other coordination), and if these were pooled, how much better off we would all be one year hence.

# References

Begun, J. W. 1992. In *Strategic Issues in Health Care Management: Point and Counterpoint*, edited by W. J. Duncan, P. M. Ginter, and L. E. Swayne. Boston, MA: Kent Publishers.

Carman, J. M. 1992. *Strategic Alliances among Rural Hospitals* (Report No. 92–003). Berkeley: Institute of Business and Economic Research, University of California.

D'Aunno, T. A., and H. S. Zuckerman. 1987. "A Life Cycle Model of Organizational Federations: The Case of Hospitals." *Academy of Management Review*, 12: 534–45.

D'Aunno, T. A., and R. H. Price. 1983. "The Context and Objectives of Community Research." In *Psychology and Community Change*, 2d ed., edited by K. Heller. Homewood, IL: The Dorsey Press.

Delbecq, A., A. Van de Ven, and D. Gustafson. 1975. *Group Techniques for Program Planning*. Glenview, IL: Scott, Foresman.

Fried, B. J., and T. G. Rundall. 1994. "Managing Groups and Teams." In *Health Care Management: Organization Design and Behavior*, 3d ed., edited by S. M. Shortell and A. D. Kaluzny. Pp. 137–63. Albany, NY: Delmar Publishers Inc.

Janis, I. L. 1972. *Victims of Groupthink*. Boston, MA: Houghton–Mifflin.

Kaluzny, A., and H. Zuckerman. 1992a. "Strategic Alliances: Two Perspectives for Understanding Their Effects on Health Services." *Hospital & Health Services Administration* 37: 477–90.

———. 1992b. In *Strategic Issues in Health Care Management: Point and Counterpoint*, edited by W. J. Duncan, P. M. Ginter, and L. E. Swayne. Boston, MA: Kent Publishers.

Longest, B. B. 1990. "Interorganizational Linkages in the Health Sector." *Health Care Management Review* 15: 17–28.

Shortell, S. M. 1988. "The Evolution of Hospital Systems: Unfulfilled Promises and Self-Fulfilling Prophecies." *Medical Care Review* 45 (2): 177–214.

Zajac, E. J., and T. A. D'Aunno. 1994. "Managing Strategic Alliances." In *Health Care Management: A Text in Organizational Behavior and Theory*, 3d ed., edited by S. M. Shortell and A. D. Kaluzny. Albany, NY: Delmar Publishers Inc.

Zuckerman, H. S., and A. Kaluzny. 1991. "Strategic Alliances in Health Care: The Challenges of Cooperation." *Frontiers of Health Services Management* 7 (5): 3–23.
Zuckerman, H. S., and T. A. D'Aunno. 1990. "Hospital Alliances: Cooperative Strategy in a Competitive Environment." *Health Care Management Review* 15 (2): 21–30.

# Appendix B

# Conference Participants

**Catherine Alter, Ph.D.**
Associate Professor
School of Social Work
University of Iowa
Iowa City, Iowa

**Fred Brown, Jr., FACHE**
President
VHA Carolinas—Tennessee
Charlotte, North Carolina

**Robert Baker**
President
University Hospital Consortium
Oak Brook, Illinois

**Ann Barry-Flood, Ph.D.**
Professor
Center for Evaluative Clinical
  Science
Dartmouth Medical School
Hanover, New Hampshire

**James Begun, Ph.D.**
Professor
Department of Health
  Administration

MCV/VCU
Richmond, Virginia

**David Berry, Dr.P.H.**
Professor and Chair
Department of Health Care
  Administration
College of Health Sciences
University of Nevada
  at Las Vegas
Las Vegas, Nevada

**Michael Bice**
President and CEO
Allegany Health System
Tampa, Florida

**Janet Bookman**
Manager, Reform Implementation
American Hospital Association
Chicago, Illinois

**Roger Butler**
Executive Director
Consolidated Catholic
  Health Care
Oak Brook, Illinois

**James Carman, Ph.D.**
Director
Health Services Management
    Program
Haas School of Business
University of California—Berkeley
Berkeley, California

**Jean Carmody**
Project Officer
Agency for Health Care Policy
    and Research
Rockville, Maryland

**Jon Christianson, Ph.D.**
Professor
Institute for Health Services
    Research
University of Minnesota
Minneapolis, Minnesota

**Edward Connors**
President Emeritus
Mercy Health Services
Morrisville, Vermont

**Paul Cooper III**
President
HealthSpring
Reston, Virginia

**Michael Daly**
President and CEO
Baystate Health System, Inc.
Springfield, Massachusetts

**Thomas D'Aunno, Ph.D.**
Associate Professor
School of Public Health
University of Michigan
Ann Arbor, Michigan

**Carol Dillard**
Mathematical Statistician
Agency for Health Care Policy
    and Research
Rockville, Maryland

**William Dowling**
Vice President
Planning and Policy Development
Sisters of Providence Health
    System
Seattle, Washington

**Jack Edmonds**
Vice President, Corporate
    Accounts
Johnson & Johnson Hospital
    Services
New Brunswick, New Jersey

**Frederick Eisele, Ph.D.**
Head, Department of Health
    Policy and Administration
Pennsylvania State University
University Park, Pennsylvania

**Mary Fennell, Ph.D.**
Professor
Department of Sociology
Pennsylvania State University
University Park, Pennsylvania

**Henry Fernandez, J.D.**
President
AUPHA
Arlington, Virginia

**Larry Gamm, Ph.D.**
Director
Center for Health Policy Research
Pennsylvania State University
University Park, Pennsylvania

**Sherril Gelmon, Dr.P.H.**
Associate Professor
Department of Public
  Adminstration
School of Urban and Public
  Affairs
Portland State University
Portland, Oregon

**Albert Gilbert, Ph.D.**
President and CEO
Summa Health System/Akron
  City Hospital
Akron, Ohio

**James Goes, Ph.D.**
Assistant Professor
Health Management and Policy
School of Public Health
University of Minnesota
Minneapolis, Minnesota

**Ann Greer, Ph.D.**
Professor
Department of Sociology
University of Wisconsin at
  Madison
Milwaukee, Wisconsin

**Barbara Harness**
Director, Section for Health Care
  Systems
American Hospital Association
Chicago, Illinois

**Richard Hayden**
President
Sisters of Providence Health
  System
Springfield, Massachusetts

**Jerald Hage, Ph.D.**
Professor
Department of Sociology
University of Maryland at College
  Park
College Park, Maryland

**Dean Harris, J.D.**
Partner
Moore & Van Allen
Raleigh, North Carolina

**B. Jon Jaeger, Ph.D.**
Research Professor
Health Services Administration
University of Florida
Jacksonville, Florida

**Lynn Hartwig, Ph.D.**
Professor
University of Southern Mississippi
Hattesberg, Mississippi

**Arnold Kaluzny, Ph.D.**
Professor
School of Health Policy and
  Administration
and Senior Fellow
Cecil G. Sheps Center for Health
  Services Research
University of North Carolina at
  Chapel Hill
Chapel Hill, North Carolina

**Kerry Kilpatrick, Ph.D.**
Chairman and Professor
Department of Health Policy and
  Administration
School of Public Health
University of North Carolina at
  Chapel Hill
Chapel Hill, North Carolina

**John Kimberly, Ph.D.**
Professor of Management and
  Health Systems
Whorton School of Business
Philadelphia, Pennsylvania

**William Kissick, M.D., Dr.P.H.**
George S. Pepper Professor of
  Public Health
University of Pennsylvania School
  of Medicine
Philadelphia, Pennsylvania

**Ben Latimer**
President and CEO
The SunHealth Alliance
SunHealth Corporation
Charlotte, North Carolina

**Peggy Leatt, Ph.D.**
Chair, Department of Health
  Administration
University of Toronto
Toronto, Ontario

**Austin Letson**
Senior Vice President
Charlotte–Mecklenburg Hospital
  Authority
Charlotte, North Carolina

**Eugene Loubier**
President
Winchester Healthcare
  Management, Inc.
Winchester, Massachusetts

**Roice Luke, Ph.D.**
Professor
Department of Health
  Administration

MCV/VCU
Richmond, Virginia

**Gerald Martin**
Divisional Vice President
Corporate Hospital Marketing
Abbott Laboratories
Abbott Park, Illinois

**Martha McKinney, Ph.D.**
Chief, Program Evaluation and
  Epidemiology Branch
U.S. Public Health Service,
  HRSA/OSF
Rockville, Maryland

**J. Alexander McMahon**
Executive-in-Residence
Fuqua School of Business
Duke University
Durham, North Carolina

**Alan Meyer, Ph.D.**
Professor
Graduate School of Management
University of Oregon
Eugene, Oregon

**Miles Meyer**
Administrator
Columbus Community Hospital
Columbus, Wisconsin

**Laura Morlock, Ph.D.**
Professor, Health Administration
  and Policy
The Johns Hopkins University
School of Public Health
Baltimore, Maryland

**Joseph Morrissey, Ph.D.**
Deputy Director for Research
Cecil G. Sheps Center for Health
 Services Research
University of North Carolina at
 Chapel Hill
Chapel Hill, North Carolina

**Ira Moscovice, Ph.D.**
Professor
Institute for Health Services
 Research
Minneapolis, Minnesota

**Eric Munson**
Executive Director
University of North Carolina
 Hospitals
Chapel Hill, North Carolina

**Neal Neuberger**
Senior Partner
Center for Public Service
 Communication
Arlington, Virginia

**Harry Nurkin, Ph.D., FACHE**
President and CEO
Carolinas Medical Center
Charlotte, North Carolina

**R. Paul O'Neill**
President
Yankee Alliance
Andover, Massachusetts

**Thomas Ricketts III, Ph.D.**
Assistant Professor
Department of Health Policy and
 Administration Deputy Director
Cecil G. Sheps Center for Health
 Services Research

University of North Carolina at
 Chapel Hill
Chapel Hill, North Carolina

**Nan Rideout**
Rural Health Consultant
North Carolina Office of Rural
 Health
Raleigh, North Carolina

**Catherine Robinson**
Executive Director
Network for Healthcare
 Management
Berkeley, California

**Sandy Robinson**
Planning Officer
Agency for Health Care Policy
 and Research
Rockville, Maryland

**C. Scott Schoenborn**
Federal Healthcare Consultant
Pfizer National Healthcare
 Operations
Richmond, Virginia

**Raymond Schultze, M.D.**
Director
University of California Los
 Angeles Medical Center
Los Angeles, California

**Richard Scott, Ph.D.**
Professor
Department of Sociology
Stanford University
Stanford, California

**Terry Shannon**
Dissemination Advisor
Agency for Health Care Policy
 and Research
Rockville, Maryland

**Stephen Shortell, Ph.D.**
A.C. Bueller Distinguished
  Professor of Health Services
  Management
J.L. Kellogg Graduate School of
  Management
Northwestern University
Evanston, Illinois

**Tim Size**
Executive Director
Rural Wisconsin Hospital
  Cooperative
Sauk City, Wisconsin

**David Smith, Ph.D.**
Professor
School of Business
Department of Health
  Administration
Temple University
Philadelphia, Pennsylvania

**Barry Stein, Ph.D.**
President
Goodmeasure, Inc.
Cambridge, Massachusetts

**Garith Steiner**
Administrator
Vernon Memorial Hospital
Viroqua, Wisconsin

**Nancy Temple**
Program Coordinator
Carolinas Medical Center
Charlotte, North Carolina

**Kenneth Thorpe, Ph.D.**
Deputy Assistant Secretary for
  Health Policy

Department of Health and Human
  Services
Washington, D.C.

**Sharon Topping, Ph.D.**
Coordinator of Sponsored
  Research
College of Business
  Administration
University of Southern Mississippi
Hattiesburg, Mississippi

**Monroe Trout, M.D., J.D.**
Chairman of the Board, President
  and CEO
American Healthcare Systems
San Diego, California

**Geoffrey Walton**
Corporate Fellow
Henry Ford Health System
Detroit, Michigan

**Alan Weinstein**
President
Premier Health Alliance, Inc.
Westchester, Illinois

**Anthony Wellever**
Research Fellow
Institute for Health Services
  Research
Minneapolis, Minnesota

**Stephen Wood**
Manager, Business Services
Blue Cross/Blue Shield
  Association
Chicago, Illinois

**Edward Zajac, Ph.D.**
James F. Beré Professor of
  Organizational Behavior

J.L. Kellogg Graduate School of
  Management
Northwestern University
Evanston, Illinois

**William Zelman, Ph.D.**
Professor
Department of Health Policy and
  Administration
School of Public Health
University of North Carolina at
  Chapel Hill
Chapel Hill, North Carolina

**Howard Zuckerman, Ph.D.**
Professor, School of Health
  Administration and Policy,
  and
Director, Center for Health
  Management Research
College of Business
Arizona State University
Tempe, Arizona

# Index

AAMC. *See* Association of American Medical Colleges

Abbott Laboratories, 57; link with Federal Express, 54–55

Acute care hospital paradigm, overemphasis on, 186

Agency for Health Care Policy and Research (AHCPR), xv

AHA. *See* American Hospital Association

AHCPR. *See* Agency for Health Care Policy and Research

AHS. *See* Allegany Health System

AIDS, in rural America, 183, 184

Airline industry, strategic alliances in, 1–2, 22

Allegany Health System (AHS), 178

Alliance pools, 22

Alliances: collaborative, in society, 69–71; customer-linked, 24; employee-linked, 24–25; hospital-driven, 92; hospital-hospital, 67; implementation, politics of, 197–98; interorganizational, 64; joint-buy, 137; joint-make, 139; lateral, 8; link, 24; multihospital, 143; multiorganizational health care, 61–83; multiorganizational opportunistic, 66; multiorganizational service, 66; multiorganizational stakeholder, 66; physician-driven, 92; pooling,

136–37; service, 8; stakeholder, 8, 24; supply linked, 24; trading, 136–37, vertical, link to health reform, 181; win-lose, 138; win-win, 137–38, 179

*See also* Strategic alliances

American Health Systems, 86

American Hospital Association (AHA): community care network concept of, 140, 165; definition of hospital consortium, 107; Hospital Research and Educational Trust at, 171

Appalachian Regional Commission, 59

Association of Academic Health Centers, 121

Association of American Medical Colleges (AAMC), 121

Automobile industry, strategic alliances in, 2, 21, 22

Backward integration, 141

BC-BS. *See* Blue Cross-Blue Shield system

Bellcore, 23

Benefits, imbalance of, as problem in strategic alliances, 32

Blue Cross-Blue Shield (BC-BS) system, 120, 130–34; in Iowa, 148; in Michigan, 148, 190

Boundary role persons, 69

Bounded rationality, 100

Budget, capped, as barrier
for strategic alliances, xii

Capital, access to, 168
Captive supply units, 5
Carolinas Medical Center (CMC), 76
Catholic Health Association (CHA):
integrated delivery network
concept of, 140, 165; proposal
for health care reform, 141
Catholic health care, future of, 180
Certified health plan, concept of, x
CHA. *See* Catholic Health Association
Charlotte Community Hospital, 74
Charlotte–Mecklenburg Hospital
Authority (CMHA), 63–83; alliance
development, 74–76; core
facility integration, 76–77;
future for, 81–83; historical
perspective, 65–68; indirect and
direct payer integration, 80;
physician integration, 77–78;
relationships of subsets to
the greater organizational
set, 68–69; unanticipated
affiliations, 80–81; urban-rural
institutional integration, 78–80
Charlotte Memorial Hospital, 74
Charlotte Rehabilitation
Hospital, 74, 76
Children's Hospital, 76
CHN. *See* Coordinated
Healthcare Network
Clinical health services
research, opportunities for
strategic alliances in, xii
Clinical outcome data,
development of, 187–88
Clinton, Bill, and proposed
health care reform, ix–xiii, 7,
11, 41, 58, 140, 156, 165
CMC. *See* Carolinas Medical Center
CMHA. *See* Charlotte–Mecklenburg
Hospital Authority
Collective bargaining techniques, 69
Columbia Health Corporation,
merger of HCA and, 178

Communication industry, strategic
alliances in, 2–3, 21, 23
Community care networks, 140
Community Choice, 148
Community necessity strategy,
182–83; distinguishing between
competitive health care market
strategy and, 177, 181–84
Community Physicians'
Network, alliance between
Wisconsin Hospital
Cooperative and, 35, 40–52
Competition, as barrier for
strategic alliances, xii–xiii
Competitive health care market
strategy, 182; distinguishing
between community necessity
strategy and, 177, 181–84
Complexity, 105, 124
Compression technology, 59
Concentration, correlation with
standard distance, 111
Concentration ratios, 108
Consortia, 22
Consortium for the Study of
University Hospitals, 121
Consortium Research
on Indicators of System
Performance (CRISP), 157, 158–59
Contracting, selective, 146
Coordinated Healthcare
Network (CHN), 151
Coordination, concept of, 195–96
Corporate partnerships, 9
Corporation for National Research, 59
Cost, as issue in health care, 71–72, 94

Daughters of Charity Health
System–West, 151
DeanCare HMO, 44
Decision making and control, sharing
of, as critical in integrated
delivery system, 171–72
Delivery, benefits of integrating
finance and, 146–48
Direct payers, definition of, 80
Double loop learning, 202–4

Drugs and substance abuse, in
rural America, 183

Eastern Maine Medical Center, 86
Eastman Kodak, 54
Economic security, as goal in forming
strategic alliances, x, 56
Economies of scale, 168–69
Education, as critical factor in
integrated delivery system, 172
Enterprise liability, xii
European Economic
Community, 53, 54

Federal Express, link with
Abbott Laboratories, 54–55
Finance, benefits of integrating
delivery and, 146–48
Forward integration, 141–42
Free rider problem, 137

HCA, merger with Columbia
Health Corporation, 178
HCFA. *See* Health Care
Financing Administration
Health care: cost as factor in, 71–72,
94; critical importance of choice in,
41–42; international marketing in,
54; market failures in, 195–96; use
of new technologies in, 61
Health Care Financing
Administration (HCFA), 60, 145
Health care reform: under President
Clinton, ix–xiii, 7, 11, 41, 58, 140,
156, 165; complexity of, 7–8; focus
of campaign for, 195; integrated
care as requirement in, 42–43; link
of vertical alliances to, 181;
managed competition approach
to, 146; and viability of
stand-alone services, 192
Health care strategic alliances,
7–14; importance of, 35,
40–52; types of, 8–9
Health care system, definition of, 179
Health maintenance organizations
(HMOs), 34, 146

Health Plan Employer Data and
Information Set (HEDIS), 159
Health Security Act (HSA). *See*
Health care reform
Health Systems Integration Study
(HSIS), 164–65, 168, 171–75, 187
HEDIS. See Health Plan Employer
Data and Information Set
Henry Ford, Health System,
148, 190; Center for Health
System Studies, 157
Hierarchical firms, 100
HMO–W, Inc., 44
Homogeneity, 105, 124;
measures of, 108–9
Horizontal integration, 92; of
hospitals, 148–50; of
physicians, 150–52
Hospital consortium, definition of, 107
Hospitals, horizontal
integration of, 148–50
HSIS. See Health Syatems
Integration Study
Huntersville Hospital, 74–75

Implementation, politics of, 197–98
Indian Health Service, 59
Indirect payers, definition of, 80
Information systems,
integrated health, 42–43
Infrastructure: developing,
167–68; local and regional
development of, 49–50
Integrated delivery systems, 156,
165–66, 194; assessing performance
of, 156–57; barriers to, 186–90;
constituencies served, perspective
of, 157–59; critical success factors
in, 171–74; delivery system
perspective of, 161–68; identifying
central force in, 170–71;
participating parties, perspective
of, 169–70; as requirement for
health care reform, 42–43; studies
of system performance, 159–61
International marketing, in
health care, 54

International Partners in
Glass Research, 23
Iowa Health Partners, 148
Iowa Methodist, 148
IPAs, 172

Johnson & Johnson–Merck
alliance, 137
Joint Commission on
Accreditation of Healthcare
Organizations (JCAHO), 60
Joint programs, 194
Joint ventures, 66

Life cycle model of development, 9–11
Loyalties, conflicting, as problem
in strategic alliances, 32

Malpractice liability, xii, 49
Managed care, 69, 87, 95–96, 146
Management and governance
structures, outmoded, 188
Management service
organization (MSO), 154, 190
Market approach,
unification of, 164–65
Mayo Clinic, 42
Mercy Health Services, 80–81, 148, 190
Microelectronics and
Computer Corporation, 23
MSO. *See* Management
service organization
Mullikin Medical Center, 150–51
Multihospital alliances, 143
Multiorganizational alliances, 66
Multispecialty group practice,
challenges in developing, 186–87

NAFTA. *See* North American Free
Trade Agreement (NAFTA).
NASA, and telemedicine, 59
National Competitiveness
Act (1933), 58
National Cooperative
Research Act (1984), 22–23
National purchasing
organizations, need for, 56

National Quality Management
Program, 156
NATO, 53–54
Network, role of physicians in, 180
Network-based practice
support, 48–49
Network building, issues associated
with success in, 178–81
Nominal group technique, setting
priorities using, 211–13
North American Free Trade
Agreement (NAFTA), 54
North Carolina Hospital
Authority Act (1943), 74

Office of Rural Health Policy, 59
Organizational impact
statements, need for, 203
Organizational research, uses of
models in guiding, 35, 36–39
Organization design, 105
Organization-environment
relations, as reason
for alliance formation, 145
Outcomes, assuming risk and
responsibility for, 166
Outcomes research, 60

PHO. *See* Physician-hospital
organization
Physician-driven alliances, 92
Physician-hospital organizations
(PHOs), 152–55, 172, 173,
190; tightness of, 153–55
Physician integration, at
Charlotte–Mecklenburg
Hospital Authority, 77–78
Physician leadership: importance
of, in integrated delivery
system, 171–72; lack
of sufficient base of, 187
Physicians, horizontal
integration of, 150–52
Physicians Plus Insurance
Corporation, 44
Points of service, 61–62

Political dynamics, role of,
in strategic alliance, 120
Power imbalance, as problem in
strategic alliances, 31–32
Preferred provider organizations
(PPOs), 95–96, 146
Premier Health Alliance, 96, 143
Primary care physicians, 45;
shortage of, 186–87
Priorities, nominal group
technique in setting, 211–13
Provident Transamerican
Insurance Companies, 87
Providers, aligning incentives
of participating, 166
Public policy, influence of,
on development of
strategic alliances, 10

Research, 199–209; basic
methodological questions in, 204–5;
managerial perspective, 199; policy
perspective, 200; priorities for, on
strategic alliances in health care,
213–17; research perspective, 199;
setting priorities in, using the
nominal group technique, 211–13;
substantive issues in, 205–9;
underlying concerns, 201–204
Research and Development
(R&D) consortia, 22–23
Resource dependence. as reason for
alliance formation,
144–45, model for, 101–2
Resources and Health Service
Administration, 59–60
Robert Wood Johnson, Foundation's
Hospital-Based Rural Health Care
Program (HBRHCP), 107
Rural areas: barriers to vertically
integrated alliances in, 182–84;
strategic alliances in, 181–84
Rural hospital networks, 99–138; areas
for future research, 111–16;
associations among structural
characteristics, 110–11; board of
directors, 110; concentration of,

108; data collection for, 107–8;
definition of strategic alliances for,
99–101; homogeneity of, 108–9;
paid director in, 110; size of, 108;
standard distance in, 109; structural
dimensions of, 103–6; structure of
strategic alliances in, 101–3, 106–11
Rural network advocacy, 50
Rural network negotiations, 47–48
Rural Wisconsin Hospital Cooperative
(RWHC), alliance between
Community Physicians'
Network, 35, 40–52

Safe Harbor regulations, 58
St. Elizabeth's Hospital, 178
Selectivity, as critical factor in
integrated delivery system, 172
Sematech, 194
Semiconductor Research
Corporation, 23
Service alliances, 8
Shared-service corporation, 43
Single corporation in
control paradigm, 43
Single loop learning, 202
Spot market, 100
Standard distance, 109; correlation
with concentration, 111
Strategic alliances, 101–3; ally
structure, 22–23; analysis of failure,
135; barriers for, xii–xiii; benefits of
integrating finance and delivery,
146–48; characteristics of, 21–25;
commitment, uneven levels as
problem, 31–32; competitive
advantages of, xi; continuums at,
134–36; cost-benefit analysis of, 4;
customer-linked, 24; definition of,
x, 20–21, 86, 99–101, 143–44, 193;
desired accomplishments of, 3–4;
effectiveness of, 13–14; employee
linked, 24–25; formation of, 9–11;
functioning of, 26–31; future for,
35, 57–62; goal achievement in, 4–5;
growing importance of, xv; in
health care, 7–14; historical lessons

learned from, 53–57; horizontal integration of hospitals in, 148–50; horizontal integration of physicians in, 150–52; ideal characteristics of, 196–97; importance of, in health care, 35, 40–52; importance of trust in, 138; industrial uses of, 40; institutionalization of, x–xi; integration, insufficient, as problem, 33; integrative, 8–9; interorganizational relations, as a result of, 1–7; key characteristics of, x; lateral, 8; lessons learned from, 31–34; methods of achieving goals, 4–5; motivation behind, 126–30, 134; operation of, 11–13; opportunistic, 23, 67; organization-environment relations for, 145; performance level of, 6–7; political dynamics in, 135–36; pool structure, 22–23; population-based goals for, xii; priorities for research on, 213–17; problem management by, 5–6; resource dependence at, 144–45; resource flows in, 136–37; role of, in health care reform, xi–xiii; service, 66; stakeholder, 66–67; structural characteristics of, 155; structural dimensions in, 103–6; as structure for integrated delivery systems, 139–98; structure of, among rural hospitals, 106–11; supplier linked, 24; tightness of alliance relationships in, 152–53; tightness of physician hospital relationships in, 153–55; transaction costs for, 145; types of, 8–9, 22–24, 145–46; typology of, 193–95; usefulness of, 25–26; as vehicle for Interorganizational relations, 1–7; and vertical integration, 144–45
Strategic decision making, unification of, 163–64
Subsets, relationships of, to greater organizational set, 68–69
Subsystems, definition of, 69

SunHealth Alliance, 26, 34, 119, 126–30, 143
Supply linked alliances, 24
Systemic networks, 9

Telemedicine, advances in, 58–60
Texas Tech MEDNET program, 59
Trading alliance, 136–37
Transaction costs, as reason for alliance formation, 145
Trust: importance of, in strategic alliances, 138; premature, as problem in strategic alliances, 32; role of education in building, 172
Trustees, role of, in integration of community health care, 172

UHC. *See* University Hospital Consortium
Ultimate payers, definition of, 80
Undermanagement, as problem in strategic alliances, 32–33
United Healthcare Systems of Kansas City, 86
University Hospital and Medical Park, 77
University Hospital Consortium (UHC), 119–25; complexity, 122; conditions of membership, 123; enhancing members welfare, 124–25; geographical relationship, 123–25; goals of, 121–22; homogeneity, 124; influence of change agents, 121–23; lose-lose alliance, 136; motivation for alliance formation, 121; rational versus political model at, 122–23; subgoal pursuits in, 136; win-lose alliance, 136; win-win alliance, 136
Urban-rural institutional integration, at Charlotte–Mecklenburg Hospital Authority, 78–80

Value-added services, 179
Value-adding partnerships, 8, 66

Vertical alliances, link
to health care reform, 181
Vertical integration, 94, 131, 139, 181,
194; barriers to, in rural areas,
180–82; conceptual issues in, 192;
continuum of care in, 196–97;
definition of, 141–43; dimensions
of, 196–97; generic elements
of, 142–43; pressures for,
140–44; purposes of, 140; and

strategic alliances, 144–45
Voluntary Hospitals of America
(VHA), 34, 67, 143

Warsaw Pact, 53
Worker's compensation, xii

Yankee Alliance, 85, 86–90,
94; goals of, *88–89*

# About the Editors

**Arnold D. Kaluzny, Ph.D.,** is a professor in the Department of Health Policy and Administration, School of Public Health at the University of North Carolina at Chapel Hill and a Senior Fellow at the Cecil G. Sheps Center for Health Services Research.

**Howard S. Zuckerman, Ph.D.,** is a professor of the School of Health Administration and Policy, College of Business at Arizona State University, and the director of the Center for Health Management Research.

**Thomas C. Ricketts, III, Ph.D.,** is the deputy director for Health Policy Analysis at the Cecil G. Sheps Center for Health Services Research and an assistant professor, Department of Health Policy and Administration, School of Public Health at the University of North Carolina at Chapel Hill.

**Geoffrey B. Walton, MHA,** is a recent graduate of the Department of Health Policy and Administration, School of Public Health at the University of North Carolina, and is currently the Corporate Fellow at the Henry Ford Health System in Detroit.